Harvests, Feasts, and Graves

Harvests, Feasts, and Graves

Postcultural Consciousness in Contemporary Papua New Guinea

Ryan Schram

Cornell University Press
Ithaca and London

Copyright © 2018 by Cornell University

All rights reserved. Except for brief quotations in a review, this book, or parts thereof, must not be reproduced in any form without permission in writing from the publisher. For information, address Cornell University Press, Sage House, 512 East State Street, Ithaca, New York 14850.

First published 2018 by Cornell University Press

Printed in the United States of America

Library of Congress Cataloging-in-Publication Data
Names: Schram, Ryan, author.
Title: Harvests, feasts, and graves : postcultural consciousness in contemporary Papua New Guinea / Ryan Schram.
Description: Ithaca : Cornell University Press, 2018. | Includes bibliographical references and index.
Identifiers: LCCN 2017027638 (print) | LCCN 2017033044 (ebook) | ISBN 9781501711022 (epub/mobi) | ISBN 9781501711015 (pdf) | ISBN 9781501710995 (cloth: alk. paper) | ISBN 9781501711008 (pbk.: alk. paper)
Subjects: LCSH: Ethnology—Papua New Guinea—Milne Bay Province. | Social change—Papua New Guinea—Milne Bay Province. | Postcolonialism—Papua New Guinea—Milne Bay Province. | Milne Bay Province (Papua New Guinea)—Social life and customs.
Classification: LCC GN671.N5 (ebook) | LCC GN671.N5 S36 2018 (print) | DDC 303.409953—dc23
LC record available at https://lccn.loc.gov/2017027638

Cornell University Press strives to use environmentally responsible suppliers and materials to the fullest extent possible in the publishing of its books. Such materials include vegetable-based, low-VOC inks and acid-free papers that are recycled, totally chlorine-free, or partly composed of nonwood fibers. For further information, visit our website at cornellpress.cornell.edu.

Teina bu'i yagu waligehao vehabadi.
Ryan Alexander, Ryan Jack David,
yagu velau alimiyai. Yauwedo.

(This book is for my namesakes.
Ryan Alexander, Ryan Jack David,
my love to you. Thank you.)

Contents

List of Illustrations	ix
Walo Velau	xi
Note on Orthography	xv
Introduction	1
1. Natives and Travelers	25
2. You Cannot Eat Your Own Blood	48
3. Hunger and Plenty	76
4. Banks, Books, and Pots	105
5. One Mind	131
6. The Weight of Tradition, the Children of Light	168
Conclusion	197
Notes	215
References	227
Index	245

Illustrations

Maps

1. Papua New Guinea and its region — 26
2. The location of Auhelawa within Milne Bay Province, Papua New Guinea — 27
3. Some of the villages in Kurada Ward, Normanby Island — 28

Figures

1. Lucy Pade sewing sago palm leaves to make roof thatch (*atovi*) in 2006 — 51
2. Noeline and baby Caleb in New Home in 2006 — 57
3. A new yam garden and yam house above New Home Village in January 2006 — 93
4. Representatives of each side count the donations at the pot-to-pot held at Wadaheya Village on August 31, 2004 — 124
5. Francis Pade after *tapwalolo* at St. Peter's Catholic Church in Mwademwadewa Village in 2006 — 133
6. The path leading up to Hegahegai Point, the original site of the Methodist mission at Bunama — 138
7. Opa Haimanu leaves the Sowala United Church after Sunday *tapwalolo* on November 12, 2006 — 144

ILLUSTRATIONS

Walo Velau

There's a story I heard in Auhelawa in 2006 about the first *polisiman*, or the village constable appointed by the Australian colonial administration in 1914. He was Didiluwa of Magetuwa Village. Part of his job was to accompany visiting Australian patrol officers on patrol through the villages of Auhelawa. He would meet them at the *maka* (marker), the border between the districts of Namoa, where he lived, and Barabara. When they met, he would salute the officers and they would freeze in place, unable to move until Didiluwa lowered his hand, releasing them from his magic. (Didiluwa was also a sorcerer.) Then the officers would come into Namoa, and they would not cause any trouble thanks to Didiluwa's powers.

I have thought a lot about this story over the years. What was it like for the people at the maka to look at each other? The *dimdim* (white, foreigner) did not know Didiluwa's language. Didiluwa probably did not know much dimdim, and yet at the maka they were able to see each other and understand something about each other. This is a book about Auhelawa, but it really tries to find these maka where people meet. I want to talk about the places and times where two ways of seeing, and two ways of life, come together. People may be look at the same things, but see them completely differently, and yet, in these places and times, they still manage to communicate, just like Didiluwa and the officers. I want to argue that we find these kinds of maka everywhere. They aren't just between dimdim and *Papua* (white people and Melanesian people). Even people in one village can be very different yet still find a way to live together as one.

My mothers, my fathers, my brothers and sisters, all my groups and all the people in Auhelawa, I want to say thank you for inviting me to live with you, first in 2004, again in 2006, and the few times I've been able to come back since then. Thank you for being my friends on Facebook. Thank you for writing me text messages telling me about how things are going at home, and your hopes and dreams for the future. Thank you for writing me letters all these years. Thank you for encouraging me to keep working and keep writing. I know that we did not always really understand each other, and perhaps I have never been able to show you the benefits of hosting a foreign anthropologist. This book is not the end, but I hope the beginning of a new conversation between us.

My family and friends in Auhelawa know that I did not write this book alone. My parents, Sanford and Joan Schram, have been talking to me about life in Auhelawa for some time, and helping out in every way they could, whether it was reading manuscripts, hearing talks I've given, hosting me on whirlwind trips to North America for conferences, or talking about plans for publication. Likewise, at many points, David Herrero, Amy Kersey, Kate O'Donnell, and other friends have read chapters and other writing that has helped me to find ways to give Auhelawa an audience. Even Clem and Arlo, Kate and Amy's sons, know how to say *yauwedo*.

I have been fortunate to talk about these ideas with many of my teachers, students, and scholarly colleagues over the years. There are too many people to name individually, but I would like to mention several people who have made important contributions to my thinking at different times. I first met Donald Tuzin at the University of California, San Diego in 2000, and over the ensuing years he became one of my most important scholarly mentors. He read not only a lot of the ideas that went into chapter 6 but also a number of research reports from the field. Since his passing in 2007, I have missed him greatly and often turned to my memories of our conversations, as well as his extensive scholarship on Ilahita Arapesh of Papua New Guinea (PNG), in the writing of this book. It is hard to overstate the value the Tuzin Archive for Melanesian Anthropology, named in his memory, has had for my research career. When I began my graduate studies, the Melanesian Archive prepared me for fieldwork. It brought me into contact with a wide range of researchers from around the world and allowed me to see my own work in a historical perspective.

As mentors and teachers, Joel Robbins and Rupert Stasch have also been invaluable sources of advice and encouragement. I also want to say thanks to Jim Lance, the book's editor and expert guide to the publishing process, and to Diane Austin-Broos, Jon Bialecki, Simon Coleman, Kevin Edahosi, Ilana Gershon, Alex Golub, John Haimanu, Courtney Handman, Jordan Haug, Naomi Haynes, Dan Jorgensen, Timo Kaartinen, Steven Kara, Bruce Knauft, Neil Maclean, Debra McDougall, Derek Milne, Francis Pade, Lucy Pade, Adam Reed, Jukka Siikala, Tom Strong, Tuomas Tammisto, Matt Tomlinson, and Terry Woronov, each of whom has either read different portions of this book, or other writings, or talked through some of the key ideas with me at different times.

Several portions of this book appeared in earlier forms: "Finding Money: Business and Charity in Auhelawa, Papua New Guinea," *Ethnos* 75, no. 4 (2010): 447–70, permission to reprint granted by Taylor and Francis; "One Mind: Enacting the Christian Congregation among the Auhelawa, Papua New Guinea," *Australian Journal of Anthropology* 24, no. 1 (2013): 30–47, permission to reprint granted by Wiley; "Indecorous, Too Hasty, Incorrect Market and Moral Imagination in Auhelawa, Papua New Guinea," *Anthropological Quarterly* 89, no. 2 (2016): 515–37, permission to reprint granted by the editor; "A Society Divided: Death, Personhood, and Christianity in Auhelawa, Papua New Guinea," *HAU: Journal of Ethnographic Theory* 5 (1): 317–37, permission to reprint granted by the editor.

Note on Orthography

The text follows the practical orthography developed by David and Daphne Lithgow for use in vernacular education in Auhelawa, and for the Auhelawa New Testament published in 2008. This orthography uses w and y between vowels to indicate separate syllables, at the beginning of a word to indicate /w/ and /j/ respectively, and uses w after some consonants to indicate labialization. Like the Lithgow orthography, I indicate a glottal stop (') when it occurs between syllables and to distinguish /w/ from /'w/, but unlike the Lithgow orthography I do not indicate a glottal stop at the beginning of a word when it is followed by a vowel (e.g. *walo* [say], *'wateya* [yam], *aba'ita* [example], and *abaita* [flood]).

Harvests, Feasts, and Graves

Introduction

A Map of the Territory

In June 2004, I had been living on Duau (Normanby Island) in Milne Bay Province, Papua New Guinea, for a few weeks. Francis and Lucy Pade had graciously offered me a house in their village and made me part of their family. The broader social environment was still unfamiliar to me. Around this time, one of my new acquaintances, a man named Kevin Edahosi, came to my house from his home in a nearby village with a map of the area. On ruled notebook paper, he had carefully traced the outline of the coast from top to bottom, indicating the points and bays. On each line of the paper, he drew a symbol for a village, and then next to it a name. Along the same line, he added notes for each named place, the totemic bird of the people living there, and whether there were people currently living there. The result was both a map from east to west of the coast, and a list of the constituent villages within the ward of Kurada (a part of the Duau Local Level Government Area). It went from Dawatai Point to Buitowolo

Rock, the approximate boundaries of this ward, and a phrase I'd already heard a few times in community meetings meaning "everybody."

Kevin and I and many other people walked up and down the main coastal road from village to village, climbed the steep rises where the land plunges down from the mountains into the sea, over the log bridges, through the groves of impossibly tall coconut palms, and along the beaches of coral and pebbles. Eventually the items on Kevin's list became as familiar as stops along University Avenue in San Diego. After I went home and began to write up my research, I read the reports written by patrolling police officers who worked in this region for the Australian colonial administration. They had also written lists of names of every place they visited, misspelling many of them. Still, the larger, older villages of each *susu* (groups related through common descent from women) were unmistakably there. When I needed a break from writing, I looked at the satellite imagery at 10.111 degrees south, 151.03 degrees east on Google Maps. All the villages on Kevin's map were within a few minutes of that point, and online I could see gardens in the inland hills, the oddly gridlike pattern of planted coconut groves, and the sharp lines of the ridges. The coastal points and bays that Kevin had carefully drawn on his map were here too, more or less the same as he had them: Dawatai Point, Buitowolo Rock, Sowala, Gogosi'i River, Patumala, not to mention other places in Bwasiyaiyai and Barabara Wards on either side of Kurada. I could see the iron roofs of the Catholic church, school, and hospital at Mwademwadewa. I imagined that I was looking at Alogawa Village where I lived, nestled among sago palms and rosewood trees, just a little to the left.

Kevin's map was like a lot of things people gave to me. They would tell a story, list their ancestors, tell me their interpretation of a Bible passage, or explain how one should mourn for one's father. They were not simply telling me facts; they too were giving me a map of the territory in which they lived. Everyone I met in Kurada, just like anyone else, was working with a model of how their social world operated and how they fit into it. And so they unfolded their maps for me. I learned that the social world of Kurada was organized mainly around susu. Kevin showed me how to record genealogies of susu, which he had learned working as an assistant for Michael Young while he came to Bwasiyaiyai as part of a two-week consultancy for a foreign mining company (Young 1995). By the end of my second, longer field trip in 2006, I had recorded lists of matrilineal descent for nearly all the susu in Kurada. Senior members of each group told me the name of the founder, where she had traveled from and settled in Kurada, her children, her daughters' children, and so on, some going back for six generations or more. They told me the ancestral name of each person had inherited in many cases, even though these are not used in everyday life. Uttering these names is forbidden to people who are not *bu'una* (relatives) of the susu, especially the in-laws and children of men. They included these in their telling because as many people explained to me, a susu's stock of inherited names is how one can verify whether or not someone really has the same descent as you, and many names are memorials to individuals of the past who founded villages and made alliances with other susu.

My research in 2004, 2006, 2010, and 2014 has been to collect these maps of the territory and to make use of the vantage they afford. It would be easy to say that these maps that people gave me were much more reliable than anything I could learn from historical records or satellite images. Yet I soon learned that these maps did not always remain folded away. Many social situations required people to explicate their models to each other, to expose their different assumptions about social processes, and fix their locations with respect to each other. Indeed, the map of the world of susu that I was learning to use was not as reliable as it might appear. In some cases, people said that their susu did not pass on ancestral names to the most recent generation, only giving young children a name at baptism or birth. When I asked why, one person said that her susu did not have all that many names to pass on, and there were so many small children now. People were tired of hearing the same names over and over again, she said. She said it with the usual dose of Auhelawa irony, but I believe she was serious. This susu had given me all of their susu's names already, for my private research.[1] There was a serious side to her quip. Several people have also taken me to caves and rock shelters high in the inland bush, far from the gardens above their villages, where prior to the Australian colonial government's ban on the practice in the early twentieth century, their susu had placed the skulls of deceased members. Many people explained to me that the skulls in these caves would normally have been arranged in a way that facilitated the recitation of the susu's history (*tetela*) but more often than not, this had been lost. One man, Aidan Cosmas, explained it this way: The caves were the books for the old people. People know how to write their genealogies in books now, so they do that instead of learning the old way of recording history. Kevin learned how to record genealogies from the anthropologist Michael Young, but in fact many people in many susu had devised their own ways of keeping track of their descent in exercise books. When I asked people why they did this, they said they did not want people to forget and they did not want people to fight over land because they did not know the history. I was learning to use the social models people created for me, but it seemed like they were beginning to question whether they could always depend on them.

One might also easily assume that this book will be a synthesis of all these models, and my ethnography would be a single, total picture of the villages of Kurada and its neighbors from one point of view. Yet Aidan's comment, like so many other things people told me, complicates this. For Aidan, these different maps do not all fit together. The people of Kurada today have many, many such devices they can use to construct a picture in their minds of who they are and how they are related. Some are indigenous and some come from dimdim (white, European) culture, like Christianity, schools, and government, and markets. So they have to grapple with the discrepancies among them. For Aidan and many others, it makes sense to place all these possibilities in a temporal order in which the precolonial past has given way to a present that is defined by membership in institutions which are global, polyglot, and transnational in nature. "Kastam i'o'ovi" (custom, or tradition, is ending), many people would say. It is a cliché in Auhelawa political discourse that they live in a "changing society," borrowing the English words. "The times are changing" (*hauga isesens*), community leaders would frequently remind people, using an English loanword (*sens*, from change). Even their own language suggests the inevitability of loss. As one man once said to me matter-of-factly, "Maybe someday we'll all be speaking dimdim [English]."

When people in Auhelawa think about how they fit into a larger system, they assume two things are true. The first is that they assume that no one else in the world sees their lives the way that they and their neighbors do, and in particular, throughout the world, most people have learned to see the world the ways dimdim people do. Given this, and second, they also assume that the written records of colonial officers and the narratives of history taught by Polynesian and Australian missionaries have more credibility as maps of the world, and hence how Auhelawa fits into that world. In these foreign frameworks, Auhelawa people live in a traditional order based on rules and with time, with exposure to education, opportunities for wage labor and cash earning, and knowledge of the world people will pull themselves out of these traditional systems. When Auhelawa people say that their customs are fading away and the times are changing, they accept this basic historical narrative of cultural difference in principle. At the same time, it remains unclear to Auhelawa how this narrative applies to them, and specifically where they are in that narrative, well over a century after the arrival of the first missionaries and colonial officers. While much has changed in Auhelawa in the last century, much also has not. Thus we cannot assume that their resignation to the inevitability of change is a symptom of a real empirical social transformation. So we must ask why Auhelawa people tell this story. What does *sens* mean to them?

In this book, I argue that Auhelawa people use their own senses of change, especially the fading or finishing of tradition, as a way to create a position of postculturalism and thus establish a new basis for their recognition of each other as members of a community. By this I do not mean that their distinctive cultural values have actually vanished. Nor do I mean that Auhelawa have moved beyond their traditional past and created something new. Rather, by this term I want to highlight how people suspend the trope of cultural difference, especially its assumed hierarchy of norm and action, and question the ways in which people's behaviors may or may not fit into a pattern. By asserting a moment of *sens*, Auhelawa make it possible to question the existence of order.

In the first part of the book, I argue that this kind of practical reflexivity is inherent in the ways Auhelawa symbolize their own belonging to a social order based on kinship. In the rituals of kinship, I show that the power to decide whether or not a person's symbolic actions count as the constitution of a relationship does not lie simply in the hands of an abstract collective but is unevenly distributed among elders and particular classes of kin. With this as background, I then examine a specific instance of the *sens* narrative. I ask why it is that Auhelawa fear that yam harvests are shrinking and people are becoming more selfish. The annual harvest of yams, the prestige crop and chief gift among susu in feasts, has become an important metaphor for moral order. A full yam house means a woman has diligently and patiently worked all year for others' benefit. This symbolism, I argue, is also the main way that people represent their earning of money through market trade and avoid the stigma of selfish haggling. It also becomes a way for people to model their membership in a wholly new kind of social unit, the Christian congregation. These analogies between harvest and new social situations might suggest that people have in fact found ways to domesticate foreign forms, reclassifying individual profit and individual faith as extensions of a gift economy. Yet, as I argue, because people have established a context of *sens*, of fading customs, and of increasing disorder, they make it possible to imagine other kinds of relationships between these cultural systems and create new grounds for mutual recognition in these spaces.

The Weight of History

To understand the Auhelawa case, it helps to reconsider the nature of historical consciousness itself. Karl Marx writes, "The tradition of all dead generations weighs like a nightmare on the brains of the living" (1972 [1852], 595). This basic conception of historical consciousness as an inheritance from the past still remains central to social theory, although it can be interpreted in various ways. For an earlier generation of social theorists, the social actor is a product of a social totality. As Louis Dumont quotes Marx saying, "It is society which thinks in me" (1980, 5). In more recent years, Marxist historiography has proven more useful to anthropologists who wish to identify the emergence of contemporary social forms by placing them in the context of postcolonial nation states and their position within global capitalism (Wallerstein 1974; Wolf 1982; Ong 1987; Comaroff and Comaroff 1992; see also Ortner 1984, 2016).[2] Rather than the social totality, relations of domination shape the consciousness of every subject.

Dipesh Chakrabarty (2000) argues that this kind of historical explanation, one in which the contemporary order is the legacy of imperial conquest and sociopolitical transformation, actually borrows from the same historicism that legitimated the Western colonial project in the first place. Like Marx, and like classical social theory in general, colonial authorities envisaged social change as a succession of stages and saw themselves as both standard-bearers and paternalistic guides to peoples who were prepolitical, irrational, and incapable of exercising liberal rights. Western social scientists and colonial administrations (as well as contemporary institutions of global governance) are both, in this fashion, blind to the alternative forms of political agency by which subalterns seek to engage and contest their domination, either in the colonial or the postcolonial era.

Chakrabarty seeks a way to identify these alternative projects of modernity and the kinds of subjectivity they involve. He argues that social analysts must reconsider how they translate political agency across distinct ways of life and incommensurate economies of value. Social and historical analysis cannot be content to detect a common political narrative underlying different sociohistorical circumstances, as if all societies served equally as affirmation of Westerners' own stories of their political origins (see Englund and Leach 2000). In this respect, Chakrabarty's critique of the historicism of difference joins with more recent debates over global indigenous politics. Here as well, scholars find that the values of indigenous peoples—especially commitments to maintaining sovereignty, perpetuating distinct forms of belonging, and maintaining relationships to natural environments—challenge the liberal conception of political agency (Blackburn 2009; de la Cadena 2010; Blaser 2013; LeFevre 2013; Muru-Lanning 2016; see Schram 2014 for a review).

In many ways, ethnography is still complicit in what Chakrabarty would call colonial historicism, because it presumes that continuity and change are objective conditions. For instance, Francesca Merlan (1998) begins her ethnography of the Australian town of Katherine by observing that most studies of social and cultural change in Aboriginal Australian societies presuppose an original social form that has been transformed.[3] Moreover, as the Australian state seeks to recognize Aboriginal communities, it too establishes a historicism of loss as the condition for self-determination. The state demands that Aboriginality "create its innerness out of its past" because this serves the interests of Australian multicultural nationalism in which the state only recognizes indigenous peoples as rural custodians of natural landscapes (Merlan 1998, 233). Against this, Merlan argues that in fact many indigenous communities reproduce their distinct cultural schemata through the materials they find in settler culture. The categories through which the indigenous subject understands herself in the contemporary multicultural state are formed through participation in spaces of settler culture. Out of their engagement with town spaces, for instance, indigenous people are able to establish an identity and membership in a distinct order. Yet these new forms of Aboriginality are marginalized because the dominant discourse of liberal multiculturalism recognizes indigenous persons only insofar as they are attached to traditional sites of occupation. As an alternative to the historicist picture of Aboriginality, Merlan writes an account of people's lives under conditions of interculturalism: that is, in which people make use of new media to realize particular visions of belonging, and in which these appropriations are valued for their double character, as evidence for both continuity and change (Merlan 1998, 231; see also Merlan 2005).

We can draw out a more general implication from this point. If we look at intercultural situations as sites of alternative forms of political and social agency rather than as evidence for a certain kind of historical change, then we must acknowledge also that people produce their own knowledge of themselves which informs their agency. This reflexive knowledge of the self is, however, not reducible to an inheritance from the past. Rather, intercultural situations create what I call a postcultural kind of consciousness. I want to give this term a very specific meaning which differs from others' uses. In her study of contemporary postcolonial Fiji, Karen Brison argues that people now live in a "postcultural world" (2007, 135; see also Rollason 2014, Trouillot 2016). By this she means that contemporary Fijians can move among a variety of social identities beyond those provided by the indigenous cultures of their birth. Rather than deriving a sense of self from networks of kinship, people now can draw on religious and national discourses as new frameworks in which to locate themselves. They can claim a self which is an integral part of a community, or which is an autonomous individual. I would like to take Brison's ideas in a somewhat different direction. Like Brison, I believe that one's sense of self is not innate but contingent. One's sense of self derives from one's practical involvement in specific situations and relationships. Moreover, one understands oneself as a self in terms of a narrative one has learned to tell about these specific situations. Yet, unlike Brison, I want to emphasize that these narratives are all equally incomplete. In many intercultural situations, it thus becomes possible for people to question the standards by which certain situations are read as instances of any cultural category or pattern. A postcultural consciousness involves not only reframing one's experiences in terms of new narratives but also establishing new criteria for what counts as continuity and what counts as change. Rather than choosing to tell a story of either one's traditional, collective self or one's modern, individual self, a postcultural consciousness creates new kinds of selves not yet foretold in any one specific narrative schema.

Scholars of contemporary societies have come to grips with one aspect of this phenomenon. As the twentieth century drew to a close, intercultural encounters revealed themselves to be more than a movement from tradition to modernity or the domination of one culture by another. In the face of multiple modernities, many posited flux, creativity, and disorder as defining elements of a new, postmodern condition and moved away from an analysis of people's experience in terms of total social systems (Kopytoff 1986; Hannerz 1987; Appadurai 1996; Ong 1999; Tsing 2009). We have not yet come to grips with the other, bigger part of postculturalism. As horizons converge, those who live in intercultural spaces not only have new ways of seeing themselves but now must themselves occupy several different kinds of historical consciousness in order to establish any one shared narrative of their collective self. We confront not worlds colliding but a shattered mirror.

For Auhelawa, the contemporary world is one of sens (change), but no single change can claim to be preeminent. Loss, continuity, domination, and transformation are all potential outcomes of sens, but the current course is still uncertain.[4] Auhelawa must produce their own social theories as a condition for their own belonging. Like the nineteenth-century burghers discussed by Charles Tilly, Auhelawa conduct their own "commonsense analysis of change" in the course of their everyday life (1984, 3). Tilly argues that the emerging bourgeoisie generalized from their experiences of rapid urbanization and industrialization to construct an understanding of society as a total system that would itself develop over time into a more complex, rational form. This commonsense analysis, he says, laid the foundations for twentieth-century social theory and its particular bias toward society as an integrated whole whose mechanisms operate at different scales. Likewise, to tell the story of what it means to be Auhelawa, people must decide the ways in which their own local histories can be fit within the scale of other people's global histories as Auhelawa have learned them. However, like many societies in PNG, Auhelawa's intercultural encounters have been diverse and uneven. Each situation requires them to engage in different kinds of reflexivity about the relationships between events and structures in order to arrive at a conclusion about where this sens is headed. No one single narrative of change, even those they have inherited from Western culture, can completely account for their present intercultural condition. In this book, I move among the different sites at which Auhelawa people produce knowledge of themselves by piecing together images, artifacts, and narratives. In spite of contradictions among these frameworks, they find ways in which these contrasting accounts can also resonate and reinforce one another. In the rest of this introduction, I sketch my main analytic lens, a general model of consciousness and agency as an emergent feature of communicative processes and practical activities, and explain why this leads me to my idea of a postcultural consciousness. The concept of a distributed consciousness has deep and tangled roots in social and cultural theory, so I want to take some time discussing the various forms it has taken. Following this, I give a brief overview of the subsequent chapters.

Indigenous Models and Social Theories

If a postcultural consciousness involves not only redefining oneself but also generating one's own ethnographic knowledge, this raises a question of long standing in anthropology. What relation, if any, does indigenous reflexive knowledge have with an ethnographer's models of social life? When, for instance, Marcel Mauss cites Eldson Best's quotation of Tamati Ranapiri for his concept of a *hau*, or "the spirit of things," it serves to dramatize the gap between the sociocentric logic of reciprocity and Western individualism (1990 [1925], 11; see also Clifford 1981). When Bronislaw Malinowski attributes the statement "He conducts his *Kula* as if it were *gimwali*" to an unnamed, presumably typical man of Kiriwina, it creates an ethnographic *effet de réel* (1932 [1922], 96; see also Marcus and Cushman 1982). Anthropologists have often had an ambivalent attitude toward indigenous models. Even if one accepts that these kinds of statements are representative, one can still see that these moments of indigenous self-observation are always placed in subordinate relation to the ethnographic observer's own categories of analysis. Malinowski argued that kula traders, in spite of this kind of talk, were themselves unaware that their partnerships formed a ring of islands, or that there was anything enduring in their exchanges (1932 [1922], 83). Tamati Ranapiri's statement is valuable to Mauss only as an example of a moment in which an individual becomes "sentimentally aware" of his place in a social totality (1990 [1925], 80). Ranapiri's apperception of social forces is, in the end, mediated by the collective representations of his society. Thus the statement is only a symptom of the fact that society thinks through the individual. As Claude Lévi-Strauss notes, both the native model and the anthropologist's own sociological model are equally removed from "unconscious reality," the deep structure of social relations, which comparative analysis should aim to elucidate (1963, 282). It would seem then that ethnographers do nothing more than appropriate indigenous voices as poetic aphorisms that confirm their own conclusions.

There is another possible perspective on indigenous models of society. Rather than appropriating the indigenous voice, one could argue that indigenous models themselves have causal efficacy. If actors themselves perceive certain relationships between normative ideas and patterns of action around them and establish this relation among them, then this order comes into being. For Harold Garfinkel (1988), the most important aspect of human social behavior is that it is "naturally accountable." That is to say, when an actor performs a particular action, she does so in ways that make it available to be seen as a response to and part of a specific type of social situation. Gregory Bateson (1972) takes this argument farther when he describes social formations as an "ecology of mind." For Bateson, individual actions are signals in an extended cybernetic network. Individual minds play a specific function within this ecology. They receive signals from other nodes in the network, then translate them into a picture of the network as a whole oriented toward a goal or ideal. The picture of the present state of affairs in the mind of the actor—a narrative or a metaphorical image of what is going on—informs the actor's own actions and thus feeds back into the system, reinforcing a particular pattern (Bateson 1958). A good example is when people form a line while waiting for service. In facing front, each new person entering the line indicates to all that the person ahead will be served first. The reading of lines as an order of precedence is not an abstract idea that exists apart from the world it describes. Rather the collection of people in the line is itself a representation of the order of precedence in its doing.[5] The analysis of action by actors is, then, what makes social actions effective, and social forms real.

Bruno Latour's (1993) theory of actor-networks also inherits this line of thinking. For Latour, scientific knowledge is created through the assembly of a network of information signals among human and nonhuman agents, mediated by objects in which the signals of one actor are transcribed and translated into codes that can be read by another. Rather than representing the world as it is, scientific observation intervenes in, elicits, and captures the combined agency of nonhuman agents. Scientists attribute these effects to entities that exist in a distinct domain of natural forces. Scientific observation identifies microbes, for example, as a source of pathology but erases the socially produced conditions that are conducive to their spread. In so doing, science attributes epidemics to the breakdown of social control, rather than seeing them as a symptom of structural domination. By the same token, social situations involve a variety of different kinds of agency, both human and nonhuman, that respond to and build on each other. Latour notes that a defining characteristic of such situations is their uncertainty; since all action is connected to and relies on others, it can never be stated in absolute terms who is doing what. Indeed, Latour (2005) argues, social scientists themselves intervene in these processes and select specific kinds of agency as being intentional, and thus being properly social, as opposed to being natural, emotional, or just random accident. If history weighs on the brains of the living, it is then because historians (or people who think like them) have provided a story that links the present to the past. If social forces constrain individual agents, then this is because these forces have been perceived as social in essence.

These approaches suggest that when anthropologists substitute their own analysis for that of the native, they blind themselves to what kind of life people actually produce for themselves. Like Garfinkel and Bateson, Roy Wagner (1991) suggests that the meaning of social action lies in its reception by observers rather than the intentions of actors, and from this he concludes that Western ethnographers of New Guinea Highlands societies misunderstand the forms of social order that Highlanders perceive in their own actions. For instance, when early ethnographers found scattered settlements, shifting residential patterns, and competitive leadership they read them as indicators of fluid social categories, as if some people were somehow less subject to social forces of integration (Wagner 1991). Marilyn Strathern (1988) develops Wagner's ideas. Like Wagner, she argues that ethnographers of Melanesia look for agency in the wrong places, attributing action to individual intentions rather than taking into consideration the network of relationships that a Melanesian actor would assume as a frame of reference and would use as a way of understanding her own and others' intentions. Both Wagner and Strathern foreground a sense that in many Melanesian societies a social actor is seen as a social microcosm, rather than being a unitary individual who occupies a place within a collective social order. Instead of assuming that individual actors are constrained by social forces, people attribute actions to relationships in which the person is always enmeshed. Individual bodies are, furthermore, the medium for these relational agencies. Strathern (1999), for instance, argues that big men are not leaders in the sense of being a particular type of social actor but people whose actions offer themselves to be read as a model of social reality at a given moment. The big man's organization of a major prestation to a rival through individual ties of exchange allows people to see these ties, and hence themselves, in a new form—as a unity, if only in the moment of the display of their gifts to their big man as an ensemble that is presented to his rival. Exchange events are a fractal image of the whole, to use Wagner's (1991) term, and social processes of cooperation consist of converting one image of the total state of social relations into another.[6]

Marilyn Strathern suggests that "scholars trained in the Western tradition cannot really expect to find others solving the metaphysical problems of Western thought" (1988, 3). Given this, she argues, anthropology must turn away from the latent assumptions about reality in Durkheimian sociology and, in particular, the conceptual dichotomy of individual and society. Émile Durkheim's theory of society treats the individual mind as raw material or as a medium onto which the thoughts of a collective mind, or social constructs, are inscribed. If there are forms of human sociality that cannot be comprehended by this framework, then, Strathern and others argue, anthropology needs a new ontology of social life. To find it, ethnography must proceed from an exegesis of people's own images of their world (Strathern 1988, 17). Eduardo Viveiros de Castro draws out one particular implication from this. Rather than confining itself to the study of people's beliefs about the world, anthropology should claim back the study of existence itself and contribute to a more inclusive ontology which admits the possibility that there is more than one kind of mind or consciousness. That is to say, he suggests that human minds, enmeshed in different kinds of networks, can participate in alternative forms of conscious being (Viveiros de Castro 1998; Viveiros de Castro 2004). Eduardo Kohn calls this an "ontological anthropology," which he defines as "the nonreductive ethnographic exploration of realities that are not necessarily socially constructed in ways that allow us to do conceptual work with them" (2015, 315). This kind of ontological anthropology would be one in which human difference itself cannot and should not be explained with recourse to a universal theory of the subject, even one based on an infinitely plastic mind and limitless capacity to acquire particular ways of seeing and thinking. Rather, in each environment people create themselves in irreducibly different terms.[7]

In an earlier era, David Schneider (1968) argued that commonplace anthropological theories of kinship themselves posited a specific concept of a person as defined by, on the one hand, essential attributes and, on the other, codes for conduct that followed from this basic substance. This was, he said, a peculiarly American (or modern, or Western) way of thinking about individuals as persons and relatives, and so, he suggested, there is no such thing as kinship except insofar as a culture represents persons in terms of a similar duality of substance and code. Today, arguments for an ontological anthropology make a similar kind of point: there is no such thing as culture except insofar as people posit a collective consciousness that constrains them as individuals. In some ways, this shift promises a privileged contact with alterity that some cultural anthropologists have long sought. In the ethnographic text, the logocentric aim of explaining society cedes to the encounter itself, and an authentic indigenous voice contributes directly to knowledge of humanity. Even among anthropologists who might be skeptical of such claims of radical alterity, it can still be said that ethnographic interpretivism has often had an ambivalent relationship to the project of social theory. The challenge posed by ethnographic description to other human sciences has always been to raise exceptions to universal rules and suggest possible forms of human experience that are difficult for scholars to imagine. Strathern's call for an exegesis of indigenous knowledge itself suggests this. And because these alternative models are not reducible to the collective representations of specific communities, they can be found potentially everywhere. Dividual personhood is not, in that sense, a trait of Melanesian cultures but a Melanesian theory (or perhaps a theory derived from Melanesia) of social life itself. Indigenous and other models of reality are, furthermore, alternative positions that the observer can take with respect to any situation or condition, each revealing and obscuring different aspects.

Ontological Alterity, Multiplicity, and Insecurity

While using ethnography as a source for empirical thought experiments is valuable, it still needs to be said that such experiments rest on a pact with the reader of the ethnographic text. The reader must commit to imagining an ideal native alone on a figurative, if not literal, island. This native spokesperson is entirely generic and exists only in the abstract. This imaginary native is often an icon of pure alterity, a perfect contrast to a similarly imaginary Westerner who analyzes the world in terms of a dualism of nature and culture. Ethnography in this mode can thus only contribute to a grand comparison of Us and Them. Yet if we take the premises of ontological anthropology seriously, then any one particular social order comes into being through an observer effect. What if ethnographic observation also has this effect? What if, more precisely, social actors employ their own ideas of difference in reading and accounting for the effects of their actions, and these models of difference also contribute to the form that people's actions create?

It would mean then that the nonreductive exploration of other people's ontologies could not be satisfied with making grand comparisons of Us and Them. We could not, for instance, conclude that Melanesian societies employ a Melanesian model of the person in contrast to Western societies' models of personhood.[8] If actors' own models feed into the form their actions create, then actors themselves can make the same kinds of grand comparisons too. For instance, while Auhelawa people frame their own worlds in terms of a map of small places, they recognize that this is not how dimdims see them. When they pass on ancestral names to children, they also recognize that these exist alongside children's other,

Christian names, and that these may have more currency, because they identify persons as unique individuals rather than kin. When one lives in intercultural spaces, analyzing one's actions always involves comparison, if not a choice between possible ways of being. Yet one of those possible ways of being, a liberal ontology centering on individual persons, is itself incomplete and contradictory as a map of social life. As such it never fully displaces the other possibility, the indigenous Auhelawa ways of analyzing action. Many intercultural spaces and contemporary situations are marked not only by ontological multiplicity but by a pervading sense of ontological insecurity.[9]

Marshall Sahlins argues that only when colonial domination results in humiliation will one's consciousness be completely redefined in terms of colonizers' values against those of one's own world (1992, 23). What I suggest here, and what I argue in this book, is that another kind of humiliation is possible (see also Schram 2016). In this second form of humiliation one's own sense of one's own being is cast into doubt, yet no single schema has yet become dominant. This is, I argue, where one finds a genuinely postcultural consciousness, an awareness of oneself not simply in an encounter with incommensurate categories of being but under conditions of both ontological multiplicity and insecurity. For instance, Matt Tomlinson (2009), writing about Fijian Methodism, describes how Christian ritual practices comment on the relationship between Christianity and the indigenous social order and thus, by extension, model the relationship between indigenous Fijian and globalized Western cultures in terms of a historicism of loss. The trauma of colonialism itself can be seen in the symptoms of many similar "colonial neuroses" (Sartre 1963, 18). What I feel is not appreciated enough, though, is that there can be creative and productive responses to ontological insecurity that go beyond simply reestablishing security, in either indigenous or settler terms.

These are, for example, the kind of responses Ilana Gershon (2012) finds in the transnational Samoan diaspora. She argues that diasporic Samoans reflexively produce their own versions of Samoanness in shifting ways depending on the institutional requirements and social expectations. For instance, in the context of seeking assistance from social service agencies, it becomes important for actors to present themselves as Samoan by virtue of their heritage and descent from Samoa—that is, as people who are defined by their origins and thus their difference. At other times they constitute their membership in this same category through fluency in Samoan, awareness of protocols of rank, or their remittances to overseas relatives. Gershon defines reflexivity as "the shifting social analysis that is specific to the social order one is committing (or forced) to enact" (2012, 167). In many ways this conception of consciousness resonates deeply with the general skepticism in contemporary social inquiry toward a model of the subject as an autonomous, rational individual. It echoes, for instance, the kind of reflexivity that Pierre Bourdieu (1977) argues the agent acquires through her habitus, and that which Anthony Giddens (1979) finds in processes of structuration. What these past approaches perhaps lack, though, is Gershon's attention to the capacity for people to pull together an alternative account of how their own social worlds work and how they fit into these social situations in particular ways, thus creating various maps of an uncertain territory.[10]

It is not merely cross-cultural encounters that are produced in this way. All social situations in some way draw on the capacity of action to comment on itself, and thus to render the flux of activity into a recognizable shape containing specific kinds of subjects and objects. For instance, in her study of addiction treatment programs in Chicago, E. Summerson Carr (2011) describes their reliance on an ideology of "inner reference" (4), which demands that program clients must show themselves to be "honest, open and willing" (1)—or to perform a transparent, sincere self—in order to qualify for social benefits. In interviews with her, however, clients explained how they learned to "flip the script" on treatment itself, or to deploy signs of sincerity in order to draw social workers into specific kinds of relationships (Carr 2011, 194). For instance, when a therapist described the program as a process by which clients earned greater autonomy as they demonstrated greater responsibility, a client countered by presenting herself and other clients as engaged in a process of rebuilding lives from scratch, learning to do things over again, and thus requiring a sustained commitment from the program over time (Carr 2011, 36). Because her audience of staff members recognized her in that moment as subjectively committed to her own personal responsibility, and thus deserving of aid, they also had to recognize that this entailed their obligations to her. Carr argues that when clients engage in script-flipping, they too participate in the same ideology of sincerity but negate the way this ideology isolates them.

In each of these situations, actors reflexively reconfigure the networks that produce them as agents, as subjects, and as bearers of particular identities. Their reflexive knowledge of themselves is not innate. Rather they achieve it by exploiting the possibilities of action's own natural accountability or inherent capacity to comment on itself in its doing. Awareness of oneself as a particular kind of actor is what Webb Keane (2015) calls the "ethical life" of the subject. For Keane, this ethical consciousness is not only socially and culturally conditioned but emerges in interaction and, in particular, through the metacommunicative dimensions of all action, or what Garfinkel calls its "natural accountability." If ethical subjectivity is a collaboration, then postcolonial ethical life is particularly fraught. In Papua New Guinea, many devices offer themselves as sites for achieving different kinds of reflexive awareness of one's individual self and one's place in a sociohistorical narrative, yet none of them seems completely secure. Auhelawa people today cannot orient themselves toward either a past horizon of tradition or a future horizon of modernity, and so they must bring together many different devices in order to make sense of who they are and where they are going.

Overview of Chapters

In the chapters to come, I examine several different situations that involve Auhelawa people in specific kinds of reflexivity about their collective order and its relation to other peoples and places. I am interested in showing how different situations call on them to make use of particular frameworks about them, and how people deal with the limits of each of these practical modes of consciousness. Given this focus, there is no need to start with any particular topic as an origin or foundation of contemporary Auhelawa life. The beginning of the Auhelawa story depends entirely on not only who is telling it but what practical problem the story helps them to solve. So instead of telling of life before their first contact with Australian colonial officials or Polynesian missionaries, I begin by looking at several key sites of everyday life that involve people in different kinds of calculations of their identities and relationships.

In the first chapter, I ask how Auhelawa establish their knowledge of a collective order based on matrilineal groups. Settlement in this region is highly dispersed, and people consider themselves related through common matrilineal descent and shared totemic affiliation to a number of groups in various places and on different islands. In this fragmented social landscape, burial sites anchor people to places as members of descent groups. Yet in looking to these sites as symbols of a corporate identity, people find them to be incomplete. As places of memory, they are indecipherable without expert knowledge of the history of their lineage. Yet when they turn to a historical framework to learn how to read these signs, they come to see themselves not simply as members of groups but also as part of a broader regional network that spread through migrations from place to place over generations. In this chapter I show how people draw on narratives of migration and reciprocal services of burial to constitute themselves as members of solidary groups of "one blood" and members in a regional network of bu'una (matrilineal relatives). Although people's belonging to place seems at first glance to rest on symbolic actions, people need to rely on another epistemic framework in order to establish why such symbols have any meaning, and why any one identity is credible. Kinship itself, I argue, rests on forms of reflexive sociality, or social behaviors that allow people to see themselves as relatives and as members of a common social order. To realize matrilineal belonging, people must construct a boundary between nature and knowledge, finding ways to read their villages and graves as traces of the past and thus establish that their descent is a natural fact.

The second chapter introduces another dominant frame for social interaction which they term "respect" (*ve'ahihi*). This primarily characterizes the relationship between cross-cousins—that is, members of a matrilineage and the children of the male members of that lineage. To explain the codes of respect, Auhelawa say "You cannot eat your own blood," by which they mean that one must abstain from sharing what one gives to another. Thus in relationships of respect, mutual avoidance leads to mutual indebtedness and a cycle of balanced reciprocity. From this basic logic comes the template for mortuary feasting and communal ceremonies of all kinds. While people speak of their respect from cross-relatives as a rule, in many instances people have choices about how they observe it. When they account for their own and others' behaviors of respect, though, Auhelawa have to rely on many different frameworks for seeing the connection between symbolic interactions, on the one hand, and the relationship between those involved, on the other. While they posit the existence of social norms, they also recognize that these situations grant one person, the recipient of respect, a greater authority to decide whether another's actions should count as such. Given this view, I argue, we must examine feasting as another site where people collaboratively produce knowledge of how the social situation fits into a larger order. Codes of respect are, in that sense, another example of reflexive sociality. As I argue, these ritual actions do not merely conform to rules or deploy symbolic resources but themselves make one person into an object of another's moral evaluation. In this way both actor and audience work together to create a model of what their relationship should be.

Feasting is, however, increasingly suspect as a means to establish a moral vision of the social world. Today people say that feasts are smaller than in the past, and the cross-relatives who should exchange and respect each other now avoid these responsibilities. Auhelawa as a whole is becoming poorer. In the third chapter, I ask why it is that the apparently successful mode of subsistence in Auhelawa today appears to Auhelawa to be in jeopardy. Why do people need to read recent innovations in gardening practice in terms of a narrative of social and material decline? Part of the answer comes from Auhelawa's experience of Australian colonial administration, which attempted to intervene in nearly every aspect of life in the name of preserving native welfare. Beginning in the colonial period and extending to today, the state's concern for individual households and their resources has always clashed on some level with the ethic of interdependence underlying Auhelawa kinship. Why should the state's vision of the social world now be more credible? To answer this question, we must examine the kinds of thinking about material resources that are afforded by garden yam houses. Yam houses are where Auhelawa gardeners store their harvests, and where people can give their membership in a household as a unit of production a material form. It is here that women have introduced a number of agricultural innovations, especially new crops that are easier to grow and thus support larger families. Through counting and sorting their yams, women also hold up another kind of mirror to themselves. In the yam house, a woman can see whether she can feed her family, pass on yam seeds to her children, and successfully demonstrate respect in feast with gifts. I argue that when women curate their collection of yams, they produce a model of their social relationships to the members of their household and others. The full yam house is not simply a sufficient quantity of food but enough of the right kind of yams, which allow a woman to create an ideal picture of her relationships in the yam house and to be confident that she can enter into these relationships.

Auhelawa believe that they can no longer produce plenty of food because families have strayed from the discipline of traditional yam gardening in favor of introduced crops such as sweet potato and cassava. I argue that people can perceive poverty only through the lens of the yam house. Because introduced plants do not need to be stored and managed as yams do, they cannot be used as a medium for representing one's household in relation to circuits of exchange. Growing these lesser crops feeds people but cannot ensure the inheritance of land. The yam house thus serves as a material artifact in which women can create a representation of their household in the image of their food stores. The yam house is, moreover, a boundary object where women can reconcile two different readings of food as a sign of household economy, and therefore two different views of themselves as mothers. In one view, mothers produce food for reciprocal exchange. In another, they ensure their family's survival. The discourse of increasing poverty is in fact a critique of mothering as the nurture of children instead of the reproduction of the matrilineage.

Having introduced people's fear of increasing selfishness, the fourth chapter explores the way people frame their everyday uses of money through the concept of *gimwala* (buying and selling with money). Gimwala connotes a purely self-interested, asocial transaction. Part of Auhelawa people's fear of increasing selfishness is that people have become more oriented toward "finding money"—that is, earning a cash income from selling as opposed to participating in reciprocal exchange and sharing among kin. In this sense, gimwala and money itself serve as methods for interpreting patterns of action as disorder and change. The stigma of money, while similar in many respects to other societies on the fringes of global capitalism, is curious given that most if not all people in Auhelawa depend on cash to meet their daily needs. The task of earning money, and bearing the stigma of selfishness, falls to women as mothers. In this chapter, I argue that women distinguish their own cash earning from gimwala by acting in ways that make market trade resemble the patient work of the disciplined gardener. In that sense, they also reframe profit as a kind of harvest. However, I also show that by modeling their purses as yam houses, Auhelawa mothers also flip the script on the discourse of selfishness. If their earnings are a harvest of cash, then their consumption on behalf of their family is a new kind of moral selfhood that is not contingent on the obligations of exchange. The translation of money into the moral discourse of gardening thus does not subordinate commodity transactions to the value of reciprocity. I then look to the ways in which women further establish this new moral self in church fundraising events. By raising funds for a common cause, people exploit the capacity of money to quantify value as a sum, which thereby serves as a symbol of solidarity of a new kind of social group, the congregation.

Indeed, the Christian congregation is an important site for creating an alternative model of social order in Auhelawa today, and it sits uneasily with the other apparatuses by which Auhelawa people see their belonging. In chapter 5, I consider the ritual of collective Christian worship itself as a rival site for modeling society. The forms of worship are oriented by a metaphor of "one mind," by which people mean that they have a unity that is based on their subjective, interior commitment yet also manifest in their harmony and cooperation as a group. In this chapter it is important to know a little more about the history of contacts between Auhelawa and Christian missions. Auhelawa ways of reading their collective state through ritual reflect a longer story of struggles by worshippers to overcome a basic contradiction in Christian belief as a basis for social relations. When Auhelawa first encountered Christianity, missionaries wanted both to liberate them as individuals from what they saw as the prison of traditional society and create a new social order that would encompass the indigenous society. Missionaries searched for signs of inward change but also prayed for a "great ingathering" of all peoples. To mediate their contradictory aims, missionaries adopted a discourse of light and darkness to signify a new era. Auhelawa today make use of the same metaphor, but for a different purpose. They instead see Christianity as a separate, parallel domain of social behavior governed by the one mind of the congregation as opposed to the selfishness of everyday life. They imagine that the sign of true individual commitment to the church can be seen in the collective action of the congregation. They enact this vision in the weekly cycle of the Sunday service and Bible reading and interpretation, which situate the event of Sunday worship in relation to a world-historical narrative. Yet in using regular Sunday worship as a site for eliciting the congregation,

Auhelawa people find themselves constantly unable to achieve the pattern they believe is sufficient for producing this group. The same contradictions between belief and practice are deferred by their form of worship, not overcome. They come closest to seeing themselves as both individual Christians and as a Christian community not in church but during the annual freewill offering, *mulolo*, when each member contributes cash to a collective sum in the name of the church. The harvest metaphor, taken out of context, again proves useful for imagining alternative modes of belonging.

In the sixth chapter, I look further at the ways people constitute themselves as members of a shared order through Christianity. Having concluded that the conception of a congregation as "one mind" does not offer sufficient grounds for the establishment of a new social order, I reconsider this problem in the context of contemporary mortuary feasting. When planning mortuary feasts, it is common for hosts to assert that they will not accept mourning gifts but will instead host a shared meal for all the relatives of a deceased. No respect relationships will be observed among feastgoers, therefore. The rationale for this change is that Christianity requires that everyone come together as equal members of one group, and Christian belief entails overturning the *kastam* (traditional rules) of respect and exchange in mourning. This kind of new feasting, called *masele* (light, as opposed to darkness), while simple in theory, is difficult to realize in practice. In many feasts today, the participants cannot agree on the significance of their acts of mourning. Their social interactions are indeterminate even when actors explicitly impose their preferred reading of the events as based on either respect or unity. I examine several examples of mourning and the ways in which people work to impose one reading of mourning over another. In particular, masele, defined by the absence of overt acts and the suspension of rules of conduct, induces a crisis of signification yet does not lead to any new form emerging. In order for Christian feasting to be possible, people have to find various ways to make room for the performance of its opposite.

In the conclusion of the book I explore how the various arguments intersect. Each chapter examines a situation that facilitates a particular kind of reflexivity on people's actions as part of a whole. Each situation occurs in its own space and time and thus figures events as part of a narrative that is more or less incompatible with other possible ways of explaining change. Auhelawa can see their lives in relation to traditional norms but also believe that traditions have lost their authority. Conversely, they can also see themselves in relation to the categories of the state and its rationality, and yet the state's narrative of modernity itself lacks credibility. Indeed, this dilemma is, in fact, quite common throughout PNG and underlies many public debates. What kind of political actors can postcultural subjects become? To answer this question, I argue that we should see PNG politics in relation to the inherent limits of the liberal model of citizenship. In claiming to be independent, liberal, modern societies, postcolonial nations have had to deal in their own ways with the challenge of multiculturalism. Unlike many African societies, PNG embraced its cultural diversity but defined difference in ethnographic terms. Since then, however, the contradictions that emerge when one's own political community depends on another culture's expert knowledge have come to the fore. Many different actors are trying to reclaim the epistemic authority over difference that has been ceded to a particular kind of ethnographic imagination. Other actors seek instead to displace the question of who can define the terms of political recognition within the public sphere and create a new kind of postcultural politics based on multiplicity instead of a liberal conception of cultural diversity. I argue that the ontological insecurity felt by Auhelawa today can also itself be a basis for a more inclusive postcolonial polity.

1

NATIVES AND TRAVELERS

New Home

Looking east across the water from the eastern cape of the New Guinea mainland, Kehelala, one sees the mountains of Hobiya and Lomabubu towering over the coastline of the island of Duau (Normanby), typically shrouded in clouds. The ridges of the mountains extend down to the water at several points, and the inland hillsides appear to be folded like a thick curtain of forests. As one approaches Duau by boat, one begins to see a patchwork of square garden plots on the lower slopes of the ridges, each in different stages of cultivation. Along the pebble beaches, one sees small settlements, each consisting only of a few houses built from sago palms and forest hardwood sitting on wide gravel lawns and terraces cut into slopes of the steeper hills. These settlements form a nearly continuous chain along the coasts of Duau, interrupted only by rushing rivers and stands of tall coconut trees. Chains of small villages can be found over most of Duau, and many other neighboring islands in this part of Milne

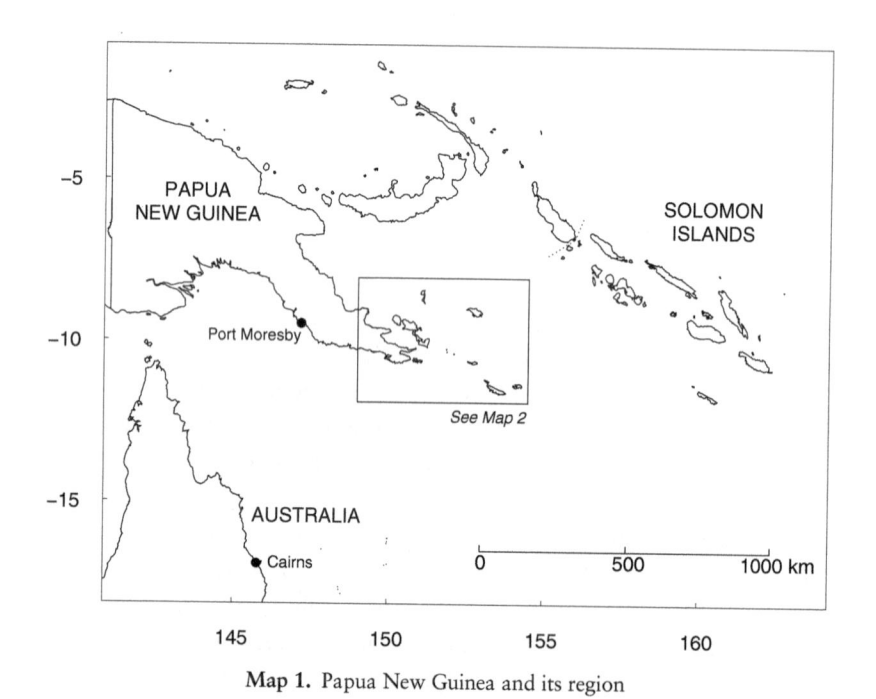

Bay Province, Papua New Guinea (Maps 1 and 2). This book is about a few links in one of these chains, the people who live under the mountain Hobiya and speak a language they call Auhelawa.

In 2004 and 2006, I was given permission to live among the residents of one of the villages of Auhelawa. I wanted to become part of this community in some small way and learn how the people there had responded to the economic and social transformations of Papua New Guinea. Members of the local Catholic parish committee suggested I stay with a couple, Francis and Lucy Pade, who had recently settled in Lucy's natal village Alogawa after they retired from their jobs as schoolteacher and nurse, respectively. Lucy had chosen a site a little ways up the hill from the beach near a creek, and the couple paid a local soccer team to clear the brush and lay down gravel to create the new village. She chose the name "New Home" for her small compound within Alogawa. This is where I lived.

There are actually a few places in Auhelawa with English names. The side of one bay is nicknamed Ela Beach after the site of the yacht club

Map 1. Papua New Guinea and its region

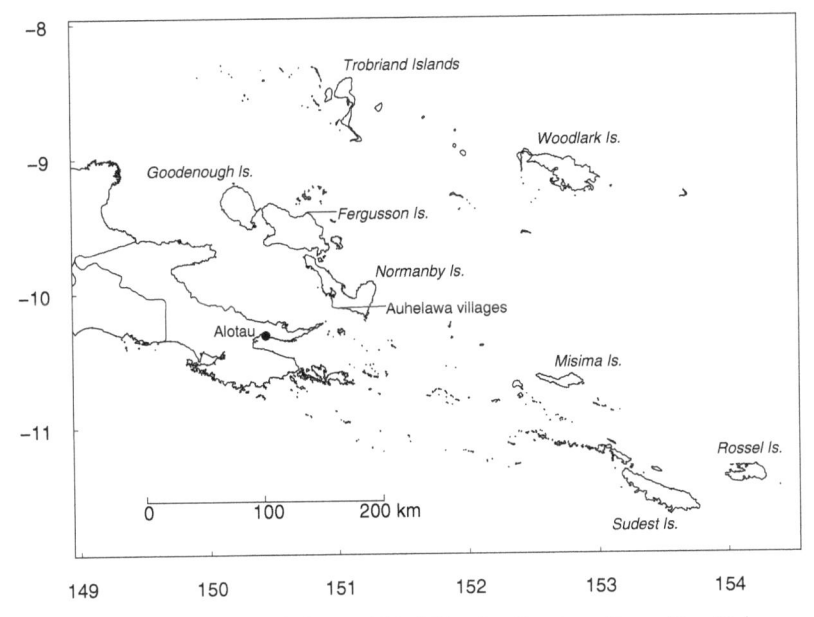

Map 2. The location of Auhelawa within Milne Bay Province, Papua New Guinea. National Statistics Office of Papua New Guinea.

in the national capital Port Moresby. Another small group of houses is named Top Town after a suburb in the provincial capital town, Alotau. New Home's name was not chosen on a whim, though. After I had been living with Francis, Lucy, and their adult children for a few months, I learned that Lucy named it after another small, recently established village on the mainland, near Kehelala. The people of Alogawa tell a story—their *tetela* (history)—of their village's founding by a woman who left Kehelala with her brother several generations ago and settled on Duau. Another Auhelawa village adopted them and allowed the migrants to live among them. Later, with their permission, the migrants founded a new village on empty land nearby. The matrilineal descendants of the woman from Kehelala, including Lucy, her siblings, her children, and her sisters' children, together form a matrilineal group called a susu, which lives together in Alogawa and makes gardens on the slopes of the adjacent inland hills. Members of the Alogawa susu inherited their own names from the founder, her brother, and, people say, her ancestors in Kehelala. Meanwhile, another line of matrilineal relatives has continued at Kehelala.

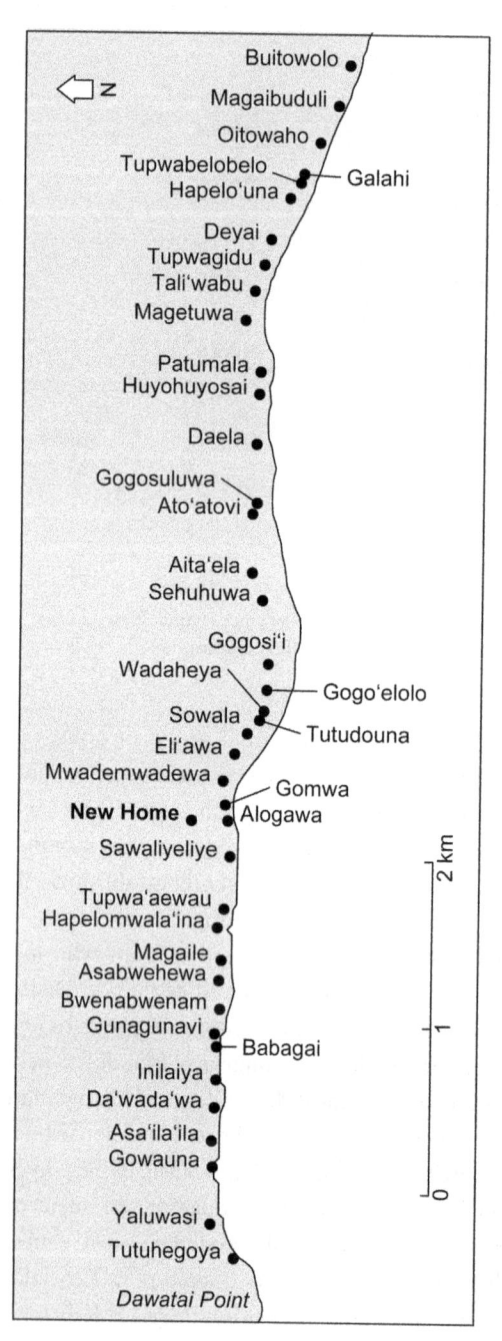

Map 3. Some of the villages in Kurada Ward, Normanby Island. Author's observations and National Statistics Office of Papua New Guinea.

During her travels as a nurse, Lucy had a chance to visit these people, and she confirmed her susu's tetela of migration and descent; she and another susu at Kehelala had the same genealogical ancestors. For Lucy, this makes her susu and the Kehelala susu related. They are not members of a single corporate group, but they recognize in each other common descent from the same origins, and they have the same matrilineal blood. They are, as Auhelawa say, bu'una. Before she retired from nursing, whenever Lucy was passing through Kehelala, she would visit her remote relative, her bu'una, to keep the relationship alive. To maintain this tie in the future, Lucy wanted to memorialize it. The Kehelala people lived in a village called New Home, and so when she and Francis returned to Alogawa, she named the compound they built New Home too.

Flash forward to 2014. I have come back to Alogawa to see Francis, Lucy, and everyone I knew from my previous visits. Simon Peter, a man from the susu at Dawatai Point, comes to welcome me back and to ask for my help. He tells me that he wants me to help him apply for historic status for one of the forest shrines high on the slopes above his susu's land. An anthropologist surveying the susu of this area as part of a social impact study sponsored by mineral prospectors once told him that the site was possibly ancient and should be preserved. Simon says he thought it could be worth millions, but he isn't interested in making money. As a leader in his susu, and someone who had a lengthy career in the PNG public service, he thinks it is his responsibility to create something to pass on to his sister's children. This shrine holds the skulls of his susu's ancestors, and because bu'una can share burial sites, it also holds many of the ancestors of their bu'una. If he did not find a way to preserve this site, he feared that this knowledge of the past would be lost. The younger members of the susu do not know the history behind it, who was buried where, and how people of Dawatai were related to them, and through them to each other and to many bu'una. If he did not protect this memorial, then he worried they might be unable to defend themselves against neighbors who wanted to claim their land. Creating a historic site, possibly with a village lodge for visiting tourists and researchers, would give the site a monetary value and make it worth keeping to today's generation. The cave must be preserved because it proves, he said, the tetela that Dawatai people tell of how they and others came to be there, and how they came to own specific lands there.

Auhelawa people are natives. Auhelawa people are also travelers. On the one hand, they belong to the villages where they were born. Sites like the shrine at Dawatai described by Simon are the material traces and memorials of a succession of generations of one susu. Yet on the other hand, many of the matrilineages of Auhelawa say that their ancestors traveled from other islands and founded new villages in the places they stopped. They now each maintain a network of bu'una links among the susu which resulted from this migration, just as Alogawa's susu does. People say that the Auhelawa language itself tells this story. It is quite different from the other languages on Duau, possessing many words that neighbors do not know but can be found in languages of other islands, at Kehelala, and on the New Guinea mainland. These are, like the names of villages and people, traces of the migrations of founders of many susu. The shrines that hold their ancestors also hold other people's ancestors as well, and thus people not only rely on the symbols of burial and memorial to connect them to particular places but also use narratives of their descent to see where their own natal group sits within a larger network of dispersed matrikinship.

As a principle of Auhelawa social organization, matrilineal descent allocates each person to one distinct susu. In that sense, descent is an essential identity based on one's origins. For Auhelawa, one's membership in a susu is strongly linked to the place of birth and tells one where one can build a house and grow food. As Auhelawa say, members of a susu are *boda ehebo* (one group) and *'wahi ehebo* (one blood). As such, the people of one susu say that they must always help one another and share what they have with one another, treating all their fellow members as a distinct class of kin. Unlike one's relationship with one's father's susu, governed by protocols of deference and avoidance, including the obligation to exchange reciprocal gifts in mortuary feasts, one's conduct toward matrikin is *besobeso* (heedless, casual) and *awawa'uhi* (lazy, purposeless). In this very simple sense, the social structure derived from a categorical distinction between those who were naturally related and all others who were not, and thus strangers (Fortes 1969). Furthermore, a person belonged to exactly one clearly delineated group and hence could see exactly how other people were related to him- or herself (Fortes 1953).

Yet one's susu is also understood to be one branch among many, each of which has over time drifted away from the origin and spread out to other islands to build new villages. So Auhelawa matriliny also includes being part of a network as well as a distinct group. Several different susu in several different places also see themselves as one (*ehebo*), yet in a different sense. These groups regard each other as bu'una. Although they each trace the descent of their members from different founders, they see their relationship to one another as based on a common essence. So they pledge to offer aid to one another freely, as if they were one susu. In the past, this took the form of visits for subsistence trade and even offers of land on which to settle (for instance, in the case of drought), as well as reciprocal namesaking of people and villages and exchanges of burial services. Yet on closer inspection, the two forms of matrikinship, group and network, blend into each other. These nodes in the network say they are one group because they have the same (*taliya*) origins, that is, they can discover parallel lines of connection in their histories. This kind of relationship of shared origins, or bu'una, connects several different susu within Auhelawa and in many other places throughout the region.

In this chapter, I introduce the people who call themselves Auhelawa and describe the spaces that organize their everyday life and their relationships to one another. I also argue that what it means to be Auhelawa is itself fundamentally ambiguous. Establishing one's own identity as Auhelawa requires that one bring together a metaphor of place and a metaphor of migration to determine where one belongs and how one is related to others. Neither group nor network provides a complete account of one's membership on its own. Every Auhelawa belongs to one susu, a group of people who are one because they have the same essential characteristics. The burial places of a susu, like the shrine at Dawatai, embody the connection of this group to a specific place and of people to one another through their shared descent. Yet, as I discuss below, this symbolization of matrilineal kinship proves to be incomplete because many people do not know how to read these monuments. Their identity must be supplemented by the narrative history of one's susu and its migration through the region. When one considers what it means to be Auhelawa, what is at issue is not so much a specifically Auhelawa sense of the meaning and value of kinship, but the fact that there are many different ways by which people can read their relationships and their place in the world in terms of a kinship order, none of which is complete on its own. Hence being Auhelawa means learning to read signs of one's relationships through a variety of lenses, particularly monuments of place and memorials of history. Let us begin as I did, and take a walk through Auhelawa.

Graves and Homes

As I settled into my new home in 2004, Kevin Edahosi offered to tour me around the neighboring villages and eventually composed a map for me. On these tours, we walked along a coastal footpath that connected all the main settlements. We traveled as far as the border of the ward of Kurada, a division within the local-level government (LLG) area of Duau, a jurisdiction covering half of the island of Normanby.[1] As time went on, we went on even longer walks to new places, and I talked to people in the wards of Barabara and Bwasiyaiyai. Because I was at New Home, I became known as a child of Alogawa among susu throughout the area who had various ties of kinship, bu'una, and affinity with Alogawa. I mainly interacted with people from the approximately thirty susu living within Kurada Ward, although I was always aware that the boundaries of these wards were more or less arbitrary.

Seen from the perspective of these walks, the whole coast of Normanby is a loose collection of small places like Alogawa, called *gogo* (or by the synonymous word *dalava*), usually translated as village. The typical village is a block of flat land usually set back from the road and the beach. The ground is cleared of brush and trees and covered with a layer of smooth, gray pebbles and gravel taken from the beach. In the villages beneath the mountains, along the western side of Kurada, the land slopes steeply down to the water, and people cut into the earth to create terraces for their houses, buttressing them with neat walls of flat stones. On the plain, especially along the eastern side of Kurada from the Gogosi'i River to Buitowolo Point, villages are set far back from the road and other villages on wide lawns of gravel. Villages vary in size from one house to as many as five. Yet as Kevin and others pointed out, if a village became much bigger than this, one family would likely settle in a new place nearby on unoccupied land of the lineage, much as Lucy and Francis did when Lucy established New Home. Even within a single village, people prefer to spread out. In Alogawa, a relatively small, compact village, the families of Lucy, her sister, and her brother each lived in compounds on one side of a small creek. On the other side, descendants from another branch of the susu lived in their own compounds. A more typical pattern is found among larger susu. The adult children and grandchildren of one woman, with their spouses and children, might occupy one named village. All the people who descend from one matrilineal ancestor, usually the founder herself, are thus distributed into lineage segments, each occupying one or more named villages and gardening in the adjacent inland areas. The *bale'u* (land) of a susu consists of a collection of named territories, some used as residential sites and others for gardening.

As Kevin and I toured along the road, we also passed many areas overgrown with grass, usually in the vicinity of a village. Each one, Kevin pointed out, was a cemetery of a nearby susu. They and other places associated with burial of the dead, including the shrines in the forest, are called *magai*. Each maximal susu will have at least one such site where all the members will eventually be buried. Prior to the colonial period, a susu would detach the skull of a deceased member and place it alongside others in a shrine in the forest of their lands. The Australian colonial administration declared early on that the dead should be buried in the ground outside residential areas, and so now for over a century each susu has established at least one cemetery, with headstones of cement laid out in neat rows.

The sites along the route we walked were either gogo or magai. Respectively, places of each type represent the branches of growth and spread of the lineage and embody its corporate unity. People spend most of their daily lives in their gogo and in their gardens, and they tend to avoid magai. Although the lands of a susu are notionally collective property, in practice each person gardens in the places where their mother made gardens, inheriting her own individual *ebe towolo* (standing places) from her mother through a filial tie. Men pass on their own gardening sites in their natal villages to one of their sisters' children whom they nominate. When someone dies, however, the deceased's susu comes together near the magai to do the work of burial. In these moments, the people of one lineage relate to each other as "one blood" and children of "one woman." They are one group because they have the same origins and they all will also return to this place at death to be buried. Inevitably, though, with the passing of generations, women also create new villages and gardens and pass these on to their children. Through the cumulative work of a single line of descent, new places are made and a lineage spreads out from its origins.

Although they think of a susu as a corporate group, in fact, each person's real tie to the susu is inherited matrifilially. Garden and residential sites are determined by one's direct tie to one's mother and mother's brothers, and hence a person of another village of the same susu must ask permission to garden elsewhere on the susu's own lands. These and other formal requests for help (*hagu*), though conducted in a spirit of generalized reciprocity, are not true sharing. People choose whom they help based on judgments of the character of the one making the request, especially that person's own willingness to help others. Not everything is available as such a gift, either. Each married couple manages its own food gardens. Requests for food in the event of a bad harvest are rare and considered shameful. A woman plants her '*wateya* yams (*Dioscorea alata*), the principal gift in feasts, from a line of seeds she inherits from her mother and must tend them carefully every year, saving enough seed to replant again next year. Yam seeds are a useful metaphor for the growth of a lineage over time, in that sense. Yams propagate along a chain of women. A susu's yam harvest is not a collective good, and neither yams nor seeds are easily transferred among members. Auhelawa say that people should remember (*nuwatuwu'avivini*) their matrikin and their solidarity with one another. As time passes and a susu spreads out and fissions, people also say that they forget (*nuwapwanopwano*) the common ancestors of one group, effectively making them two new groups.[2] The magai of a susu thus hold this memory and allow people of many villages to see themselves as part of a larger unity.

Monument and Memorial

As someone nears death, her susu gathers in her natal village to prepare for her burial. Husband and wife periodically shift residence between each other's natal villages, and if a husband is living in his wife's village, he is taken to his natal village at this time. People talk about this as an *asiyebwa*, a word meaning a grave illness but used euphemistically to mean that the susu anticipates the immanent death of one of its members. During the period leading up to death until the burial, people of other susu avoid the village of the dying person, and a generally somber mood settles as word spreads from person to person. The word itself, usually uttered sotto voce, also implies this sudden shift into a period of ritual mourning. Death sets off a series of rituals, each accompanied by a feast, discussed in detail below. In this chapter I describe the relationship among death, burial, and people's sense of membership in a susu. When someone dies, the susu comes together as a corporate group to create and maintain the memorials of their relatives.

Although no longer practiced, the placement of skulls in a shrine, called a *totoleana* or *duluva*, remains salient for people today as a way to think about the relationship between death and the susu.[3] As Simon did in 2014, many people have offered to take me to their susu's duluva over the years and show me the skulls still held there. Often I would ask people about the cemeteries by the side of the road, but our conversation quickly veered to a discussion of exotic practices which my interlocutors had never witnessed themselves. In their view, I could not understand what people did today unless they explained what people had done in the past. As my interlocutors explained, the matrirelatives of the deceased choose several men from another branch of the same susu to serve as *galiyauna* (sextons). The galiyauna clean the corpse, and then place it in a shallow stone tomb within a circular platform of stones called a *da'eda'e* in the center of the main village of the susu. They cover the body with stones up to the neck, and cover the head with a clay pot. They then lie on the platform resting their own heads on the pot, listening for the sound of the body separating from the head. When the head detaches from the body, the galiyauna clean away the flesh from the skull with their teeth and wash the skull clean in the pot. The skull can now be enshrined as a memorial to the deceased as an ancestor of the susu. A party of galiyauna, accompanied by a senior woman of the susu, transport it to the cave. Most caves are located very far from the villages of the susu, deep in the forest above the land used for gardening. On the steep slopes of the mountain ridgelines, one finds many rock outcroppings. Skulls are usually placed in the deepest of these to shelter them. After the skull has been placed among the others, the party leaves, reciting poetic chants as they descend to farewell the spirits of the susu's ancestors, called *mwadimwadi*, who inhabit the forest around the shrine. (The mwadimwadi also hover near other magai of the susu, including modern cemeteries.)

The body is reburied in another small grave in or nearby the village with the bones of dead of the susu.

Even though this form of burial is no longer practiced, many people described what the galiyauna used to do in sensuous detail to me. An in-law of Alogawa, Simon's brother, Philip, liked to mime the actions of the galiyauna—lying with the corpse, tearing the flesh from the skull with his teeth, and so on—all with one eye on my reactions. Philip and other people who explained this procedure to me were quite clear that they wanted me to understand what it felt like to be a galiyauna, and hence why being chosen as a galiyauna demanded a sacrifice on behalf of one's susu mates. To act as a galiyauna is a supremely generous and noble service. When galiyauna sat with the body and prepared the corpse in the past, they could eat only burned garden food and were forbidden to eat meat. They drank only salt water, which was supposed to purge the germs they were said to acquire from contact with the body. Moreover, all others from other susu were forbidden to approach them because their contact with the corpse and grave made them part of the magai. When someone dies nowadays, galiyauna clear the brush from the susu's cemetery and dig a grave for the body. They build a coffin and, after a Christian service, take it to the cemetery to bury it. During this time, as in the past, the galiyauna become magai and observe the same food taboos. Some drink salt water also as a purgative, although there is much less direct contact with the deceased's body. During rites of mourning, the galiyauna sit apart, and others avoid contact with them. The mwadimwadi also hover nearby, and when the galiyauna carry the coffin from the village to the cemetery for burial, mothers of the susu bring their young children to the coffin to touch it, even ducking underneath the coffin between the galiyauna on either end with a toddler or baby in arms, to introduce the spirits to their children. Much later, when the susu has organized another mourning feast and purchased dry cement, the galiyauna return and erect a cement headstone over the grave. The name of the deceased is painted on the headstone, and the grave is covered with flowers. After they finish any work in the cemetery, the galiyauna receive gifts of meat, fine food, and shell valuables in honor of their heroic labors. The only way to fully repay one's debt to a galiyauna is by reciprocating the service when one's immediate matrikin dies. The galiyauna role is thus also part of a ceremonial partnership between segments of one matrilineage, knitting them together as a susu.

While the media of the memorial have changed, modern graves also attempt to preserve the memory of the person and locate the person as a member of the immortal susu. Even though these magai lie right along the main coastal road, people treat them with the same ambivalence as remote forest shrines. After the grave has been completed, the cemetery becomes overgrown and totally obscured from view. Owners of the cemetery don't want to see it, let alone enter it, because it will remind them of the people who have recently died. The only reason someone could have to enter a magai when there is no asiyebwa is, people say, to secretly ask the mwadimwadi there for magic. People gossip that young men hide out in magai when they want to brew homemade beer called "jungle juice" because they know they won't be disturbed. The very places and artifacts that represent the susu to itself often appear to people as mysterious ruins of a lost past. Their matrilineal kinship and their bu'una are all somehow stored in these sites, yet by being kept in this way, their significance is obscured and alienated from the people they represent. This is true for forest shrines as well. I found that many people had never visited their own susu caves. Trips to the shrines require one to announce one's presence to forest spirits, who are, in a mysterious way, also spirits of those buried there. The experience of the shrine is rare and special. When people took me to their own susu's cave, or explained to me the traditional ways of burial, they would often tell me that it was supposed to be a memorial to preserve the history of the susu and to establish its identity. Yet when I asked if they knew this history, most said they did not know the complete story and said they did not want to mislead me. That is to say, while they may have known most of it, they did not consider their knowledge to be authoritative because the "full story" had not yet been passed down to them yet (Briggs 1984, 15–16). Only a few elders of the susu, sometimes only one person, knew who was buried where, and how people today were related through descent to the skulls in the cave. These elders could narrate a story that identified the skulls. The elders also hold on to their information and selectively choose the place and time to impart it and the person to whom they entrust it. Basic knowledge of the susu's history is widely known in and outside the susu, but the exact details of how memorials link people to ancestors is not, and thus not really present as the context for everyday life. For example, although everyone agreed that totoleana are magai, and that the spirits of the ancestors hover near them, they did not agree on how the skulls in a shrine should be arranged. Some said that the skulls should be placed in neat rows, with each line representing a line of descent from one woman. Others told me that skulls are placed so that all of them are visible. What people mostly agreed on was that a new skull is placed in front of those that preceded it, and that skulls should be decorated in ways that make them identifiable. A susu will place a rare valuable like polished pearlshell or a stone ax blade next to the skull of a rich, important person's skull to signify its status. Also many people said that the spirit of such a prominent dead person enshrined in a cave could push away the other skulls. The spirit of a warrior would be strong enough to knock away all the other skulls near his skull to clear space for himself. When people visited shrines and found the skulls in disarray, this is how they explained it. No matter what one expected to find in a shrine, there was no guarantee that it would be there. Although recognized as symbols of the lineage as an immortal corporate body, shrines are mysterious. Like other magai, they sit on the periphery of people's everyday experiences. The information they are said to contain is assumed to be there, but they do not have personal contact with it, and hence their status as unambiguous evidence of a connection to place is uncertain.

Learning to See Kinship

Although people tried to show me how the Auhelawa social landscape was put together, I struggled to see it the way they did. A susu seemed to be a descent group localized in one or more villages. But what was the difference between branches of a maximal descent group, each also called susu, and a susu as a whole? What, furthermore, was bu'una and how was this category of relationship different from that of susu members? Matrilineal descent seemed to encompass both a sense of a corporate group and a dispersed network, but I could not see how these two distinct modes of relationship could be part of the same idea. When people explained to me why they told lineage histories (*tetela*), it became somewhat clearer. In light of this narrative of migration and descent, a susu appeared not as an enduring corporation but as the product of historical change. Susu were both structures for organizing relationships and nodes in a network that formed over time as branches split off, migrated, and settled elsewhere.

If I found the right people in each susu, I could learn the complete history of that susu and how it was connected to its bu'una lineages elsewhere. Each tetela began with the lineage's *ebe laoma* (origin, place where it comes from) and a story of how one or two people first left that place at some point in the past. In some ways, these stories of departure all seemed to be derived from a handful of mythic tropes. It was common to hear of a young girl who went out in a canoe or down to the beach and was swept away, arriving on a distant island shore, and then was adopted by a susu already living there. In other stories, people departed after a fight with their kinspeople over the distribution of meat. Still others were more matter-of-fact: "We left because of a famine" or "We ran away because we were raided by our enemies." Stories then proceeded to tell of where the susu settled, and some would note several places in a series, before finally telling of the arrival of one or more men and at least one woman in Auhelawa. This woman is the *mumuga* (founding ancestor) of the susu, and today all branches of the susu should be able to trace their matrilineal genealogical descent back to this one woman. The image created by these narratives of a wandering susu helped clarify how matrilineal descent could create both groups and networks.

Yet in another way, tetela raised new questions for me. When I began to ask to hear the tetela of each susu, I was thinking of them mainly as genealogies. I hoped that they would be mostly open to anyone who wanted to know them. While tetela are not secret, I quickly found that people wanted to know why exactly I needed this information. At the same time, many young and middle-aged men told me that they too had undertaken what they called research on their own susu to identify all the branches and bu'una with whom they shared graves. I thought that I was asking for a narrative account of the unilineal descent of a group. I assumed that this would be noncontroversial because it described something that people themselves presented as natural and unchanging. Yet once again I found that there was more at stake than the symbolic codes for people's social classifications. People believed membership in a susu was natural, but they also believed that their own knowledge of the basis for their membership could potentially be faulty. Thus they felt they needed to confirm it by collecting information. People assumed that one's bu'una could potentially be anyone, living anywhere, waiting to be discovered. Moreover, every single specific claim about a susu's history was open to challenge as "false" (*oyama*). When I asked about tetela, many people avoided the risk of being exposed and said they did not know the "full story." Some also insisted that other people "did not know their own history" and could only tell me lies, but they knew the truth. This is probably why, when a young man researches sources of new knowledge on his own descent, other people often call it "politics" (*politiki*). Like candidates for office looking for pledges of support, these men are asking not simply if two people are related, but that one will affirm the claim of relatedness by another. Even though what they sought to hear was supposedly a descriptive statement of a set of biological facts and historical events, exposing this information to specific people at specific times was controversial, since they could then take up that information into their own account of who belonged to which group and which groups were associated as bu'una.

Robert Hertz (2006 [1960]) argues that secondary burials, like the practice of detaching and enshrining the skull in Auhelawa, are a symbolic expression of the dead person's dual nature, the flesh representing the biological individuality which ends at death, and the bones symbolizing the society as an eternal structure (see also Metcalf and Huntington 1991; Bloch 1993 [1971]). Auhelawa people speak of their susu as one blood, meaning a perduring, unchanging unity. Their magai are sacred ancestral sites that symbolize the triumph of the susu over death itself (see Macintyre 1989). This view, however, requires one to make an assumption about the nature of kinship. For early British social anthropologists, the principle of unilineal descent is the foundation of social order because through it, every member of society is allocated to a specific position within a distinct, clearly bounded group, and this group is perpetuated throughout time through clear lines of succession (Radcliffe-Brown 1952 [1935]). Descent groups provide a permanent structure to society because the facts of kinship have, in a sense, the force of law. In such societies, one's social identity is determined absolutely by the filial tie to one parent, in Auhelawa, the mother. Yet when Auhelawa enshrined the skull of a fellow susu member, and when they today inter a body in a grave in their susu's cemetery, they may intend to create a symbol of their unity as matrilineal descendants of one woman, but they inevitably create another cipher of the past. Burial and enshrinement inevitably provoke questions about one's true matrilineal identity.

After the burial or enshrinement, the magai recedes from view. The connections that it symbolizes risk being forgotten by those connected to it. When people do encounter it as a site of memory, they may realize that they do not possess enough knowledge to understand how exactly this magai connects to them in particular. Through the decoration and arrangement of skulls in the shrine, or the creation and decoration of modern gravestones, a susu not only ties itself spiritually to a place but also tracks its history. Here one must rely on the tetela of the susu as a framework for deciphering the signs of identity. Notably, this framework does not posit ancestral presence nor sacred power in the usually forbidden sites of burial. Rather, the same sites are now read as an iconic trace of past actions. The magai and burials are evidence of the past, not sites for performing unity (Parmentier 1987). In this sense, a tetela figures the susu as a product of accumulated historical events but does not construct the susu as an abstract whole beyond those events. Matrikinship is still natural, but as a material fact about individual people. Because any bu'una of a susu can be enshrined or buried in its magai, over time each of these material symbols of susu unity becomes a palimpsest tracing the connections among different susu. Moreover, learning to see kinship in a historical frame also means relying on people who possess this history in full. In their perspective, the present susu and its villages and lands are merely an episode in an ongoing process in which the lines of susu and bu'una shift.

In the same way, although two susu may associate themselves with the same species of bird as a totem, this itself is not sufficient to make the two susu each other's bu'una. Of the seven species of birds that are totems in Auhelawa, most susu associate with one, *manihubu* (wedge-tailed eagle), yet not all of these susu regard all other manihubu as bu'una. They look instead to their lineage histories for common descent, use of common burial sites, shared migratory origin, the adoption of one's ancestor by another susu, or past agreements to serve as galiyauna or provide burial sites as different reasons for their bu'una relationship, which would most often entail having the same totem as well. For instance, Francis and Lucy each come from susu that associate with manihubu. When they went to the resident Australian Catholic priest to be married, he queried this. "I thought in your custom, people with the same bird aren't supposed to get married," he said. They happily replied, "No, we checked our stories. We are the same bird from different places, so we are not related."[4] That is, they confirmed that although their susu had the same totem, each told tetela histories that did not coincide. Francis's mother's susu originated from one place, and Lucy's another, and they had no magai in common. Likewise, two susu who pass on the same ancestral names to their children would also consider each other to have a remote matrilineal connection that would validate their bu'una. A totemic bird at first glance appears to be a symbol that stands for a category, just as magai are intended to create a material sign that stands for the idea of a permanent descent group. But like magai, a susu's totem cannot be reliably read in this way. It is at best a clue that two susu each possess the same characteristics derived from the same source in the past. The link between the bird as a sign and this category has to be combined with other evidence of matrilineal transmission and past actions to confirm this connection.

It may seem as though totemic categories are, if not a mode of symbolic classification of susu, a shorthand that people use to approximate more complex genealogical connections recorded in people's tetela and memorialized in burials and shrines. Indeed, the rule of exogamy that Francis and Lucy followed, and to which all marriages must absolutely adhere, is really based only on genealogical distance. If two people have no ancestors in common in each other's tetela, then they are considered unrelated and hence marriageable. As we have seen, bu'una is more than being related genealogically, and memorializations of bu'una through reciprocal namesaking (e.g. Lucy's relationship to New Home) are not simply reiterations of an existing ancestral tie, although people do think about them as being this. Galiyauna are taken from different branches of the same susu or a bu'una susu, and since this service is reciprocated, the institution of galiyauna reinforces a tie among matrirelatives that might otherwise be forgotten. However, one can also choose anyone who is not otherwise prohibited from entering one's magai (e.g., an affine or the children of men, called *natuleiya*) as a galiyauna, and this service would be reciprocated, tying two otherwise unrelated groups in a new relationship of bu'una.[5] In the same way, many tetela claim that a founder of one lineage was adopted by members of another, unrelated lineage, and that on this basis their matrilineal descendants not only each have the same totem but also are bu'una lineages. Moreover, bu'una relationships can be disrupted by marriages, which require the families of each spouse to treat the other as affines. Indeed, on rare occasions a susu can simply declare itself to have a different totem and enter into a relationship of bu'una with another susu of the same totem. In the one instance of this that I know about, this was decided simply because one small susu thought it was marginalized in the community without bu'una to support it. All this is to say that having a shared totem can really be reliably read only as a trace of one of many events in the past.

To see themselves as part of a descent group and social order based on kinship, Auhelawa people must learn to utilize two different frameworks for reading the signs of these relationships. One framework is based on place, like the villages, gardens, and burial sites where they live and work alongside their susu mates. Yet this proves to be incomplete on its own and calls forth another framework in which they see their kinship group as a product of change over time. Turning to the historical stories in which signs of kinship are read as evidence of past actions, though, is incomplete on its own as well, since these stories are not all universally known. While not secret, they are passed on selectively by those who know the full story of the susu and its burial sites. They pass on this information to junior relatives of their own choosing. More important, any one story of the susu itself can be forgotten and so must be associated with a material token as a memorial. These two frameworks are thus not simply alternative ways that people can relate to their own identity and position in the social order. People must learn to use both at once to see the full picture.

There is, moreover, a general principle underlying the movement between them. People reason logically about why particular signs can be read as evidence for shared matrilineal descent. When two strangers from different islands meet and discover that they, or their matrilineal relatives, have the same ancestral names, they infer that at some point in the past the original "owner of the name" transmitted this name matrilineally to each of their ancestors as that owner's namesakes. They may even be able to confirm the vertical transmission of this name through two separate paths by comparing their separate tetela. Even if they cannot trace these parallel lines through genealogical ties, they can still conclude that they are part of the same category, matrilineal relatives, and hence each other's bu'una based on the existence of the same inherited name alone. Auhelawa people use the term *taliya* to denote a logical identity. Their relationship of unity and mutuality—one blood, one group—is derived from their sameness (*taliya*). In the same way, separate susu can claim to be bu'una because each has a different ancestor enshrined in the same cave. They stand in a similar relationship to one cave as a sign of their descent from an ancestor, and this similarity supports the inference that they are the same in substance, even if they do not know the details of how they might be genealogically related. So too do separate branches of one susu, living in different villages but with one known founding ancestor, also see themselves as united as one blood. This also helps clarify the most curious form of bu'una. When I asked for a definition of bu'una, people would say that it meant "one group" but could be based on many things that two people shared, an ancestor, totem, or a migratory homeland. Then they would usually add that if two people's fathers were brothers, then they would be *taliya natuleiya*, children of different male members of the same matrilineal susu, and that too was a kind of bu'una. Certainly this kind of bu'una has nothing to do with matrilineal descent, real or putative. It is formally the same as other kinds of matrilineal bu'una. Each of these patrilateral parallel cousins stands in a similar relationship (*natuleiya*) to the same susu, and so they posit a oneness between them. Two taliya natuleiya each have to give their own gifts to their fathers' susu. They may also invite each other to be galiyauna for their own burials. Men and women who are taliya natuleiya are cautioned not to marry each other since this would make them and their siblings affines and hence eliminate any bu'una relationship. Their bu'una relationship is more than simply seeing the similarity and positing a relationship of unity as a representational construct. Once seen, it can potentially become like any other kind of bu'una. As already mentioned, other kinds of bu'una are not simply discovered either. Rather, like Lucy and the people of East Cape, the discovery is ratified by reciprocal namesaking, visits, and other acts to cement the tie of bu'una anew so that it will not be forgotten again.[6]

Some would argue that Auhelawa kinship is best understood not as a fixed, overarching structure but as the result of a process where people's individual symbolic actions, like namesaking, burial, and making villages, performatively create bonds among susu members (Carsten 1995). This would also explain why knowledge of a susu's tetela is so guarded. To tell the story and to use the story to decipher the monuments of the susu in the magai is in fact to legislate the membership of the susu and its bu'una. Auhelawa people may say that they help their fellow members of their susu and their bu'una, but in many cases it seems like their fellow members and bu'una are simply those to whom they extend help. Yet, such an approach to kinship must still reckon with the fact that Auhelawa and many other cultures regard the kin relationship as an objectively distinct kind of fact. Marshall Sahlins writes that "while people often decide what kinship relationships are appropriate to them, they do not thereby decide what is appropriate to their relationships" (2011a, 6). That is, although each culture symbolizes kinship in distinct ways, defining its own set of categories, everywhere one finds that some of these categories, whether achieved or ascribed, and whether distinguished by birth, residence, or food, these categories usually involve what he calls a "mutuality of being" (Sahlins 2011a, 10). For Sahlins, this ethos ultimately is what all forms of kinship have in common. It certainly applies to the Auhelawa belief in the meaning of their susu membership.

It would not be right to say that the Auhelawa kinship order is simply an universally known and unquestioned map of the social world, since people do challenge and contest what others claim, and hence whether relationships in fact exist. At the same time, people do not simply enter into agreements with others and seal with them symbols of kinship either. If kinship is a particular kind of mutual recognition of a relationship, it is neither given automatically nor achieved through intentional acts. Even the one rare case in which a susu changed its totemic bird and became bu'una to another susu would not have been successful if other people did not see this and accept it and its consequences as valid. Similarly, within one susu, members recognize each other as a specific kind of kin through a stereoscopic effect in which both people need each other's information in order to see the full picture and their own individual place within it.[7] To see the sameness on which the inference of oneness rests, one must step outside one's own narrative of oneself and see it in terms of the other with whom it coincides. When people accuse each other of "lying" (*oyama*) about their history, in debates over land, for instance, this is not so much conflict as it is part of a process of discovering moments where people's knowledge of themselves aligns with others. (And indeed, people assured me that in spite of the heated arguments in public meetings on land, most people in the audience knew enough of everyone's else's tetela to know who really was what they claimed to be.) Tetela were, moreover, not fixed statements of what people believed about their susu's ancestry. Each tetela is the product of a method of storing and transmitting knowledge of the past, including finding these points of alignment with others and incorporating this into a susu's stock of knowledge about itself. Once I heard a story about "a time when the sky sneezed," and the sky became black, what Auhelawa call a *bwaneta* (catastrophe). I asked an older man who had explained Auhelawa's ancient history to me if he knew any stories of this bwaneta, and he said he didn't know, but "ebe tatetela mata talobai" (If we tell histories, then we will find it).

Writing about the denial of recognition of Australian Aboriginal forms of belonging in contemporary Australia, Elizabeth Povinelli (2006) argues that the liberal social order rests on a discourse that imagines only two kinds of identity, the autology of the independent individual or the genealogy of one's origins, family, and ethnicity. One either creates one's own identity or derives it entirely as a legacy from one's past. People's various feelings of obligation or commitment are thus rendered as either being their own choices or their slavish loyalty to their community. What liberal discourses of identity miss is the intrinsically porous self, involving mind, body, and emotions, on which Aboriginal people—and many other people excluded from liberal publics—ground their sense of belonging in a community. So too Sahlins argues does the mutuality involved in all forms of kinship create not a bounded totality but what he calls a "transpersonal praxis" (2011b, 230). The liberal misrecognition of kinship, besides being present in many forms of older ethnographies of cultural difference, could now be said to influence Auhelawa, as they increasingly feel the need to translate the concepts of susu and bu'una into terms that are intelligible to the state and on the basis of which they can claim property rights to their lands (Schram 2014). More generally, though, what Povinelli argues is an ontologically distinct form of life I argue is an effect of the techniques of vision available to people in a specific social situation. Specifically, people are able to see their susu as one branch in a vast, ongoing migratory movement over the island region through the stereoscopic vision achieved when they merge the frameworks of place and history. It is the case that Western discourses of difference, including Western social theory, erase this kind of transpersonal praxis, seeing only an inherited legacy. However, this is not entirely because of the limits of its language, but because these kinds of belonging only emerge when people engage in certain kinds of practical reflexivity about their own relatedness.

This stereoscopic effect is an example of a postcultural way of finding a basis for social order and connection to a community. I don't mean to suggest that this kind of kinship is what forms after a culture has passed away. Nor do I mean to suggest that culture itself is no longer relevant as a theory of human ways of life and needs to be replaced with something new. Rather insofar as classical concepts of culture are fundamentally based on a hierarchy of norm and action, we will not be able to fully understand how Auhelawa people find grounds for recognizing each other as part of the same order. Of course, anthropology has undertaken a vocal, passionate critique of the classical Durkheimian model of culture in some form or another for over fifty years. The symbolic turn and Povinelli's own argument for a new ontology of belonging are themselves only two attempts to move beyond culture. What I find in Auhelawa, though, is not simply more evidence in the brief against classical holism. This is a society in which people have to come to grips with the limits of their folk theories of order and themselves produce and circulate knowledge that not only describes their relationships and the obligations entailed but also explains them. Tetela are not ethnographies, and perhaps it is too simple to say that they are attempts at social explanation, but nonetheless they do share the same motivation. Moreover, Auhelawa share tetela in ways that allow them to find alternative bases for mutual recognition among people with whom they may not actually have much in common. Yet in so doing, they strive to create a world of mutuality and prevent all forms of connection from becoming merely contracts between individuals, which they sign with ritual actions. In the next chapter, I expand this argument to include the bilateral circle of kin on whom all people in Auhelawa depend and argue that we see the same kind of circulation of knowledge underlying the ritual exchanges among patrilateral kin and affines in mortuary feasts.

2

You Cannot Eat Your Own Blood

Asiyebwa

June is the coldest, wettest time of year in Auhelawa. In June 2006, many people had not harvested their annual crop of yams and were still subsisting on lesser crops, breadfruit, and nuts during this lean period of the year, *tagwala*. On Sunday the 18th, the congregation of St. Peter's Catholic Church in the mission station at Mwademwadewa Village stepped outside and huddled under the awning after the service. They gossiped and chewed betel nut while waiting for a break in the rain. Then a woman's piercing wail and loud cries shot through the air. All fell silent. A small procession passed on the road along the beach in front of the church and the assembled crowd. The crying woman led a group of men bearing a body on a bier made of thick bamboo stems and lashed together with vines. They continued along without pause. No one in the crowd said a word. They knew from the woman's *woe* (loud wail) that the man had died and the procession was taking him back from his wife's village in

Bwasiyaiyai to the place he was born, in Sehuhuwa Village. After they had passed, the church leaders conferred and canceled the planned celebration of several students' first communion. People left quickly and quietly. An asiyebwa, a euphemistic word for serious illness and death, had come to Sehuhuwa, and so all wished to respect their mourning.

The next day, on the 19th, I attended a feast at Sehuhuwa Village with my adoptive family. We had come, along with other members of Alogawa's lineage, to mourn for the man borne by the procession. When we arrived, many other people of Sehuhuwa and other villages were already there, sitting in several different groups. We sat together, at a remove from the Sehuhuwa residents, and started preparing food to cook as well. Others arrived from other villages, some bringing baskets of yams, others bringing rice and other packaged food purchased at local trade stores. Because many people's gardens were not ready for harvest at this time of year, few could bring 'wateya (*Dioscorea alata*), the type of yam usually given to other lineages in mortuary feasts like this. Fortunately, this was an *aemehelino* (literally, flowing tears), a feast usually held immediately after the death to end the pall of *malahilili* (the period between asiyebwa and the burial), and so formal gifts were not needed yet. As we were sitting, Lucy's cross-cousin, Lorenzo Mesaki (the man from Wadaheya Village who first brought me to Auhelawa) came over to the group of visitors and reminded everyone to write their names on their cooking pots. Lucy had brought cooking pots, and it wasn't until then that I noticed that she wasn't using them. The people of Sehuhuwa were going to be using them to cook, sitting in their village along with members of their susu from Wadaheya and their bu'una susu from the neighboring village of Aita'ela.

Our group cooked our gifts, including rice and tinned fish I had just bought from the local trade store. We served it on several banana fronds laid out in a long column. Some of the Sehuhuwa residents came over to eat the rice and drink cups of tea we poured for them. We, however, sat back and did not join them. A few minutes later, Lorenzo's sister, Zita, ordered the people of Sehuhuwa and Wadaheya to bring over food they had cooked for the visitors and serve it. As the hosts of the event served individual portions of yams and rice into plates, I noticed that many people, visitors and hosts alike, had gathered together under a tent in the middle of the village for a Bible service led by Emmanuel, the Auhelawa

Catholic eucharistic minister. He and a few of the other Catholic attendees read a Bible passage, sang a hymn, and then the congregation listened to Emmanuel's sermon and prayer. (And, as during many religious observances in Auhelawa, both Catholics and members of the United Church participated in this *tapwalolo* [worship] as one group.)

After Lucy and I left, I asked her why she did not cook in her own pots. She said, "It's my prohibition" (*Bwabwalegu*). If she had cooked food she would serve to the hosts in her own pots, then the pots themselves would be forbidden to her. They would contain traces of the food she gave as her gift, and so any food cooked in them again would also be forbidden. Lucy's gift of food to the people of Sehuhuwa is also called a *bwabwale*, albeit a minor one, in this case meant only as a small meal for the hosts during the burial. When one gives this or any kind of bwabwale, people say "you cannot eat your own blood," meaning you cannot eat what you give. It was just one more prohibition which Lucy must follow in the villages of Lorenzo's susu. She could not enter their grave sites, or in the days between the death and the feast itself, their villages. When she appeared in their villages, she wore dirty clothes, and did not comb her hair. When other mourners with closer ties to the deceased arrived, they wailed (*dou*) in a keening, often melodic, voice, sobbing uncontrollably until they were met by the hosts who cried with them, embraced them, and then finally both stopped. All of these ritual behaviors of avoidance and deference are called *ve'ahihi* (respect), which is what natuleiya should show to their patrilateral cross-cousins in feasts of mourning. When I bought rice and tea to give to the Sehuhuwa people, this too, Lucy said at the time, was because of my ve'ahihi for the hosts.

Lucy cooked Sehuhuwa people's food in their pots, and they in hers. As the prohibitions on pots suggest, bwabwale is a gift in a cycle of reciprocal exchange. One cannot eat one's own blood, and one's recipients cannot eat theirs either, and so each must give to the other, and each must receive from the other.[1] This is a gift that creates a debt. Indeed, at a feast at Sehuhuwa held the following Saturday, guests brought many more baskets of 'wateya, many of which were not cooked but transferred to the hosts. Some of the baskets that Alogawa and others brought were a *maiha* (return) for baskets they had received from Wadaheya in the past. Others created a new *vaga* (debt). Sehuhuwa and their "supporters"—co-totemic relatives—also brought yams for Sehuhuwa to give to visitors.

Figure 1. Lucy Pade sewing sago palm leaves to make roof thatch (*atovi*) in 2006

At the heart of this feast and any mortuary feast is an exchange, and a step in an ongoing cycle of exchanges, between people of two lineages related through men. Even at the hastily arranged aemehelino held in Sehuhuwa, hosts and guests sat apart, and each prepared food for the other. You cannot eat your own blood.

When people say "You cannot eat your own blood," are they pointing to a social norm that precedes their action? Or are they making an observation of a pattern they see in their own and others' actions? Because people do not "eat their own blood" by abstaining from the rice they serve or by offering a basket of yams, they frame their interaction with another person as the giving of a gift and the creation of a debt, as opposed to sharing—for instance, offering betel nuts or tobacco to a friend who asks for them. Anthropologists have historically treated patterns of social behavior like these as something governed by rules. They have focused on the cycle of exchanges that such patterns create and explained it as a function of an underlying social structure that reproduces itself as a whole and reinforces these patterns as components of that whole. In this kind of analysis, Lucy and Lorenzo are simply conforming to rules. They are acting as would any two cross-cousins in the same kind of situation. Their fulfillment of this normative expectation reproduces the total system of which they are each a part.

Another school of thought has also influenced anthropology. It would build its analysis on the individual acts of respect, including gifts, that Lucy pays to Lorenzo. Rather than try to infer the rules that govern these acts, this approach would instead assume that Lucy and Lorenzo both see such actions as having specific meanings and treat Lucy's actions as a form of communication to Lorenzo that shapes how they relate to each other as part of a social world. There is another important part of this scene at Sehuhuwa that both of these approaches neglect. Lucy commented on the events to me as they happened. Lorenzo reminded his visitors about how to prepare their gifts. Other participants also made commentaries on other people's behavior. All this talk made use of a particular language of exchange. It suggests that the stories people tell about the events, both during and after, also determine the consequences of people's actions. Where then does the social force of respect really lie?

As discussed in the introduction, Roy Wagner and Marilyn Strathern argue that one cannot understand something like an Auhelawa feast if one assumes in advance that one can separate the abstract rules for Auhelawa feasting, on the one hand, from the actions that follow from them, on the other. If one makes this assumption that rules and actions are distinct, then one commits oneself to a view of social life as like an invisible social contract to which all parties have tacitly agreed in advance. Strathern and Wagner each argue that analysts must start instead by recognizing that the actors in this situation make their own assumptions about how social interactions work, and especially who is included in an interaction. In particular, Strathern emphasizes that for the people she studied in PNG, reciprocal exchanges create a sense of obligation for donors and recipients because each side in the exchange sees herself as an incomplete person without the other (1988, 271–73). Auhelawa feasting then is not best described as an event in which two people come together and each individually conforms to social rules of giving and receiving. Rather this is a situation in which people as a complementary pair perform one action to advance an ongoing cycle of reproduction.

While this line of argument is useful in some ways for rethinking many common assumptions about exchange, I would like to take their general point further. When Lorenzo reminds his visitors to write their names on their pots, he treads a fine line between everyday life and the special protocols he and his visitors are currently observing. In his comment, he and they are *both* individuals with personal property (pots) *and* kin who are bound in particular kinds of complementary relationships (debts). Although people generally say that they give gifts and show respect in specific ways because they must, when we look more closely, we see that they actually bring together many different accounts of who they are, how they are related, and why this determines particular courses of action. Thus the question of why people say "you cannot eat your own blood" cannot be solved by appealing to the ontological alterity of the Auhelawa person, but by the epistemological problems which they themselves perceive in how to interpret their own behavior, and how they arrive at solutions by creating a specific account of what is happening.

As I argue throughout this book, the relationship between norm and practice, in this case between the expectation of veʻahihi and its demonstration in action, is always presumed but never certain. People always assume they are doing something according to an established rule, but they cannot know the full consequences of their actions. In mourning feasts, people say that the visitors must show ve'ahihi. They also say that the hosts must reciprocate in various ways, but more important, people also say that the hosts must watch the ve'ahihi of visitors and then decide if it counts. The social efficacy of gifts and respectful actions, then, rests not simply its conformity to patterns but in its judgement as such, particularly by the recipients. In this chapter, I argue that when people display respect to cross-cousins in feasts and in everyday interactions, they act in ways that invoke a specific metalanguage of social relationships. When a person engages in appropriate forms of avoidance of the father's susu's lineage properties, like magai, they present themselves as being respectful of the father's susu. When they show deference to the members of the father's susu, especially on occasions of mourning in the father's susu, they likewise frame their relationships with their cross-cousins in terms of mutual indebtedness and frame the interaction with them as the actions of a complementary pair. The metamessage carried by each of these symbolic acts of avoidance and deference effectively frames this scene in this way only if the acts are also recognized by their recipients. One person may offer a gift to a cross-cousin and choose to abstain from sharing in it, but whether this offering becomes a debt hinges on whether or not the recipient judges the actions of the donor to be ve'ahihi. Arguably this is what Lorenzo was doing implicitly when he reminded the visitors to the feast to label their pots. Thus the efficacy of ritual behavior in a feast comes not from the symbolism of the actions that make it up but from their incorporation into a story about the actions and the larger situation. Moreover, while many people contribute to this story, it is largely affirmed by the recipients of the actions. Thus to understand why people exchange and why people practice respect, we must look not for rules in the abstract, nor to individual actions. Rather, we need to think about action and interaction in ecological terms. In an ecological approach to interaction people act as audiences for each other and feed information about each action back to the actor as the interaction takes place. As in the previous chapter we find that no one single lens for the reading of symbols is complete unto itself. In interactions between cross-cousins, this allows each to negotiate their exact relationship. In later chapters, I build on this finding to examine how people recruit other narratives as lenses with which to read actions in new terms and to establish an account of why feasts are shrinking and why reciprocity is weakening. In this chapter, I examine how people create paternal kinship in everyday life and in feasts.

Father and Child

As noted earlier, Auhelawa regard people related through women as naturally similar and believe they should share resources and support each other, whether they are of the same susu or any kind of bu'una. This also means that their relationships to fellow susu members and bu'una have no expectations of ve'ahihi, unlike the relationship of people related through men, and particularly between children and their father's susu. Each person thus has a bilateral kindred, consisting of mother's relatives and father's relatives, and one behaves toward each of these classes of kin differently throughout one's life. Learning the boundaries of these two classes begins early, starting with how parents teach their children to treat their father. Basically, children must "fear" (*mehe'uhi*) their father and, because of this fear, obey him. Fathers are not particularly stern. Indeed, many are very attentive and doting. But as his children are members of his wife's susu, there is a fundamental difference between him and his children, so each must treat the other differently than they do their own matrikin (see also Battaglia 1985). While this principle is often stated as a set of prohibitions, children's treatment of their father is really more of an elaborate politeness code. They must never use his name, it being the property of his susu. Instead children must always address and refer to their father as *tamagu* (my father) or *Taubada*, a loanword common from the colonial days basically meaning *Sir*. They must not walk in front of him when he is sitting but instead walk behind him or around the group in which he is sitting. This rule, however, is really only observed in the breach. Generally young children who are passing in front of the father or his relatives will bow their head and duck past quickly while loudly exclaiming "Ex-cuse!" with a characteristic high tone on the last syllable. Children are taught a certain set of manners and that manners are important, but they need only to acknowledge their own lapse for it to count as good behavior. Their father, likewise, as an affine of his wife's susu, must avoid uttering his wife's name or any of her matrikin's names, including his children's, usually calling them by a nickname or *natugu* (my child). This is in addition to the many similar prohibitions on bad language and temper that he observes as a son-in-law, as well as a general positive attitude to garden work. Violations of these are not serious but do merit criticism from his wife's matrikin.

As mentioned, a husband and wife will usually first reside in the wife's natal hamlet, where the husband is a *wohiwa* (male affine) and thus required himself to respect (*ve'ahihi*) the magai of the wife's susu. Later, the married couple also builds a house in the husband's natal village, where the wife then becomes a *hinevelam* (female affine) and must herself pay the same respect. The couple then periodically shifts between their residences, making food gardens in each place and, as people say, allowing each to visit with their parents and kin equally. Children thus spend roughly equal amounts of time living in their own natal village and their *magai tama* (father's grave), their father's village. There they are natuleiya (children of male members) of the father's susu and must avoid physical contact with its *magai*. Here they live alongside their *nibai* (cross-cousins). In this context they also encounter their father's brother's children, whom they call taliya natuleiya (natuleiya of the same susu), who are classed with siblings and matrilateral parallel cousins as *gelu* (friends, siblings). All of one's gelu and nibai are important peer relationships throughout one's life, although they each play different roles. Nibai have an asymmetric relationship in which one's father's sister's children act in a way as surrogate fathers who look out for and can admonish their mother's brother's children. Children thus are socialized into a world consisting of two distinct sides, and one in which their father's susu is marked as an object of special attention. The child is, however, not just learning rules but also acquiring a kind of self that bears responsibility for its conduct toward others, especially its father's susu.

Children's attunement to this social landscape, rather than obedience or good behavior, is what parents value. Indeed, they look for signs of this awareness even in infancy. When I returned to Alogawa in 2006 for fieldwork, my sister Noeline had given birth to her first child, a son named Caleb. Caleb was naturally cautious around the village's pig, which usually roamed freely during the day and slept under one of the houses at night. As Caleb learned to crawl, his mother and he would play a game while sitting under one of the village houses. Caleb would wander away from her, and when he started to go under a bench or look behind a closed door, his mother, sitting behind him, would grunt like a pig, and Caleb would immediately whirl around and scramble back to her arms. Soon she could replace her grunts with the word "pig" and he would react the same way. Noeline and other adults described Caleb's reaction as mehe'uhi (fear), but they took it as a sign of his intellectual development. When he showed fear, he showed he was aware of his surroundings. The word "fear" is based on the word for eye (*mehe*), and Caleb's wide-eyed gaze was the main sign of his fear and his awareness. Whenever he stared at anything, like the moon or the village pig, this too was taken as his fear and another sign of his awareness. Children's growing awareness and appropriate responses were linked in people's minds to

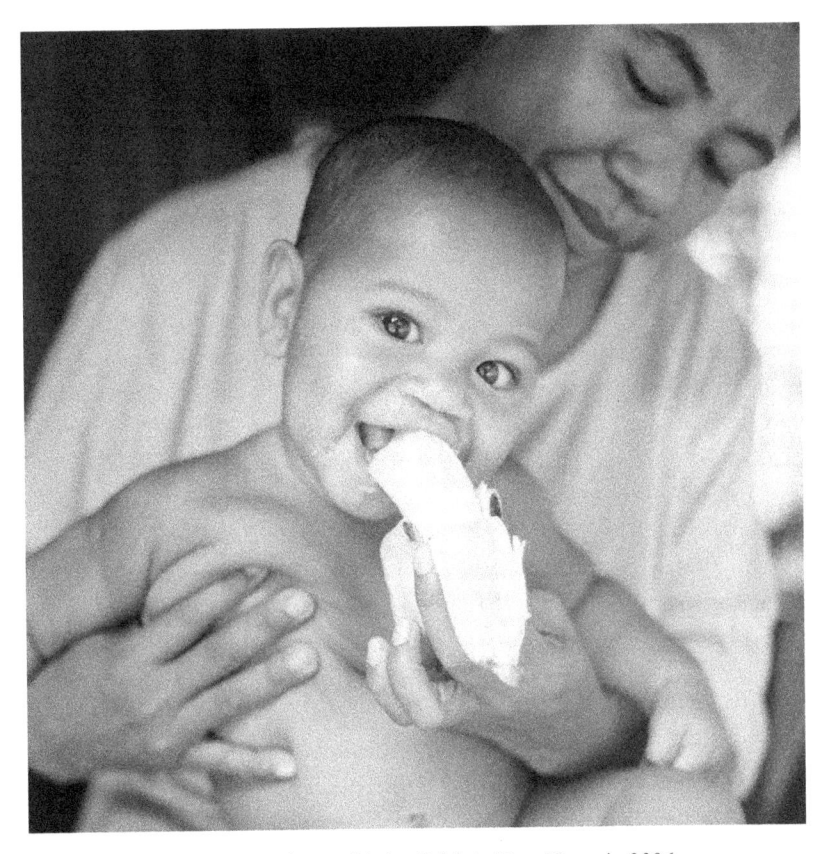

Figure 2. Noeline and baby Caleb in New Home in 2006

their understanding of language, often well before children can speak. Parents often carry on playful conversations with children as young as Caleb, reading meaning into every babbled syllable (compare with Ochs and Schieffelin 1984). Naughty toddlers who do not listen to instructions, by contrast, are said to have no fear in the same sense, and their fearlessness is linked with slow learning.

Older children are expected to be attentive to social space in the same way. Once when wandering through a village to church, I saw children climbing a lemon tree unsupervised. The children gleefully ignored my initial paltry attempts to admonish them—"Are you supposed to be doing that? Is that safe?"—then I remembered how I'd seen other adults control children and said, "Is this your village?" They immediately climbed down and ran home. In fact, as our group cooked the meal for the hosts in Sehuhuwa in June, children from another village were horsing around loudly. A senior woman in our group working nearby turned to them and said sharply, "Teina magai havam?" (This is the grave of your what?) Her rhetorical question implied that this was the children's *magai tama*, a place where they should behave with restraint, unlike in their *susu*'s village, where is acceptable to act *besobeso* (carelessly). Although children are not expected to act with the same degree of respect as adults, they are taught the locations that require respect, including where their father's *magai* are. Similarly, young children are taught to respect their father by avoiding contact with the top of his head, remaining physically lower than him, and especially to excuse themselves when passing through the space in front of him. Not only are they learning the basic sociospatial categories of their world, but children are also acquiring the appropriate dispositions associated with these spaces. Proper behavior toward the father also indicates that a child has acquired the capacity to feel *hinimaya* (shame), which is needed to know when to act with respect toward people beyond one's own *susu*. A child's father is an other, not only because he belongs to a distinct category but also as a representative of the wider social world. As such, he serves as a site where children demonstrate their moral competence (see also Brison 1999).

One's father retains this role even after one reaches adulthood, marries, and lives apart from the parents. As an adult, one should regularly make a special trip to visit one's father at home and spend time with him, especially if and when he is sick. A man's health is influenced by this kind of attention and care by his children. Fathers offer advice and counsel to their adult children on marriage and householding, and his children should heed this out of the same sense of shame. The surest way to stop an argument or a fight is for a matrikinsman of one of the belligerents to place a hand on that person and utter a kind of oath called *walo'apu'apuni*, saying "Your father is already dead. Do you want me to die too?" When I observed this once, the man to whom it was addressed was so shamed he immediately collapsed in tears into the arms of his susu mates standing nearby.

The death of one's father is then an important episode in every adult's biography. When one's father dies, one must mourn as a visitor to the feasts held by members of his susu, wailing over his body as a sign of respect to them. When a man dies, his children and wife are looked after by his susu during their mourning. In the past, this would require them to observe harsh taboos on self-feeding and self-care, which were done instead by the man's susu. Today it is more common for a man's children to mourn him by abstaining from washing, combing their hair, wearing clean clothes, and eating rich, savory food. Usually when a man is buried, the wife and children offer gifts to his susu, and the susu releases them from these taboos. After the burial, then, the children must begin to prepare their bwabwale gift to their father's susu. The bwabwale gift for one's father is, as one man told me, "the biggest thing you will ever do in your life." A man's children will give at least one large, live pig to his susu, as well as several baskets of 'wateya yams, each containing twenty large, premium tubers usually weighing about one kilogram each. (Auhelawa call this quantity "one pound" in English, presumably after the shillings in a pound sterling.) If these expressions of ve'ahihi are accepted by the man's susu, as they usually are, they will permit the children to visit the village again, free of all mourning taboos, and will offer them usufruct rights to some of the sites where the father had gardened in his natal territories.

When one completes the ceremonial mourning of one's father, one enters into a new kind of relationship with one's nibai, both the father's sisters' children and one's classificatory nibai (FMZDC and potentially FMMZDDC, or anyone who called one's father *bada*, or maternal uncle). These people are always treated with respect and fear, and are respected sources of advice as adults. They also become important exchange partners, as one's respect for them impels people to make supplementary gifts to them when any member of their susu subsequently dies. The nibai then reciprocate the bwabwale and other later gifts in feasts held by their natuleiya, giving exactly the same type and number of gifts as maiha (return) for the vaga (debt) given to them. The relationship to one's patrilateral nibai is asymmetric, and indeed in the fashion of Crow kin terminologies, they and all the members of the father's susu are collectively called "my fathers" (*tamaguwao*) who in turn call the children of their male matrikin natuleiya, derived from *natu* (child). It is important to note also that this relationship is doubly asymmetric. Not only are one's metaphorical fathers treated with deference, but they also hold the power to decide whether one's deference, avoidance, mourning, and gifts count as ve'ahihi and make the decision as to whether they accept one as a metaphorical "child"—that is, an exchange partner and holder of usufruct rights to their matrilineal lands. If a child is obligated to respect and to mourn her father, then the job of the nibai is to watch her behavior and decide what it says about her, and then finally to lift the taboos of mourning. The relationship among nibai then is not simply hierarchical but also characterized by an unequal distribution of epistemic authority. One's father's sister's children in that sense stand in for society at large as arbiters of the efficacy of one's own social actions. As we see in the next section, this special privilege becomes decisive in the ways people use the rituals of mourning to accomplish specific aims.

Lucy's Fathers, Cosmas's Children

The ideal picture of fathers and children is usually stated in terms of rules and thus assumes that every person always has two clearly delineated classes of maternal and paternal kin from birth. In reality, many people do not, and so they have to create them. If an Auhelawa woman, for instance, marries a man from another part of the country who comes to live in Auhelawa, he will usually be taken on as an adult adoptee of another, unrelated susu, allowing him to reside there and make use of their gardening lands and villages.[2] Thus when the normal cycle of household formation is impractical, people rearrange things so that the new household has two villages in which to reside and the normal range of gardening sites. People can also create a paternal relationship to a susu through their own actions. Lucy's relationship to Lorenzo is a good example. Lucy's father was named Makadonia. He was from the susu of Sehuhuwa, and Lorenzo's mother's brother. Makadonia and his wife, Eteli of Alogawa, had Lucy around 1950. In 1954, a new Catholic mission school was founded in Mwademwadewa Village, near Alogawa. In 1958, Makadonia and Eteli brought Lucy to an Australian priest living at the mission to be baptized. The priest estimated Lucy's age to be about eight years old. Makadonia eventually became an elected representative of the ward of Kurada within the newly formed local government council of Duau and, after that, the president of the council. As a leader in Kurada, he encouraged people to support the Catholic mission, which was bringing services such as education and health care to the community.

When Lucy was still young, Makadonia left her mother and married another woman. When Lucy tells the story, she uses words like "divorce" and "marriage." These terms require some qualification. Auhelawa marriages are a formal bond between two people and a formal affinal relationship between their respective susu. As mentioned, the in-marrying spouse is treated as an outsider and must demonstrate his respect to his parents-in-law through hard work and marked deference. The parents-in-law for their part heap scorn and demands for work on their children's spouses, male or female, and monitor closely how they behave. In Auhelawa eyes, even after two people are married, the parents-in-law and the susu can refuse their child's spouse and chase them away if they do not approve of him or her, and marriages break up because of the interference of the susu. Later in life, marriages often dissolve over adultery as well as other problems. I am not certain exactly why Makadonia left his first wife, but I do want to note that his remarriage to another woman after having a child was not uncommon. Lucy's mother quickly remarried another man from the village of Patumala and had several more children with him. Lucy was accepted by him as a child and was treated the same as her step-siblings.

In her life, Lucy chose to care for both of her fathers. She grew up in Alogawa and Patumala with her mother, stepfather, and step-siblings. Along with her step-siblings, she demonstrated respect for her father of Patumala and his susu, including frequent visits to them when their members were ill. This was expected of her as a natuleiya of Patumala. Lucy also sought to build a relationship with the sister's children of her birth father, Makadonia. Even though she had not lived in the village of

Sehuhuwa with him and her mother, she wanted to show that she was their natuleiya too. In addition to mourning for Makadonia and giving gifts of bwabwale, she also contributed to other feasts that they hosted by giving new gifts and wailed with other mourners for Sehuhuwa's deceased relatives. This was not expected of her but something she chose to take on. The Sehuhuwa susu received these gifts and accepted them as appropriate signs of respect. In return, her cross-cousins, including Lorenzo, began to reciprocate these feast gifts to Lucy at Alogawa's feasts, and the cycle continued. Lorenzo and his siblings decided that Lucy could continue to make gardens on their lands. They eventually offered the same usufruct to one of Lucy's sons, their *tubuni* (grandchild of a male member). Lorenzo ran the largest trade store in the area and owned a boat, with which he shipped goods and carried passengers from Duau to the provincial capital town of Alotau on the mainland. He gave shares in the business to his susu and to Lucy. Lucy's husband, Francis, and Lorenzo at various times loaned each other's businesses money to make orders when sales fell short. When Lorenzo proposed to build a public memorial to Makadonia, the first elected council president of Duau, he named Lucy to the committee overseeing the funds he had raised. Lucy looks on this relationship with pride as something she has developed, and indeed, she has a reputation for being a "good" person, someone who is respectful to both of her fathers' susu.

Another example of how individuals cultivate a relationship to their father's susu through acts of respect comes from Alogawa. Lucy's mother's brother Cosmas lived by himself at the foot of the hill near the beach at Alogawa. He had been married twice, and his second wife had died some years ago. In his old age he had become quite frail and walked with a walking stick. He no longer went to the garden to work, although he regularly attended the nearby Catholic church for mass and other religious services. He was nicknamed Taubada Doudouna (Crying Old Man), not because he was sad or cried, but because he would tease children by making menacing faces, and this would usually make them wail with fear. His children from both marriages were now all adults, most married with children of their own. Two of his daughters had married men of other provinces and permanently relocated. One of his sons was a man of Sehuhuwa named Aidan. Before my arrival in Kurada and over the course of 2006, Aidan came to Alogawa regularly to visit his father and work for him. Aidan built a small sleeping house low to the ground so that Cosmas could climb in and out easily. He also built an outhouse nearby over a creek, so that Cosmas would not have to walk all the way down to the surf to relieve himself. Aidan chopped firewood and brought food from his garden in Alogawa to Cosmas. Aidan's wife also frequently came to Alogawa to tend the garden and cook for Cosmas. Both of them frequently stopped by New Home on these visits. Aidan joined the work party of Francis's sister's children and children who cleared his and Lucy's new yam gardens. At Francis's request, Aidan was one of three men I hired to build my house in New Home too. Whenever Aidan was around, Lucy remarked to me and many other people what a good son he was for all the things he did for Cosmas, especially compared to his mostly absent siblings.

When we take into consideration Aidan's and Lucy's ways of showing respect to their fathers' susu, we are forced to revise our understanding of why people pay respect and why they give gifts. Lucy could explain her own behavior in terms of rules—"You cannot eat your own blood"—but as I learned more about her life, she revealed that there was more to it than simply obeying these rules. She saw herself as cultivating a moral relationship with people she called her "fathers." By first appearing in Sehuhuwa's feasts, mourning with them as a natuleiya should, and giving them gifts each time, not only did she ensure their reciprocal gifts in Alogawa's feasts, but she was converting her garden wealth into moral standing with them and with everyone who witnessed this. Others interpreted her behavior as a strategy to convert these same acts and gifts into rights, specifically to the produce of Makadonia's gardening sites. Indeed, the lands of Wadaheya and Sehuhuwa where she has gardened over the years are desirable spots. The village gardening lands lie on plains, as opposed to the steep hillsides of Alogawa, making them more accessible and better suited for some crops. Aidan too, in Lucy's account, converted his care for his father into moral prestige. And Alogawa permitted him to work their land as well. (Others mentioned that Aidan hoped that Cosmas would also pass on his magical knowledge.)

Ve'ahihi as Strategy and as Performance

Given this, one might turn to Pierre Bourdieu's (1977) theory of social action. For Bourdieu, ve'ahihi looks like part of a habitus. A habitus is a learned way of using one's resources, including one's body, as instruments of effective social action. Bourdieu rejects the Maussian concept of reciprocity as a law that people unconsciously obey. Yes, he says, when people exchange gifts in feasts, we can see an ongoing cycle over time. But, he argues, we cannot then assume that the sequences of action are reversible, or that all the actions that make up the cycle are simply conforming to a "mechanical law" (Bourdieu 1977, 9). Likewise, just because in every feast people come together, and some offer food which they do not eat, we cannot then conclude that a rule precedes the actions that conform to it. When we think of a social order as an abstract system of such rules, Bourdieu says that we ignore that the donors of gifts can never know whether or not their gifts will be reciprocated (1977, 12). From the donor's point of view, every gift is also a gamble that the recipient will recognize the gift as a debt. Gifts can potentially be refused when they are simply given back right away, and gifts can be stolen when the recipient takes forever to reciprocate. Given that these failures of reciprocity are both possible at any given moment of exchange, donor and recipient can and indeed must choose the timing of their gifts and countergifts. What appears to the clockwork repetition of routine patterns is in fact the combined outcome of different strategies for acquiring the recognition and in some cases honor of being a generous giver and a responsible recipient.

Bourdieu answers the question of why people give gifts by saying that the giver embodies the logic of the system as a habitus, which he defines precisely as "[a system] of durable, transposable dispositions, [which are] structured structures predisposed to function as structuring structures" (1977, 72). This means that the actor internalizes the objective structural rules of their society, yet not only as constraints on their own free choices. Rather, Bourdieu argues that society influences the body, and not the mind, of the actor. A person's socialization, he says, consists primarily of training her body to conform physically to her social environment. As she is trained to behave and respond in certain ways, the actor gains a mastery over her own body. Her habitus is determined by the social environment but is predisposed to serve as a template, a structuring structure. When social rules are embodied as a habitus, rather than internalized as knowledge, the body and its capacity for action become a resource that the actor can use to gain prestige. The actor learns to see the world in terms of opportunities to achieve particular aims by drawing from a repertoire of styles of embodied actions. With respect to the gift, the giver is one who possesses a habitus of exchange in which other actors are opportunities to acquire prestige. The giver learns to time the presentation of gifts in ways that maximize their social impact. Recipients of others' gifts also possess a habitus in which they have learned to respond to gifts the have received as opportunities to reciprocate at a time of their choosing. They have learned that they must maneuver between reciprocating too quickly, in which case one appears to be eager to end the relationship, and reciprocating too slowly, in which case one demeans oneself in others' eyes as a debtor. The recipient's habitus is trained to find the right time in which satisfying the obligation to pay one's debts will also consequently confer the most esteem on the person.

In reconceptualizing reciprocity in terms of habitus, Bourdieu does not mean to suggest that all social action results from conscious, perfectly rational choices (1977, 172, 177–78). While he faults structuralist accounts of exchange for their lack of attention to choice, he is clear that no actor has absolute freedom to choose a course of action. Rather they experience the constraints of the social system as a field in which they naturally know how to play the game (Bourdieu 1977, 167–68). By learning to see the world through certain embodied capacities, one also becomes blind to other possibilities. Moreover, even as they embody social patterns, actors do not also have perfect awareness of the implications of their choices. In Bourdieu's terms, actors misrecognize the real consequences of the gift (1977, 171). They see it as moral conduct and to a lesser extent a competition for prestige among equals. Yet in orienting themselves to this kind of field of play, they fail to see how they unwittingly reproduce the total system of gift and countergift as a perduring structure. In particular, Bourdieu is eager to show that the morality of the gift motivates the practice of reciprocity, yet as a habitus it also reproduces a form of structural domination. Actors accumulate prestige in gifts which reinforce their advantages in strategic exchange.

We can think of the behaviors that Auhelawa class as ve'ahihi, especially the ways they comport themselves and express affect in the presence of their father's kin, as being the expressions of a habitus of kinship. In Bourdieu's framework, Auhelawa people do not simply learn the social boundaries of susu and their codes of behavior in the abstract.

Rather they learn to feel shame in the presence of the father and his susu and ways to respond to this feeling through deference and avoidance. Indeed, Auhelawa talk about this feeling of shame in terms of the body. Natuleiya cannot be loud, expressive, and boisterous in the presence of their father's susu, especially during times of mourning. Only among their own susu, can they act besobeso. Control over one's body also pertains to sharing. As a natuleiya one must learn to abstain from what one gives to one's father's susu, again in contrast to the free sharing and help that one learns to expect of one's matrikin. Demonstrating control over one's body and its intrinsic potential to shame the father thus becomes a resource one can tap in order to modulate and control the relationship to the father's susu. Bourdieu would also emphasize that actors can convert this resource into material gains—for instance, the rights to use land—and furthermore convert their material capital in the form of land rights into "symbolic capital" within the field of feasting exchange. The conversion of "symbolic capital," for Bourdieu, is "the most valuable form of accumulation" in societies based on small-scale agriculture (1977, 179).

For that reason, the concept of habitus has a limited applicability to ve'ahihi in Auhelawa. Bourdieu's chief examples for the habitus of reciprocity comes from his observations of reciprocal gifts of hospitality and labor among male Kabyle peasant householders in Algeria (Silverstein 2009). Unlike Auhelawa, these men would give and receive gifts of different kinds and in general appear to have a greater freedom of choice over how and when to offer gifts and reciprocate what they had received. The habitus of reciprocity is matched with a world in which men have greater independent control over their household's resources. Auhelawa households as units of production will be examined in more detail in the next chapter. Here it is enough to say that every household has a number of competing claims on its food supply, one of which is feast gifts. Also, since the occasion for Auhelawa exchanges is usually someone's death, one does not have time as a resource to the same extent; people cannot choose when they reciprocate gifts. In fact, the hosts of most major Auhelawa feasts postpone them until the next harvest season, when all who attend will be able to provide gifts. The opportunity to time one's gift is simply taken out of the equation by convention. Compared to the grand spectacles of PNG Highlands pig prestations like the *moka* and the *tee*, Auhelawa mortuary feasting is not a scene of competitive exchange (compare with Strathern 1971; Feil 1984). When people give bwabwale, a different kind of misrecognition takes place. When they give bwabwale, Auhelawa see themselves as making a choice to fulfill an obligation, not to advance their careers as big men. They wish to secure recognition and continuing support of their father's kin and acquire the material benefit of land use rights that come with this support; their respect maintains their moral standing in the eyes of others. They misrecognize the fact that this apparent moral agency reproduces an egalitarian order of complementary and interdependent relationships between descent groups.

This is not to say that Auhelawa themselves do not see the potential for strategy and competition in feasts. For instance, there are men and women who are skilled in gardening. Typically they are members of large susu and thus have a great number of junior relatives and affines in their village who can provide labor to plant and harvest many more gardens each year than the typical household. Thus these gardeners can proudly give many gifts at feasts and host large feasts for their susu, which draw in many groups of natuleiya. Their exchanges of yams go beyond what most people have to do in the course of their lives. These wealthy men and women, *wasawasa* and *alawata* respectively, can give and receive competitively because they have the resources to meet any challenge to reciprocate. Only true wasawasa and alawata can confidently stride into a feast with a major gift. For normal people it is more common to hear the euphemism that an upcoming feast is a heavy burden (*vitai*). It is often the case that a person is not able to amass a sufficient quantity of 'wateya to give as bwabwale, and so must borrow from others. Wasawasa and alawata have the means to make formal loans, called *sagena*, to those who need them in these cases. Unlike a ceremonial presentation of bwabwale in which a mourner presents the gift to the recipient without being asked, a person seeking a loan will go to a rich person "empty-handed" (*nima'a'avana*) and ask to take a pig or a basket of yams. The rich person can then demand repayment at a later time, and it should be given immediately. Asking for a sagena is risky, because the lender can ask for its immediate return at any time, and failure to do so is not only shameful but liable to make one a target of revenge sorcery. Receiving a sagena subordinates one to the donor, much as Bourdieu suggests for many Kabyle exchange relationships (1977, 190). For this reason, my informants saw sagena as an absolute last resort. A more common solution for someone needing pigs and yams for a major gift is instead to ask for *hagu* (help), the kind of generalized reciprocity among members of a susu. While these gifts are not strictly balanced, asking for help entails the possibility that one will be asked for another kind of help in the future. Through exchanges of help, everyone's burdens are met, no one loses standing in the eyes of either their exchange partners or lenders, and the system overall maintains a steady state.

More important, even though self-interest and competition, on the one hand, and institutional rules and obligations, on the other, are each available as ways to think about feast exchanges, these are not the only frame Auhelawa use to interpret their own and others' reasons for giving gifts. They also cite the emotion *hinihinini*, a word closely resembling shame (*hinimaya*). Hinihinini is an irresistible urge to mourn with one's father's susu and to give gifts even when they aren't required. Under its sway, people do whatever it takes to give gifts and pay respect to their father's susu. Auhelawa thus have at least three different frameworks—rules, self-interest, and emotion—by which they can account for the reasons for people's ve'ahihi, none of which captures all that is going on in any one feast. Each account identifies in its own way who it is that really acts, why they do so, and why it is that those actions have consequences. If accounts appeal to rules, the actor is an individual whose choices to act are effective insofar as they conform to the appropriate codes of behavior for a specific social category—for instance, a mother's brother's child who pays respect and a father's sister's child who receives it. Accounts based on self-interest construe the same situation as one in which individuals deploy certain kinds of actions and objects as symbolic resources to accomplish a goal, to convert these symbols into another kind of resource such as prestige, land, or secret magical knowledge. Finally, in accounts based on emotion one frames the feast as an expression of inner feelings of particular people already tied in various ways to each other. For Bourdieu, all such representations by actors are simply various kinds of misrecognition of the habitus acquired in this specific field of action. I would, however, note two things. First, each account rests on a different theory of agency and locates the efficacy of social action in different places. Second, in each feast, the recipients of the actions themselves develop their own account of what is going in that moment, even if implicitly they decide whether they count as sufficient grounds for the nibai relationship itself to continue. As an audience the recipients of respect may have many reasons of their own for making whatever judgement they reach. To my knowledge, no feast host has ever turned away their natuleiya. It appears that all have an interest in keeping things as they are, removing the burdens of mourning from the visitors, and resuming their normal relationships. Perhaps that is because any feast host knows that they will be someone else's visitor. The outcomes of feast exchanges are not, in the end, derived from the moves and countermoves of strategic actors in a particular kind of field, because each of the actors must also take the perspective of the others in order to understand themselves. In one feast, hosts hold superior epistemic authority as judges of their visitors. Yet everyone at some point occupies the other position, and in the aggregate all people in Auhelawa eventually participate in not only creating a moral order through their actions but also in evaluating how others fit into this moral order. It makes sense, then, to bring people's mutual participation in the value of others' actions into the analysis of gifts in feasts.

Erving Goffman's theory of social action can help in this regard. For Goffman, institutional rules only create order when they provide the actor with meaning. People follow rules and reproduce patterns when they see how these rules lead to some value or goal that is held by the society as a whole. In a paper on the concept of face, he lays out his social theory of action (1967a). He says that most social theory presents patterns of action as if society and social behavior were like the actions of a student in school (1967a, 42). The teacher prompts the student, and the student responds in the way she has been taught. If the student performs correctly, she gets a reward, and if she does not perform according to the normative pattern, then she is penalized. Social life, especially at the interpersonal level, is a game in which people reproduce the patterns they have learned, but it is not a "hard, dull game" like the student's many tests (1967a, 43). Instead parties in an interaction both work to help the other person achieve the desired end, the successful replication of the socially normal, and hence socially meaningful, pattern. In this respect Goffman differs from Bourdieu. As the interaction unfolds, each party indicates in ways large and small, how they think the other party is performing their expected role and thus gives them a chance to correct or adjust themselves along the way and fulfill the pattern they intend. In some ways these responses and feedback from the other party can be subtle gestures, a wince or a smile, that signal how one's action is being received (see also Bateson 1958). They can also be explicit requests for clarification and confirmation. In either case, if social life is a performance, it is one in which the players are also simultaneously an audience for one another. Actors each take turns in the scene, and each comments on how it is going. Social action thus is never simply an iteration of an ideal, normative construct. It is always done in ways that are subtly self-aware and constantly gearing itself toward the information that comes from its reception in the unfolding interaction. At the same time, the performance of social action is not solely driven by a single actor as an embodiment of social forces. It is, rather, a collaboration in which actors offer themselves to be read by others so that their actions can be recognized as efficacious.

Goffman never wrote about the question of gift exchange as a distinct type of social institution. Nonetheless his theory of symbolic interaction can help clarify what happens when people give bwabwale. In developing this theory, Goffman confined himself mainly to what he considered to be the particular conditions of modern mass society. In particular, he believed that urban society was composed of autonomous individuals who were more or less anonymous to one another and thus needed to create their sociality through interpersonal interactions. In his thinking, however, mass society is not simply a rational and disenchanted order free of traditional rules and ideas. Rather, it is a type of society that embodies a distinct set of values but nevertheless still uses the same mechanisms as any society large or small to express and instill these values. As he says, if traditional societies treat certain things as sacred, in modern society, each individual is sacred as a person (Goffman 1967b, 47). Each individual is seen as an instance of the society's ideal person. For this reason, an individual's actions reflect on her capacities in relation to the ideal individual as a standard of value. People strive to present themselves in ways that demonstrate them to be competent, responsible, and self-sufficient as individuals, and to a great extent, many codes of behavior come to support this self-image and presentation to others. Thus, as Goffman would say, modern, mass society demonstrates that the individual person is treated as sacred when people respect the personal space of strangers, avoiding unnecessary physical contact, and by the same token greeting new acquaintances in a gratuitously ceremonial, highly scripted way.

Yet as much as Goffman gains critical distance on mass society by treating it as if it were a traditional society based on strict rules of conduct, his theory of action is not reducible to a Durkheimian concept of a functional system of rules. Rather he shows that in any society patterns of conduct are themselves symbolic codes of communication, and that every interaction is itself a circuit of communication between several interactants who all know the same basic codes and seek together to establish the message in their actions and interactions. This approach in general is also relevant to understanding ritual behavior in Auhelawa.

In Auhelawa, the interaction between members of a susu and its natuleiya are defined by what Goffman would call the face of the participants, especially that of the natuleiya. One's face is one's image as it is seen by others. When one violates expectations of a situation and reveals oneself to have misread how one fits into the situation, one's face is threatened, and if no attempt is made to repair the situation, then one could appear diminished in the eyes of others. This is not to suggest that one is not on display in other contexts or that people do not evaluate each other in other situations. Rather these interactions among people of different susu threaten them with shame more than other situations, and this shame can change the nature of the relationship. If one behaves inappropriately in these situations, it will be read as evidence for taking the wrong "line" on the situation or misunderstanding the state of one's relationship to other people (Goffman 1967a, 8). In these cases failure to perform means that one does not have respect for the father's susu, which in turn means one is a bad person. Given this backdrop, in Goffman's framework, natuleiya have to work to ensure that their actions toward the father's susu also communicate their respect for the father's susu. It is not enough to simply do what is expected, because one's actions are being read in terms of one's attitude toward the relationship.

For instance, natuleiya cannot utter the name of their father or the members of their father's susu. In many cases, one simply avoids this using a teknonym for the prohibited person's name, saying "N's son" where N is a person of another susu whose name is not prohibited. Yet many techniques of avoidance are more obvious. For instance if the name being avoided is one's own father's name, one often says "my danger" (*agu woiyawa*), meaning that to utter the father's name is dangerous and so should be avoided. When referring to a person with a prohibited name, one can use filler words *naniwa* (something) and *naniwa haidova* (something somewhere) in a mock display of searching for the name. In many instances, if someone does not volunteer the name to the person speaking, that person might pick a nearby piece of gravel from the ground, toss it in the general direction of someone who can speak to get their attention, and say "You say his name!" Thus it is often not enough to simply avoid uttering prohibited names; one also announces in so many words, "I am observing a prohibition" (see also Stasch 2003). Avoidance of names and graves, like respect in general, is not simply a pattern of behavior correlated with the social boundaries of susu. Because interactions outside one's susu in the presence of the father's susu have such important consequences, one needs to ensure that these routine patterns are recognized for what they are.

Giving a bwabwale gift is likewise embellished with ceremonial actions that serve to communicate what kind of a gift it is and where the giver places itself in relation to the donor. Giving bwabwale possesses an important characteristic of social action for Goffman, which is that actors externalize and make visible what they believe themselves to be doing through their own bodies (2009 [1971], 9). When acting, actors exhibit their own attitude toward the action through their posture and expression. Goffman calls this a body gloss. In this case, natuleiya wish to create a debt (vaga) with the father's susu which will impel a return gift (maiha) at a later time. This kind of reciprocal relationship is logically predicated on an opposition between sides, and so donors adopt an externalization that suggests this precondition. During mourning, for instance, natuleiya have to make visible and audible their respect for the father's susu by wailing and abstaining from cleaning. They tangle their hair and wear dirty clothes, making it immediately obvious to anyone who sees them that they are mourning the matrilineal kin of their father. By marking themselves off as distinct, the natuleiya circumscribe the gift in a totalizing, asymmetric opposition. One either pays respect or is paid respect. Each action of respect by a mourner is done with the owners in mind. In this way every act serves to signal the direction in which the bwabwale is moving and thus works to establish that it is a gift that creates a debt. For Goffman when an actor adopts a particular externalization, other people in the situation respond with their own body gloss that indicates their response to the performance of the self entailed in the actor's externalization. When natuleiya appear before the father's susu, they wail and sob. The owners of the death respond to this display by joining in wailing, indicating that they accept and affirm the context the natuleiya have asserted. Each of them calls out to the deceased person by a different kin term and thereby indexes their complementary ties to one another. When the mourners give a bwabwale to their father's kin, they also refuse to share in eating it. The gift itself, like the many other things associated with the father, becomes an object of avoidance and thus communicates again the boundary between the two groups.

Respect and Reflexivity

When Auhelawa initially explained the rules of respect and mortuary feasting to me, they would often say, "Our custom is hard," and then go on to illustrate this by saying that if a wife dies before her husband, the husband is simply evicted from the wife's village, and his children can only visit him in his own natal village. Although mostly true, this characterization omits something important, especially in Goffman's analysis. When a man mourns his wife as an affine, giving his own children another kind of bwabwale and paying the same kinds of respect to their susu that they will ultimately do for his, he makes himself conspicuously present in his own abstentions. He does not, in fact, simply disappear from the lives of his affines and children. His avoidance is not then the end of the relationship. Rather, by practicing avoidance and giving gifts, he acts in ways that make himself as a person an object of others' gaze and evaluation. Writing in a similar context, Stasch (2003) argues that a person's observance of rules of avoidance can be taken up as an object of discourse by its recipients and thus turned into a basis for a connection to that person. Stasch notes that avoidance is never simply the absence of a particular prohibited action. Rather than being a binary code of action or inaction, the practice of avoidance also offers room for exaggeration and play, and thus the manner in which people observe these rules itself sends a metacommunicative message about the present state of the relationship to those implicated in the rules. For instance, if contact with one's mother-in-law is prohibited, then the overt ways in which a child-in-law moves in domestic spaces in the presence of the mother-in-law themselves carry a message about their relationship. Auhelawa do likewise with the variety of circumlocutions they employ to avoid uttering the names that are prohibited to them. I would take this one step farther. Avoidance in particular is what Harold Garfinkel (1988) would call a naturally accountable action. It is always done with the gaze of others in mind. In his avoidances the widower offers himself as a visible model of what the social relationship is and should be. His gifts and his actions are, in the context of the feast as a ritual, a prospective metaphor for the consequences he seeks. His face is at stake; he is vulnerable to the judgement of others. But more important, by acting in these ways—and similarly by abstaining from food, wailing, and acting deferentially—the actor invites the participation of his audience. What they create together need not be face in the sense of a coherent individual personhood, as Goffman may have intended. Actor and audience meet in the territory of a moral self that is by definition part of a complex web of kinship connections. This order is not the outcome of any one single actor or action, but it is produced collectively through the ritual of feast and exchange. To come into being, it needs both Lucy to bring gifts and Lorenzo to remind her to write her name on her pot.

Thus Auhelawa exchanges create relationships not because people acquire a specific habitus, but because through their interaction they enter into specific kinds of reflexivity about their own actions. Rather than being conscious reflection on the patterns they see, these modes of reflexivity are embedded in specific situations (see Gershon 2012). As such, people depend on the media available in those situations to achieve together a specific view of how their actions fit into patterns and thus build relationships and the social order writ large. In feasts, the gift is not only the instrument but also the mirror of people's moral selves as kin.

As mentioned above, one of the ways that Auhelawa do reflect on the underlying logic of feasting is to see a strategic dimension. They imagine that wasawasa and alawata can meet any challenge of exchange and capitalize on the opportunity to turn their wealth into greater prestige. However, when people do imagine this possibility, they see it only in retrospect. That's how it was in the old days. Today, they say, the population is too large. There are too many children to feed, and so people offer less in feasts as gifts. They imagine a world in the not-too-distant future when people do not exchange in feasts, and each household looks out for its own interests. The people I knew in Auhelawa quite often adopted this other kind of reflexivity in which they cast their own social order in historical terms and predicted a gradual decline of their material and social well-being. This kind of reflexivity is also keyed to specific social situations, specifically the garden and the annual round of planting and harvesting. In particular, the yam house serves as the main device by which each gardener represents her economic well-being, social standing, and indeed her moral worth as a mother. Here too women find new ways to cultivate an alternative moral self, and it is to that struggle I turn in the next and following chapters.

3

HUNGER AND PLENTY

Are There Farmers in America?

Sometime in 2006, I went to the market to purchase some *gabulu*, a stinging nettle leaf rubbed on the skin for aches and pains. Women usually sold it by the bundle near the mission, but there wasn't any that day, so I decided to sit around with the sellers on the gravel lawn in front of St. Peter's Church. As I walked down to them, a neighbor, a senior woman of Eli'awa Village, was apparently in the middle of a discourse on proper marketing ethics: "We plant everything, cabbage, spinach. God put all of it here as a blessing to humanity. They aren't there for you to sell for 50 toea, 60 toea. Only sell them at a low price like the rest of us."[1]

A woman sitting nearby shot me a look and smiled. "Oh, you know her. Toktok," she said. (Her nickname means "talkative.") I approached two women sitting together. One struck up a conversation with me, "Any time you go to Alotau, Ryan, you load *hada* [betel nut] and market, and you'll find money." The woman sitting next to her then asked me something seriously, "In America, people market things, don't they? Some of them are 'like us' [*dova ai*], 'poor' [*pouwa*]." I said yes and started to tell a story about from my childhood in rural upstate New York, when I went driving with my parents to buy summer corn from a roadside stand. But her friend, not listening, answered instead, "Oh no, they might sell store goods, but not hada." That didn't satisfy the one who asked me, so she turned to me to confirm it, saying, "Some dimdims don't have money, right? They're 'poor'? They are 'farmers' [*fama*]? Toktok echoed from the back, "Yes, some dimdims have no money."[2]

Were Auhelawa families really poor? Many people told me that they could no longer produce enough food in their gardens. They said that everyone's harvests are not big enough to feed the growing population. In particular, they said that people cannot produce enough prestigious 'wateya yams to eat at home and to give to affines and patrikin in mortuary feasts, and so feasts have shrunk. In fact, Auhelawa see evidence of agricultural decline all around them. Many Auhelawa look back nostalgically to a time when people planted only four traditional crops and could sustain themselves, grow great harvests, and offer major gifts in feasts. As one senior man versed in the knowledge of gardening told me, "Today no one is a big man; we are all cassava-eaters." Indeed, this man is correct in at least one respect. Most families grow and eat cassava, sweet potato, pumpkin, and several other nontraditional crops now. Why would that be seen as a sign of poverty and decline?

I didn't see any evidence for this decline myself. Families seemed well fed, and when I conducted a household survey in 2006, all families had planted several gardens, and no one reported being hungry or short of food. Certainly New Home had plenty of food to feed all the residents, including myself.[3] While the birth rate and the population overall has steadily grown, as elsewhere in PNG, gardeners have adopted new crops like cassava and sweet potato (Bourke 2001). After they have harvested yams, they plant sweet potato and cassava in the old garden. At least from the outside, it seemed like the changes to Auhelawa subsistence largely complement and augment the traditional system. Compared with other areas in the region, Auhelawa seems to be faring well in spite of demographic pressure (Foale 2005). I had learned to trust what people told me, even when it didn't make sense, especially when it came to the arts of gardening. On this matter, though, I found it difficult to do so.

Auhelawa may know intuitively how much food they can grow, but they also learn about themselves from the many state agencies which observe and measure them. For example, early in my fieldwork in 2004, the PNG government launched a program to issue birth certificates for every child born. They began by enrolling all children under eighteen years to issue them with certificates retroactively. In Auhelawa, a team of health extension workers carried the enrollment forms from village to village and house to house. Seeing an opportunity to familiarize myself with the demographic structure of Auhelawa, I went along with the extension workers. For each parent they interviewed, the workers filled in a form for each child, writing the name of the mother and the father as well as the child's birth date and several other pieces of information. Each family's number of children was, in this way, recorded and associated with a presumed married couple, the child's mother and father. The child census, like so many government surveys, presupposed a particular kind of social landscape of households, relatively similar and independent groups, in order to measure the population. Many of the questions made no sense. Because Auhelawa's population is distributed across a chain of small settlements along the coast, the questions of the parents' "clan" and "village" did not easily translate. The survey team improvised some convenient answers: the totemic bird species for clan and the name of the largest nearby village of the mother's susu for village. For father's and mother's occupations, they filled in "subsistence farmer" and "housewife" without a second thought. It looked to me like bureaucratic rationality run amok. The picture of families created by the forms bore no relation to the reality that Auhelawa experience and that I was already learning to see. The forms assumed that the world consisted of neat little groups that were all alike, and people were simply shoehorned into these categories.

Yet over time, I've come to see that these statistical pictures, though clearly skewed, still have weight locally. As I spent more time in Auhelawa, I started to understand that people have also learned to think of themselves as forming a population that can be counted and whose parameters can be estimated. In some contexts, people believe it is very important to see themselves collectively in relation to the same statistical patterns of growth and decline that interest state institutions. For instance, on a return trip to Auhelawa in 2014, I sat in on a meeting of parents and teachers at Hapelomwala'ina Elementary School. The school usually takes in students starting at age five but recently had announced that classes were overenrolled for the next year. The government had recently eliminated school fees and promised open enrollment to primary school, starting with kindergarten (called elementary prep in PNG). Yet the government had not planned for the number of eligible children, the teachers announced. The audience of parents asked questions about how the government could have ignored the self-evident fact that the population of children was growing so quickly. After all, one elder woman said, everyone knows that young women have many more children than in the past and get married much earlier. She went on to remark that young women and men chose to sleep together too quickly, too often, and without the parents' permission or knowledge, and then the women became pregnant. The crowd, perhaps slightly scandalized by such frank talk at a school meeting, chuckled, and eventually the woman was asked to stop. Yet this woman was not saying anything anyone there had not heard before. During most of my field work in Auhelawa, the growth of the population was a chief topic of gossip. The older generation often remarked that there were too many children in Auhelawa now, which was their way of saying that young women did not control their sexuality, either before or during marriage. My adoptive grandfather told me that a young wife today starts out pregnant, and then as soon as one was delivered, another one was on the way. Indeed, some women remarked that these younger women had children stupidly. In past years, women drank herbal medicine to prevent pregnancy or to make oneself infertile after having a few children. Today women did not do this, they said, and the population was growing out of control.

When people gossip about a growing population, they are also entering into a discourse of development and progress that has existed since the colonial era. While over time, this discourse has taken several forms, it has consistently framed the health and well-being of people as a function of their patterns of behavior at the level of a coresident group of parents and children. This framework is, as one might expect, strongly associated with the institutional contexts in which Auhelawa engage with the state. Auhelawa are interpellated into this position when they bring their infant children for checkups at the monthly clinic or when they enroll their children in school. Yet these are not the only places where one may find this framework. Another place where one grapples with seeing oneself as a member of household which is either rich or poor is in one's own gardens, and especially in one's *vatavata* (yam house), a structure each gardener builds near a garden to store the year's harvest. Gardens and yam houses are, much like surveys of households, particular kinds of apparatuses in which people are compelled to see themselves as a unit and as a component of an encompassing social system. As I argue below, gardens and yam houses are also places where people reconcile and balance competing orientations. They serve as sites for cultivating different dispositions toward domestic work and acquiring different kinds of agency as mothers and kinswomen. A gardener can read her harvest as either a sign of her material wealth or poverty, or a sign of her capacity to engage in prestigious reciprocal exchanges beyond the household and matrilineage. Depending on the categories she uses to frame her relationship to her harvest she can have plenty of food or not enough.

In this chapter I ask why these two readings of harvests are so salient. Why do the introduced crops on which people have come to rely represent hunger instead of prosperity? Why do new family forms seem to imply the breakdown of moral order? One possibility is that through food and children, people in Auhelawa are working out an inevitable contradiction between the need to feed one's husband and children and the need to be a good kinswoman—that is, the contradiction between one's membership in a conjugal household and a matrilineage that must relate to other matrilineages. People have adapted to social and political changes by adopting new crops that require less labor but pull people away from the production of prestige crops used in feasting. Women as the principal laborers and managers of gardens embody this change. Tensions between household and descent group are a commonplace of anthropology of matrilineal societies (Malinowski 1935; Fortune 1963 [1932]; Macintyre 1987; Foster 1995; Bolyanatz 2000). From this perspective, Auhelawa grapple with a basic "matrilineal puzzle" (Richards 1950, 246). One might thus argue that women acquire a habitus geared to this structural cleavage between the conjugal family and the descent group that determines people's gardening regime and thus shapes how they see the new crops that are adopted. I argue, however, that the moral habitus of the garden is not simply an embodiment of a matrilineal social structure and its history. Rather women make use of yams and gardens as symbolic media that mediate historical change as a dilemma between two rival conceptions of motherhood. Yam gardening is oriented toward reciprocal exchanges between people of different lineages. Crops in secondary gardens are devoted toward feeding the household and constitute relationships through sharing. In their yam houses, women find ways to balance these competing orientations by counting and sorting their wealth into a map of their relationships that can be read both as a picture of a household as a component of a matrilineal order.

One can think of the changes in Auhelawa gardening as a kind of agricultural intensification. Ester Boserup (2007 [1970]) has argued that technological changes in agriculture, including new crops, influence the social organization of farming labor. She argues that the change in many African societies from shifting cultivation to plough cultivation was also a transition from a "female farming system" in which women were primarily responsible for food production to a system driven by male labor, and in which women were relegated to purely domestic duties (Boserup 2007 [1970]). In Auhelawa, I see an analogous conflict between different ways of securing a livelihood, each linked with two distinct conceptions of mothers, the matrilineal mother and the domestic mother. The matrilineal mother gives birth to and raises new members of her susu, giving them membership and political and economic rights in this group. In the same way, the matrilineal mother's yam harvests do not merely signify her wealth or her capacities to sustain herself but also represent continuity and perdurance in a line of yams, children, and rights to particular gardening sites. The domestic mother, by contrast, gives birth to children as part of a heterosexual union. Her care for these children is a component of a sexual division of labor within this conjugal unit. When children and food are measured in relation to this kind of relatively autonomous unit of consumption and production, they highlight the biological health and development of the children as signs of success and self-sufficiency. Through the lens of domestic mothering, population growth is a corollary of a woman with too many children. In some ways, the domestic mother comes into Auhelawa in the early days of Australian colonial administration, when the government took on the protection of native welfare as one of its key missions, but only in a narrowly defined sense. The colonial ideology of families did not replace indigenous concepts of women's work but laid bare contradictions already there. Women now reconcile these competing appraisals of their work in the vatavata, a house in their gardens where women store the annual crop of yams, and where they can create a diagram of the demands on their work and see how well they are able to meet them. The yam house is both a mirror of oneself and a prism by which a woman can align the colonial ideology of domesticity and the expectations of reciprocity. Thus yam harvests are powerful metaphors for public morality and powerful devices for women to mediate the moral contradictions they occupy.

Colonialism, Population, and Poverty

The government surveys I observed in Auhelawa are just the latest version of a process of statistical measurement that began in the colonial era. Britain declared the Protectorate of British New Guinea in 1884 over the southern coasts and eastern islands of New Guinea, including Normanby Island. The stated purpose of colonial policy was dual: to open the territory to development, and to safeguard the welfare of the indigenous peoples (Edmonds 2006). One of the colonial administration's chief concerns was the possibility that women of indigenous societies there were having fewer children. While there is evidence for modest population decline in some areas, it is difficult to generalize from it (Bayliss-Smith 2014). At the time, some observers noted that introduced European diseases probably accounted for much of the loss of population, yet nonetheless most officials spoke about depopulation in terms of the extinction of an inferior race. The prejudices of the time seemed mainly to be the source for the fear of depopulation. Margaret Jolly (1998), for instance, argues that class-based discourses of mothering in Britain developed in Pacific island colonies into a discourse of mothering in which white society needed to instruct indigenous women in the right way to care for and raise children and in the value of motherhood generally. Similarly, Adam Reed (1997) argues that colonial policy in Papua was grounded in a discourse of sexuality in which indigenous Melanesians lacked discipline to control themselves and to contain desire within the institution of a monogamous heterosexual conjugal relationship. In any case, what Europeans at the time seemed to assume was that any human society would always have a tendency to grow through natural fertility. Men and women would always marry and have as many children as possible, leading to greater numbers. For them, human societies were always based on a natural foundation of monogamous heterosexual conjugality and a gendered division of labor, which extended directly from women's procreative capacity. If a population declined, it was because this natural logic had been disrupted. Thus in considering possible responses, policymakers automatically applied the conjugal household as a lens with which to see population and responded accordingly.

Yet the bias toward the domestic mother was not simply a cross-cultural misunderstanding. It derived from the nature of state power as it was expressed in the ways in which colonial agents related to indigenous subjects. Michel Foucault (1991) argues that modern state power comes into being with the creation of a new concept of a population over which the state has control and responsibility. Statistical measurement, blessed with the authority of scientific objectivity, becomes one way in which people and communities are constituted as a mass, a population. As a population, they become politically inert. The state takes on the role of managing people as they are known in aggregate through quantitative measures. Being comparable individual units, subjects only have variable characteristics and tendencies. Policies apply to people only as units within an overall trend across the population that the state seeks to manage. The administrations of British New Guinea and, and after 1906, the Australian external territory of Papua were each charged with the task of protecting native welfare, and each conceptualized this as a feature of the population as a whole.[4] In that sense the fear of depopulation itself is an artifact of an epistemological framing of indigenous peoples common to Australian and British elites at this time. To protect Melanesians from this perceived risk, the state first had to constitute the peoples of this territory as a population that could either grow or decline. Two early lieutenant governors, William Macgregor and J.H.P. Murray, put in place policies that did much to enable this framing. Although they differed on some points, Murray saw his own administration as building on the foundation laid by Macgregor. Murray describes their process of spreading the influence of government as "the policy of the oil stain" (1933, 7). First, bases were established and patrolling officers and native police assigned to work outward to convert the people they encountered into law-abiding communities. Following initial contacts, patrols would regularly visit these communities in a series, taking censuses of each district. As its influence spread, the administration imposed native regulations on the settled communities, requiring them to bury dead in cemeteries, to maintain clean villages, to build large houses, and eventually to plant useful trees such as coconut palms. Regulations required that each adult man plant a certain number of palms as part of a collective plantation within his community with the intention that the coconuts could be sold to traders for cash to make copra, a valuable source of energy at the time. By drawing natives into a cash economy as smallholders, the administration hoped to create a tax base that would fund its operations. They would guard native welfare by transforming native societies, bring them into an economic system in which individual households would generate the revenue for providing health care, education, and infrastructure to the territory.

Macgregor and Murray both believed that depopulation could be reversed by bringing natives under a colonial government. They both used tax policy as an incentive for women to have more children. For every man who supported a woman with at least four children, the head tax was waived. Every woman who was raising more than four children was given a card with which she could claim a baby bonus for each child above four (Reed 1997). (Given that both men and women received a benefit from children, one could argue that the baby bonus also created an incentive for men and women to enter into a monogamous marriage centered on raising their children.) Even as doctors requested more money from the colonial government to improve medical care and public health of natives, Macgregor and Murray maintained that they could protect native welfare by encouraging different kinds of domestic behavior (Lambert 1934; see also Bennett 2014). The colonial government even used propaganda to encourage a higher birth rate. On patrols through the area, officers inquired about venereal disease, lectured people on the importance of having children, and in one case distributed pamphlets on the matter.[5] The administration used native tax revenue to pay for an English newspaper for Papuan peoples, the *Papuan Villager*. Over the years, the paper published a number of articles aimed at changing behavior that the government thought inhibited population growth. Items promoted methods for growing more and different kinds of crops, encouraged people to build big houses and to "be proud of your village" by cleaning it up.[6] Native tax funds were spent on medical services, too.

The government built native hospitals, including maternity hospitals. It also paid money to Christian missions to establish hospitals and schools. This reflected a long-standing belief in the colonial administration that the missions served the government's aims by adjusting natives to colonial laws. In missions, people were taught to regulate their own behaviors as individuals. The benefit to the colonial government of Christian conversion was that native peoples also became the right kind of unit for the colonial accounting regime.

Murray (1933) was particularly interested in what he considered a scientific approach to government and created the office of the government anthropologist in part to collect information on people, which would aid in the making of native social policy. The government anthropology department, for instance, including one or more researchers and several research assistants, was funded by the Native Tax Fund, as was the *Papuan Villager* (Territory of Papua 1949 [1936]; Young and Clark 2001, 13). By law, native tax revenue was spent only on native welfare (Territory of Papua 1949 [1936]). In the writings of the government anthropologists, one can also see an effort to represent native people and native welfare in terms of the behavior of individuals and households. In several reports, the government anthropologists W. E. Armstrong and Francis Williams address the responses to and effects of native taxation (Armstrong 1922a; Armstrong 1922b; Williams 1933; see also Young and Clark 2001, 13). They each affirm what appears to be the conventional wisdom regarding taxes: that they are accepted insofar as people understand that they are dedicated for government services, and that they motivate people to earn money and, thanks to the baby bonus, have children. In other ways, their approach to social customs and institutions is influenced by not only government priorities but also the administration's attention to natives as a population. Hence the cultural attributes of indigenous communities are interpreted in relation to how they function to maintain the health of a population, as opposed to the reproduction of a particular kind of social order.

In colonial policy, mothers were the means for reproducing life but not people whose health and life had value in their own right.[7] The perception of depopulation presupposed that women would, under normal circumstances, naturally have healthy pregnancies and deliver and care for healthy babies. Any indication that women did not automatically adopt the position of a domestic mother was assumed to mean that something had interfered with the natural logic of heterosexual fertility. Although the threat of depopulation proved to be exaggerated, the colonial apparatus of census and taxation brought Auhelawa and their neighbors into a system in which they learned to see themselves as naturally members of households centered on heterosexual marriages. As the first government anthropologist W. E. Armstrong wrote, the census is "a mechanism of a new order, which, as it were, 'catches hold of each native by his name and never lets him go'" (1922b, 34). The same can be said for the baby bonus cards by which people could claim to be exempt from tax and obtain set benefits for each additional child. By becoming members of a colonial state, Auhelawa people learned to see themselves as countable units, measured in households, and linked to specific territories and groups. From this point on, people were regularly called on to be counted as part of these population measurements. Even now after independence and the end of the head tax, government officials still regularly canvass the coastline of Normanby, stopping in at each house and counting the people, their children, their possessions, and other facts about them as individuals. Thus Auhelawa people have learned to measure themselves as households, centered on a heterosexual married couple, including a domestic mother.

Respect for the Yams

For Macgregor and Murray, indigenous subjects lived in material poverty, but their sense of this poverty extended to include their health and well-being. Poverty was a sign of people's cultural and racial vitality. Depopulation in particular represented the moral qualities of men and women as spouses and parents. Thus it might be easy to conclude that Auhelawa see themselves as getting poorer, since for so many years the state has related to them as a population that needed some kind of intervention in order to improve. Yet when Auhelawa take up this discourse themselves, they also have to translate it into the terms of their own agricultural regime. In the Auhelawa agricultural system, poverty and wealth include both material conditions and social capacities. Each person is a gardener, a member of a susu, a natuleiya of the father's susu, and likely also an affine for another susu. Someone who is rich is one who is capable of not only meeting all of her needs through her own gardening but capable of satisfying the expectations of many others to provide gifts in feasts. The discipline of gardening and the tools used to cultivate, reap, and store one's food for the year also provide a lens by which people can engage in their own measurements of themselves.

As mentioned earlier, a marriage is a formal bond between people of different susu and thus also an affinal relationship between a person and the susu of his or her spouse. Each spouse must respect the susu of the other as their "spouse's grave" (*magai mwane*). The domestic household exists at the juncture between the lineages of each spouse and as such is defined by the intersection of their economic interests in each of their susu and the lands they can access for gardening in each susu's territory. A married couple works in the garden as members of their respective lineages as well as members of a conjugal unit that cares for and raises children. The gardening system reflects this dual division between home production and social production at the most basic level. Each year, a married couple will tend several gardens. Some of these will be newly dug gardens, known as *oya* (the generic word for garden), with rich, fertile soil for the growing of two species of yam. Others will be plots from which the last year's yams were harvested. After the yam harvest the oya becomes a *yaheyahe* (a lesser garden) when it is replanted with secondary crops for the family's own consumption. Once a yaheyahe has been harvested, it is allowed to revert to the forest and lie fallow, ideally for many years.[8] This kind of system is common for the region of the island and seaboard societies of Milne Bay Province. Malinowski notes that Kiriwina *taytu* yam gardens, called *kaymata*, are distinct from taro gardens, known as *tapopu*, and secondary crop gardens, called *kaymugwa* (Malinowski 1935, 58, 256). Most of the food of the kaymata is grown to given to others. Taro and secondary crops mainly provide for a gardener's family during the hunger period when the yams have all been consumed or given. Moreover, kaymata are laid out in such a way that the gardener makes separate plantings for his affinal tribute and his wife and children's own consumption. A similar kind of distinction between foods grown for household consumption and prestige foods can be found in descriptions of several gardening systems of the Milne Bay Province region (Austen 1945; Young 1971; Kahn 1986). While Auhelawa's gardening practice is not exactly the same as its neighbors, all these systems are structured by the same unequal division between home production and social production. As I describe below, the harvest from the Auhelawa oya is also recursively divided into greater and lesser parts for gifts and for home use respectively, just as in Kiriwina. This principle of recursive unequal division, starting with the separation of oya and yaheyahe and continuing to the division of the yam harvest, is the central principle of Auhelawa gardening.

Each year a married couple makes several oya (new gardens). Each spouse maintains rights to make gardens in one or more "standing places" (*ebe towolo*), gardening sites in their natal susu lands that they have inherited from their mother and possibly uncles. Each spouse has also inherited the yam seeds of their mothers, which they will plant in their yam gardens of their susu. As affines, they also must pay respect to the matrirelatives of their spouse by working in their gardens. If one of the spouses' fathers has died, then the child will have had to show respect to the father's susu as a natuleiya, and if this has been accepted, then that person may exercise usufruct on his ebe towolo as well. Typically, a couple will make a new garden in its respective ebe towolo of its own lineage's territory, and one or both of the spouses will make a garden on part of the father's ebe towolo. If one's father is alive, it is also still possible to receive permission to garden in his ebe towolo as well, as Aidan did before Cosmas died. Thus a household makes use of gardens in several different sites in the vicinity, while it occupies only one village as its main residence (usually first the wife's natal home and then, after some time, the husband's).

New gardens are usually cleared beginning in October, and the clearing away of bush (*daibi*), digging up of the soil (*tudai*), and planting (*peli*) of a household's new gardens should ideally be finished well before Christmas but often can extend until early February. The work of clearing and digging is done by men. One common way for this work to be organized is as an exchange between affinally linked villages called *iliwa*. The husband summons his male kin and joins with his wife's male kin to dig the couple's gardens in each of its villages over several days. Women of the village cook food, also called *iliwa*, to feed the workers. In reciprocation, the men of the wife's village form a party and go to their in-law's village to clear his gardens, for which they again are fed in return for their work. The daily movement of large groups of men carrying heavy iron spades in the hot sun back and forth between villages characterizes "the season of work" (*paihowa yana hauga*) at this time of year.

Once the gardens are cleared and dug, a woman plants her yam seeds in her gardens and her husband's seeds in his gardens. Each row (*laba*) of the garden is planted with the portion of seed set aside for each child of the couple. There are several named varieties of 'wateya, and a gardener may have seeds for several different types. She plants each of these in separate rows. In addition to 'wateya (*Dioscorea alata*) people also plant another species of yam called *halutu* (*Dioscorea esculenta*) in its own rows or, if there is enough space, in a separate garden altogether. 'Wateya and halutu are the most important food crops; all households reported that they planted at least one new garden with yams of both species, and most planted all their new gardens with yams. Yams require a large investment of labor and usually the best and most fertile land. They must be planted in a newly cleared garden, and they must be given adequate space to grow and receive regular weeding. Yet despite these apparent disadvantages, people work hard to have as large a harvest of yams as they can and preserve as much of it as possible for seed for planting next year, thereby increasing their harvest year on year. Successful harvests allow people to meet exchange obligations and gain renown as good gardeners but are not meant to provide the food a family will eat on a regular basis.

'Wateya and halutu also present a special problem as a food crop. They require approximately seven months after planting to produce tubers and for the tubers to grow to their maximum size. If properly tended over this period, they will produce tubers abundantly all at once, then die. Harvested tubers will remain dormant and can be stored for nearly a year before they germinate and need to be planted again. During this time, they must be kept dry so they do not develop rot. The seasonality of the yam means that people who rely on it for food will experience roughly equal periods of abundance after the harvest and lean times from the planting of next year's gardens. To avoid hunger, yam gardeners must work hard in the garden and exercise proper management of their stored wealth after harvesting.

Auhelawa represent these constraints imposed by the yam's biology in terms of a strict gardening ethic called *enao*. Good gardening, in essence, mandates that people keep time with the yam, the development of which follows its own schedule. People who explained gardening to me usually started with the importance of timing work properly to coincide with natural seasonal changes. For instance, the blooming and falling of rosewood flowers alert people when to start a new phase of the gardening cycle, as does the movement of the Pleiades (*gamayawe*) across the sky. Gardeners must scrupulously attend to these natural "signs" (*ila'ilala*), because humans are not set by natural rhythms. Rather, people must use their minds to interpret the signs of the season, understand them, and respond appropriately. Gardeners cannot be lazy at their work lest they miss a crucial window for necessary tasks. Auhelawa gardeners readily admit that they are not always eager to work in the garden. The result of this, they say, is that they are late in doing their garden work and thus do not achieve the best harvest from their garden. Good gardeners are aware, attentive, and diligent all the time, an ethic that Auhelawa describe as a kind of punctuality. People believe that it is most important to attend to changes in the garden itself and read them as signs of the growth of yams. To read the signs on yam plants requires, of course, frequent trips to the yam garden to inspect the plants. Garden "visits" (*taubo'e*), using the same term used to denote a social visit, are one of many ways in which Auhelawa say that they respect yams. By this they mean that they treat their yam plants as if they were people (*tomowa*) and show them the same care and respect that would show humans. If a gardener fails to show respect to the yams, then they wilt from shyness and fail to grow. This begins during planting. When planting yam seeds, the gardener ceremonially washes (*vehuguvi*) her seeds in the juice and oils of leaves from selected bush plants and trees. This treats the seeds with a "medicine" that makes them grow big and produce many tubers. Whenever one arrives in the yam garden, one greets the yams by saying "Good morning!" and encourages them to grow, speaking gently to them as one would to children. This respectful relationship to the yams resembles the kind of respect one pays to fathers and cross-cousins, and indeed, as in those relationships, it also grants the recipient the power to decide whether or not the respect paid is sufficient.

After the heavy work of making the gardens, gardeners plant and tend their yams alone. Most men and women plant their own seed lines in separate gardens on their lineage ebe towolo, performing vehuguvi over each seed and reciting magic formulae over them. Even though many people professed not to believe in magic spells, they still washed the seeds with the right leaves and prayed to God to bless them. This practice is very private, and few people wanted to discuss it with me, except maybe to suggest that they did not perform it but others did. The magic and art of planting 'wateya comes from one's mother or father and is dangerous to others to see or attempt if it is not transmitted to them. Each lineage restricts this knowledge to its members and its natuleiya.

In the same vein, people generally act discreetly with respect to other people's garden work. They respectfully avoid looking at and asking about other people's gardens. It is inappropriate to ask about another's crops and to tell other people about one's own gardens. If someone needs to mention what they have grown, she refers to her crops with dysphemistic words for immature growths and bad tubers. Most people say that people become jealous of others' gardens and thus avoid revealing what they grow for fear it will be stolen or they will be afflicted with witchcraft. Yet revealing what one has also obligates one to share it, and this applies to garden produce as well. So if someone were to see another harvesting, the gardener might hide and later discreetly leave a basket of food for the viewer to take away.

The practice of yam gardening is thus not merely a work ethic of individuals or the household. Working in the garden is done mostly in social isolation yet for the benefit of others who will receive the food, either as gifts or as part of the routine sharing among relatives. People depend on their own work in the garden, but their success or failure has social consequences. Gardening therefore requires an orientation of submission of one's own individual agency to the collective order. For instance, as tubers mature in the ground, small premature tubers called *bwalesi* push through the surface. As food, they are regarded quite ambivalently. People say they are slippery and flavorless, yet they appear at the very moment when people are most eagerly awaiting the new crop, having struggled to get through tagwala, the hunger period. People ideally should deny them to themselves and choose to wait until other people are harvesting. If a family has no other food, though, it will secretly feed bwalesi to its children. After preparing them, women take care to throw the peelings into the sea so that their neighbors do not find out that they have eaten yams before the harvest.

This ethical orientation toward the harvest is also expressed in terms of time. As mentioned above, people talk about their own gardening work in relation to watching the signs of seasonal change and the signs of their maturing plants. Throughout the year, they focus their attention on these changes and respond to them. This culminates in the harvest of new 'wateya yams, which is signaled by the falling of dried leaves from the yam vines. Yet unlike preceding stages, social factors ultimately determine the exact timing of the harvest. People do not simply harvest their 'wateya when they see these signs. Ideally, they wait until an appointed time when other neighboring households will also harvest. I was told that it was traditional for one person, a wasawasa (rich man) to fix the date of the harvest for all of the households of one area. No one could explain to me how this traditional custom operated in practice. Yet the idea that this should be the norm is important in its own right. When I asked people when they planned to harvest, they often said that they should harvest "in May" (mentioning the calendar month) because that is the proper time of harvesting. They also often said that they were late because they had planted late, which suggests that they were comparing themselves to other families. When they remark on their lateness, they assume that everyone's harvests should take place at the same time. Many people said that people merely watched when other people started to harvest and then harvested themselves. No one wanted to be first.

A woman harvests her family's yams from each new yam garden they plant. As the work of cutting and clearing new gardens is the domain of men, so planting and harvesting of yams are the domain of women. Throughout the life of the garden, the woman has been caring for the plants as if they were children, treating them with sensitivity. In harvesting, she continues by carefully digging up each plant by hand and stroking away the dirt from each tuber. Typically each ebe towolo has one yam house nearby which the woman of the family will use to store the yams. A woman will place her yams in this house one by one, taking care not to bruise any. Storing yams is a crucial part of how a woman manages the harvest so that a family can contribute yams as gifts to feasts, feed itself, and plant seed tubers in the next year's garden. Yams are classified according to their quality, variety, and the line to which they belong. The largest yams are called *'wateya mohili* (real yams). They are approximately one kilogram or more and are free of bruises and rot. These are reserved as gifts to be given in feasts hosted by affinally and patrilaterally related lineages. A harvest will consist of several of these perfect specimens and many

Figure 3. A new yam garden and yam house above New Home Village in January 2006

other tubers ranging in size of one kilogram to small marble-sized yams called *ma'ama'a*, or bad yams that turn red when cooked called *belabelala*. (There are also some tubers that are too immature to be harvested, called *yabayaba*, are left in the ground.) These inferior specimens cannot be replanted or given, so they can be eaten by the family freely. Most yams fall somewhere in the middle and can either be eaten or replanted so that the seed material in the head of the tuber will germinate. A woman strives to eat as little of this harvest as possible at home and preserve as much as possible for gifts and for seeds to be replanted next year. The family eats the smallest yams first, gradually eating larger tubers while also earmarking certain yams for certain purposes. An abundant harvest of yams, then, does not guarantee that the gardener's household will eat well. Rather, all harvests, large and small, are managed so that the best tubers are reserved as gifts, and other tubers are replanted as seed in the yam lines of each child, while the family eats as little as possible of what remains. Finally, when the time comes for new gardens to be planted at the beginning of the hot, dry season, the remaining seeds are planted in new gardens, and tagwala begins.

As part of the management of the harvest, the woman separates the yams she has harvested into piles in the yam house. Ideally a woman will plant one row in her garden for each child she has. The harvest from each row is placed in its own group in the yam house. After several years, when the child is married and ready to start planting her own gardens, she will inherit the seeds from her pile in her mother's yam house. Other rows in the garden are sometimes planted with special varieties of 'wateya. For instance, one important variety is called *pwane'ahu*, which tends to be long and spindly rather than round. Pwane'ahu are also separated and placed in their own pile in the yam house. Halutu are a distinct species of yam, which are also stored in the yam house. While planted in the same garden, they are also planted in their own rows and placed in their own piles in the yam house. Halutu can vary in size, and a harvest will produce some of impressive size. Yet these are not used as feast gifts, and so their classification is not as elaborate. A woman will separate the big *halutu ai'aina* (halutu with plenty of food) and save them as food for guests in the village. For instance, she can cook halutu ai'aina as a meal for workers who perform iliwa. The family will eat through the supply of halutu from the smallest to largest until it is time for the next year's garden to be planted.

As a woman organizes the 'wateya and halutu in her yam house, she thinks ahead to all the upcoming memorial feasts to which she must contribute a ceremonial gift. For each of these *paula* (jobs), she sets aside yams. The interior layout of the yam house is a picture of the woman's relationships to her children and to other kin. When the harvest is sorted, a woman closes the door, and if she has a padlock, she locks it, too. Only one person, the gardener, should be allowed to enter the yam house. Women's involvement in food production has been cited as one reason for their relatively "high status" in the Milne Bay region (Lepowsky 1990, 175; see also Lepowsky 1993; Mallett 2003; Kuehling 2005). What has not been emphasized, however, is the value created by classifying, organizing, and accounting for the harvest. Not only does a woman have material control of her family's food supplies, but she is also responsible for inventorying and curating this collection of material tokens and the values they represent. When Auhelawa men and women explain why only a woman can withdraw food from the yam house, it is said that men would irresponsibly take the wrong food or too much of the wrong kind of food. A good gardener knows every yam in her store and can make rational decisions about what to eat and when.

To summarize, a couple divides its gardens and the food they produce between the conflicting aims of producing for social obligations and producing to feed one's family. The new gardens of the year are planted with prestige crops, which are intended primarily for gifts. The previous years' gardens are planted with secondary crops for home consumption. This distinction is recursively applied several times to the harvest from new gardens as well, creating a hierarchy of yams in which the better part of the harvest is committed to outward transmission over home consumption. Within the yam garden, people plant two species, one reserved for gifts and one that cannot be given as a gift. 'Wateya are also divided into categories based on future use, as specific gifts and as seeds for children, and the small yams, which cannot be used for these purposes, are marked for the family's food. Halutu are also divided, with bigger and better tubers reserved as meals for guests and smaller tubers marked for the family's consumption. The purpose of gardening and managing harvest in this way is to create "plenty of food" (*ai'ai bahuna*). People who are exceptionally good at producing food are "rich men" (*wasawasa*) and "rich women" (*alawata*). Yet wealth is not possession of a sheer quantity of food. Since food has to be allocated to one or the other of these conflicting purposes, wealth means having sufficient food to balance all these demands and to be able to replant yams the following year. As Kenelm Burridge (1975) suggests for big men in general in Melanesia, wasawasa and alawata are exceptional in the sense that they can transcend the contradictions between home production and social production in a society in which egalitarianism and reciprocity are norms.

Yet much as one sees with exchanges in feasting, most people do not treat their gardens as an enterprise for acquiring prestige. Instead, they strive to keep up with the regular work demanded by enao and to show respect for the fickle yams that cannot grow unless soil, rainfall, weeding, and care are all sufficient. The respect relationship in the garden is in that sense much like respect between cross-cousins. It is not so much that there are routines one has to follow, but that the whole relationship to one's yams is colored by self-conscious diligence and patience for the seven or eight months between planting and harvest. Ultimately the yams decide whether the gardener was adequately respectful, either by producing abundance or withering and dying. When the yams are finally harvested, this enao then extends to the careful storage and management of a limited supply, ensuring both enough for the next planting season and for one's gifts to others. In that sense, the gardener brings their moral orientation of respect into their own garden and uses it as a framework for their daily work. This demonstrates the moral aspect of enao, and it has an influence beyond the yam house as a template for other kinds of action by women (see Munn 1992).

Gardening is not simply enao. There is another, completely different approach to food production called *lauyaba*. If enao is a moral orientation to others through the production of yams as gifts, then lauyaba is what one does for one's daily meals. New gardens receive the most elaboration in the minds of gardeners, since this is what defines them as gardeners and as people, but this is not the only source of food for families. A gardener must also provide food once the yam seeds have been planted, and the lean time begins. In this time, people rely on other crops that produce throughout the year. In this way, yaheyahe complement and supplement the cultivation of prestige yams. Thus every year a family tends new yam gardens and harvest food on a regular basis from secondary gardens. Many families also visit sites of yaheyahe from previous years.

Even after these gardens have been left to revert to bush, many food plants continue to grow in them. These kinds of untended gardens are called *ya'waya'wala*. The main crops planted in yaheyahe are sweet potato (*kumwala, anu'anule*) and cassava (*tapioko*), yet any kind of food can be planted here. New gardens are almost entirely devoted to yams, with bananas planted only on the edges, and so anything else that a gardener chooses to cultivate tends to be planted in yaheyahe.

Unlike new gardens, people collect food from yaheyahe as it matures and when it is needed for the day's main evening meal. A woman will usually make a trip every other day to the yaheyahe to "collect bad food" (*lauyaba*). Work in the yaheyahe is oriented toward oneself and one's household. This is perhaps why people use a dysphemism for this activity; the work of provisioning one's household is the antithesis of the moral work of creating plenty through enao. Likewise, one's harvests from secondary gardens are characterized as yabayaba, meaning they are nothing, not important, no better than rubbish.[9] Work in secondary gardens unfolds in its own daily rhythm. No patience and careful planning over the whole year is required. Nor does growing secondary crops require self-control. Everyone has several yaheyahe from which they take food regularly. Indeed, this lesser sphere of home production makes the higher sphere of prestige production possible. Yet this kind of activity is intrinsically selfish and asocial. Gardening practices thus offer people two distinct frameworks with which to perform themselves as particular kinds of persons. While these two patterns of work complement each other, they also embody contradictory values. Gardeners must move between these different moral personalities, expressed in different temporal rhythms of gardening work, in order to meet all their obligations. This struggle influences the way people think about changes in gardening and explains why Auhelawa read these changes as signs of decline.

New Food

The preceding discussion of gardening in Auhelawa may make it sound like it is a stable system, but in fact gardeners consider gardening to have changed a great deal. People say that in the past, before the arrival of Australian and Polynesian missionaries, Auhelawa only grew four crops, 'wateya, halutu, *weda* (taro, *Colocasia esculenta*), and *pona'e* (a native species of *Musa* banana). Yet as I learned in my 2006 survey, nearly everyone in Auhelawa has moved far from this idealized image of tradition.[10] Nearly all those interviewed said that they planted 'wateya and halutu in new gardens, and tapioko and kumwala in their yaheyahe. The frequency with which I heard this response, especially from respondents with many gardens who were clearly getting bored with answering questions about each one, suggests that a new norm has emerged in which yams are grown in new gardens and these new crops are planted in old gardens.[11]

Auhelawa identify many of the foods they eat today as "new," by which they imply that they have a foreign origin and were introduced in the colonial era or later. When asked where these new crops came from, most people immediately replied that they were brought by the first missionary teachers from Polynesia. Many words for these crops and plants are bear their origin in their name, for instance *wa'ai samowa* (Samoan breadfruit) and *weda biti* (Fijian taro), as is also common for the names of varieties of native crops. Even halutu is said to be an introduction, not by missionaries but by people from the north of Normanby Island and neighboring Fergusson Island, where it is the prestige species.

Auhelawa consider new crops to be significantly different from 'wateya and other native crops.[12] These new crops require little work and can grow in poor-quality soil. They produce food within a few months. Like the fruit and nut trees that people also identify as foreign, these new foods supplement the diet during tagwala. Hence most people believe that missionaries brought these crops as a way of helping Auhelawa people take care of themselves and improve. Yet these crops cannot be used as gifts in feasts, and so they can only be eaten at home. New foods are not yams, and so by definition they are yabayaba. People harvest them for home consumption as they need them. Yet as much as they are a major part of everyone's diet, new foods also carry a new kind of stigma of being too easy to grow. Because sweet potatoes, for instance, require so little work, people say young women today do not learn the techniques of gardening and managing yams. They have grown up on sweet potato and cassava, and so this is all they know about garden work.

People also recognize that they rely on sweet potato and cassava for food throughout the year, and they link this to declining harvests from their yam gardens. I have no direct evidence that yam harvests are smaller than in the past. Auhelawa overwhelmingly hold the opinion that they are, or at least other people besides themselves are not able to grow enough yams from new gardens to both feed their children and make feast gifts. People observe that couples have more children now than in the past, and that women begin bearing children at younger ages. Faced with the need to support bigger households, families grow more sweet potato and cassava, which produces more food with less land, time, and effort. Meanwhile the gifts people give one another in ceremonial feasts have become smaller, feasts less frequent, and people generally more selfish than in the past. Auhelawa share a consensus that most people in their communities are poor. Yet as with wealth, what this seems to mean is that people lack the social capacity for exchanges that comes with a well-stocked yam house. They may be able to meet their basic needs, but they can only sit at home being private (*privat*) rather than "acting proud" (*gagasa*) by contributing to feasts. As an informant told me, "Today no one is a big man; we are all cassava eaters."

In her work on agricultural change Boserup (2007 [1970]) dismantles twin misconceptions of small-scale, family-based agriculture. One prevalent image at the time of her research was that family farms were organized in terms of a natural, universal division of labor rooted in the gender roles of the family. In fact, she shows that there were at least two distinct social organizational types of farming system: one in which women did most of the work, and one in which men did most of the work. Women's role in agricultural production was usually uncounted in studies at the time, leading to a skewed picture of lazy male farmers and unproductive subsistence forms. Second, and related to this, was that family-based agriculture was traditional in the sense that farmers merely followed unchanging patterns they learned from their ancestors. Boserup also shows that small-scale farming can be quite dynamic and able to respond to changing demands on the system, especially demographic pressure. So-called traditional farmers actually were very practical and receptive to innovations. Furthermore, agricultural intensification also had often dramatic social consequences for the family and the broader society. While Auhelawa gardening is not strictly comparable to the African and Asian cases in Boserup's study, these principles nonetheless apply.

Boserup is interested in how female farming systems are transformed into male farming systems. She argues that, in the case of African societies, colonialism and absorption into a market economy favored this change and led to a loss of women's status. Auhelawa gardening is highly gendered, and arguably women do most of the work, even as the system has changed. Even though it might make sense to call Auhelawa agriculture a female farming system, it seems more accurate to say that Auhelawa gardening includes a system in which women as cross-cousins and affines perform the gardening labor and another system in which women labor in their roles as mothers and wives. Women have always played both of these kinship roles and straddled the different spheres of value in which they participate, enao and lauyaba. In each of these roles, women's work as food producers and food managers is not merely practical. By giving different kinds of food, women constitute different kinds of kinship. The practices of yam gardening differentiate not only different categories of food but different spheres of nurture. By giving yams as feast gifts to one's affines and father's kin, one performs a relatedness of complementarity. By preserving seeds to transmit to one's children, one links them to one's matrilineage. By contrast, home production serves to nurture children physically. Commensality at home partakes of a sphere of sharing that creates kinship solidarity, which is distinct from yet also necessary to the production of kinship and descent through different kinds of reciprocal exchanges. Agricultural intensification is not associated with the rise of a male farming system that displaces women's control over resources. Instead, colonial governments provided a patriarchal narrative in which women were framed primarily as mothers within a conjugal household, whose work in the garden was an extension of their care for children. Auhelawa women gardeners have since had to reconcile this relatively new conception of themselves with their status within a matrilineal order in which they create wealth for exchange and preserve a line of yams to ensure the continued social capacities of their descendants. In a general way, an Auhelawa woman embodies the changing politics of kinship in a colonial and postcolonial society. More appropriately, though, women have drawn on existing and new resources as a set of devices to mediate the tensions between being a matrilineal mother and a domestic mother. Their gardens, yam houses, seed piles, and "new" crops are together a mirror through which gardeners see themselves as moral beings who can, with the right kind of effort, avoid poverty and find plenty.

The Yam House as a Boundary Object

The value of both traditional and nontraditional crops lies not simply in their nutritional utility but in their symbolic weight as well. Many anthropologists have discussed the symbolic value of food in many societies, including and especially in Papua New Guinea. Donald Tuzin (1972), for instance, discusses the yam as a symbol of many values of maleness among male Arapesh gardeners of Ilahita Village. Yet to be clear, for the Ilahita it is the idea of a yam that is a symbol of male virtue. Categories of food provide a symbolic language for many categories of kinship and society in Ilahita and elsewhere (Wagner 1977; Kahn 1986; Schieffelin 2005 [1976]). I would like to take this idea one step further. What is at stake is more than just the symbolism of different kinds of diet. Each actual harvest and the work that goes into producing it are also a medium for women to engage in a reflexive process of framing their families in terms of different kinds of economic and social values and, to a certain extent, attempt to mediate conflicting values expressed in the idea of the yam garden as a symbol. The conception of a traditional precolonial gardening system assumes that the only kind of gardening work is enao. At the same time, there has always been a tagwala, since the growing cycle of yams requires that seed be replanted and other foods sought until the next harvest. While informants suggested that banana and taro served this role, Auhelawa people have always eaten a variety of cultivated green vegetables, wild fruits, and wild nuts too. There has always been something else besides enao people have done to make ends meet. It may be better to say that enao encompasses its opposite, lauyaba. Enao is both the patient cultivation and preservation of yams for others and the sorting of good yams from lesser ones, which are acceptable to eat at home. A good gardener has plenty of food stored to meet any demand, but even good gardeners feed their children bwalesi in secret. Today, and indeed as long as anyone can remember, there are yaheyahe where one goes to lauyaba. This residual category of subsistence is, moreover, where gardeners innovate their practices, planting not only cassava and sweet potato but a wide variety of many different kinds of food, including beans, squash, corn, new species of banana, and pineapple. If yams are symbols of the matrilineal order of kinship, then these new, bad foods are a symbol of what that order excludes. The complementary opposition between enao and lauyaba thus serves as a handy way for gardeners to think about how their socioeconomic landscape has changed. As contemporary gardeners, women balance these two sides of gardening, in the separate kinds of work but also within the division and budgeting of yams, which is itself part of enao. If food is a symbol, then the opposition between different kinds of gardening work is a way people can classify and organize otherwise disparate roles they play to form a coherent whole.

To say that Auhelawa gardens are part of a "female farming system" is correct in that women do most of the work. More important, though, is that women, as mothers and wives, manage the harvest. Through their storage and sorting of their harvests in their yam houses, they produce information. The mental labor of women gives value to yam harvests as much if not more than women's physical labor. Women take the sheer quantity of tubers and, by piling them up in various patterns, calculate how much food the family has to eat, how many feast gifts the family can offer, and how many gardens they can plant the next year. The yam house computer stores information about the number of children this woman cares for, represented symbolically as a pile of seed yams. One woman explained the system this way: "The yam house is like a bank. You put money in, and then you take money out." It may seem that this woman is comparing yams to money as wealth, but what I would add is that by highlighting debits and credits, she is also talking about yams as a measurement of value. Like an abacus or a khipu calendar, the yam house is a material artifact that facilitates thinking in and through the environment (Hutchins 2005). A good woman knows every yam in her yam house by memory, but it must also be said, a good yam house allows a woman to remember every job she has to do. Unlike digital computers, and for that matter unlike banks, however, the yam house computer also represents wealth as more than sheer quantity. It also encodes the qualities of social connections between children and their mother, and through her, their lineage. Yam varieties are cultivated and passed on, and the specific varieties of yam give an identity to the line and the hands through which it passes. In this sense, the yam house computes a network of kinship relationships through the internal accounting of food stores.

A collection of yams stores information about a household that can be read in more than one way. It allows a gardener to see not only what paula can be performed, and what varieties can be propogated, but what remains to be eaten today. In the same way, one's gardens embody both concrete, ongoing claims to ownership and usufruct of land (that is, different kinds of relationships) and places to go to find food for the daily meal (that is, economic resources). The old and new foods grown in the family's gardens and stored in the yam house together form a boundary object, which coordinates the often divergent roles of matrilineal and domestic mothers. Susan Leigh Star and James Griesemer (1989) define a boundary object as a device that carries messages that move among distinct economies of signification. As communication media, boundary objects need to be robust enough to retain their information even as they move from one audience in which a certain context for them can be known and into a new audience that wants to coordinate with the first audience but does not know what they know or assume what they assume. Star and Griesemer are most interested in how groups with disparate knowledge, like scientists and the public, can coordinate their activities. A map of a national park, for instance, will consist of several symbolic layers. Some of these, like ecological zones, will make sense to scientists but be obscure to most visitors to the park. Other layers will be clear to the public, like picnic spots, but less interesting or relevant to scientists. The map itself, the material paper marked in a systematic way with geographic information, is a boundary object. Its job is to coordinate these two groups even though they use the same map to access different information. Through a boundary object, research on ecology within a park can inform choices about picnicking, without ecologists needing to pick scenic areas or picnickers needing to know about the health of the park's ecosystem. In the same way, the sorting of yams in the yam house creates a map of a household that can be read in different ways.

The yam house is read two different ways but by the same person, a gardener who inherits the legacies of colonialism, and has two disparate narratives of herself as a mother. Yam houses are private spaces. Women do not want it to be generally known how much they have to eat. Yam houses are secure, tied shut, and often locked. In this limited sense, the yam house is also an example of Star and Griesemer's (1989) boundary object. Unlike a map, yam houses do not robustly encode kinship relationships for external audiences. Few people will ever access a yam house from which they do not eat. When the woman who manages a particular yam house comes to withdraw food, she may be coming as a domestic mother on a᷄ lauyaba or as a matrilineal mother getting ready to present a bwabwale gift. Within the space of the yam house, she can alternate between the possible readings of its contents and see herself in either position. Still, these readings are not merely back of the envelope calculations. When this woman comes to the yam house, the weight of many dead census forms weighs on her brain like a nightmare. She sees what food she has, she performs her domestic calculations, and, I suggest, she uses this computational process to make a measure of her own socioeconomic standing. Some women mentioned to me that they did allocate some of their harvest for market sales in a separate pile. But more to the point, all women must calculate what they feed their children. In this process they choose new food over old food. In so doing, they come to embody the history of agricultural change in a certain way. From my perspective, having so many foods is a kind of agricultural innovation. Yet in the yam house women would not experience it in that way, just as they see their yam stores not as a fungible economic resource but as a foundation for effective social action.

The moral thinking that the garden enables also informs other new situations in Auhelawa, and I turn to these in the next two chapters. Money and commodities have circulated in Auhelawa since the early days of the colonial period, and daily life is impossible without either. Yet the earning of money for home consumption, though universal, is also highly stigmatized. A woman selling in the market is, by definition, not working in the garden. Money is both a symptom and a cause for the rise of selfish domesticity people see. Here too women straddle the contradictions that have emerged through the encounter between different cultures. In the next chapter, I argue that women shield themselves from the stigma of greed by creating a form of market trade in which they can see their purses of money as being like a little yam house. Rather than subordinate money to the same gift economy that structures the management of yams, however, they turn the harvesting of money into a site for an alternative moral imagination, in which their patient collecting of money in a personal fund exempts them from the expectations of generous sharing.

4

Banks, Books, and Pots

Gimwala, or Immoral Money

Once, while walking to meet someone, I passed a group of people in their village tying up a pig and packing baskets with food. I stopped and asked them what they were doing, and they explained to me that two of them, a husband and wife, were about to walk across the island to visit bu'una to trade these items for yams. Days later, I talked to someone else about it and asked if this was like a marketing trip. The woman I asked said, "No, this isn't a market." She went on to explain to me that this was a form of exchange based on the partners' existing relationship. In this case, the husband's susu had a bu'una susu on the other side of the island. She herself had recently taken a dog to her bu'una elsewhere on the island and received yams from them. This kind of exchange is a way for trade partners to help each other, and only if it was easy for them to do so. Marketing, she said, involved putting one's produce on the ground on display for all to see. People come up to you and pay for what they want with money. Because she emphasized that trade partners remembered each other and the help they had given each other in the past like kin, it was clear that for her market selling was the opposite: anonymous, impersonal, and self-interested. She ended by saying that today people were more likely to go to a market to find money than to practice these older forms of help.

The woman's elaborate explanation resembles a quotation in Bronislaw Malinowski's (1932 [1922]) ethnography of ceremonial exchange in the Trobriand Islands, *Argonauts of the Western Pacific*. He quotes a Kiriwina man remarking derisively on another's exchange of *kula* shell valuables, saying "He conducts his *kula* as if it were *gimwali*" (1932 [1922], 96). Malinowski presents this quotation as evidence of the formality and decorum of proper kula exchange, and more generally its instituted aspects. Just as one can hear the sarcasm in the Kiriwina man's voice, my informant also seemed repelled by the idea that trade with bu'una was a "market," or what Auhelawa also call gimwala. She made it sound like women selling in the market were no better than beggars. Gimwala has historically meant a kind of barter among unrelated people just like what gimwali meant this to Malinowski's informant. In Auhelawa today, gimwala refers specifically to buying and selling with money. Just as gimwali should never be confused with kula, Auhelawa contrast gimwala with anything connected to traditional forms of partnership, including trade among bu'una. These are not merely different institutions though. Gimwala and markets carry a distinct stigma. Indeed, as my previous conversation with women in the local market showed me, people thought that only poor people sold goods in markets. Were there, they wondered, Americans who are poor and have to search for money this way? Overall, people told me that women who sell in markets in Alotau and the mission station at Mwademwadewa—and it is predominantly women who sell—are just wasting their time that should be spent working in the garden. Earning money makes you poor.

As we saw in the last chapter, rightly or wrongly, Auhelawa worry about their growing population and declining harvests. This they fear is making everyone selfish and privat (private). Being selfish is in one sense built into the gardening system. People must give up much of their harvest as seeds, and once these are planted, the period of feasts ends, and people become privat during tagwala when they lauyaba in their secondary gardens. Even when people choose to eat some of their yams, they are also choosing not to store them or reserve them for gifts. At the beginning of the yam harvest, people cheat by selfishly eating bwalesi in secret. This little deviance is, arguably, a way to remind themselves that the yams to come should be used wisely as feast gifts. Yet one also hears about selfishness in a different sense. People say that others do not care to participate in feast exchanges, because today everyone is "looking for money" (*mani hibehai*) by selling in marketplaces. Money is thus another sign of decline. Money represents the opposite of the values of gardening. If people are earning money, they are earning for themselves and not working for others, as they are necessarily doing in the yam garden. If Auhelawa are all cassava eaters, it follows for Auhelawa that they are also all money earners too. Auhelawa's response to money is, to an extent, very common in societies based on subsistence production. Anthropologists have documented many societies in which people limit the circulation and use of money, especially among their fellow community members, with whom they also share and engage in formal reciprocity (Shipton 1989; Evers and Schrader 1994). Likewise, the general attitude among Auhelawa is that selling in the market is a waste of time and somewhat shameful.

Yet when they demean the market and money, Auhelawa are not exactly telling the whole story. Rural farmers in many societies throughout Oceania build on their secure tenure of fertile land to grow cash crops like coffee for export (e.g., Barclay and McCormack 2013). Quite possibly many more people in PNG plant betel palms and pepper vines to raise a crop of "green gold"—the mildly narcotic, and highly addictive, betel nuts and pepper which are as indispensable as a morning cup of coffee for many people of PNG, including most Auhelawa (Sharp 2013; Sharp 2016). Likewise, in my 2006 survey, I found that nearly every household in Kurada engaged in some money-earning activity, usually market trade in the mission station or in the mainland town of Alotau. While it is common to stigmatize money, people depend on their modest, regular earnings. Money is a second harvest in at least two senses. People sought to invest savings, materials, and effort into a profit-making enterprise that would grow and provide a regular cash income. At the same time, they avoided talking openly about money, like harvests, for fear of gossip and criticism.

Since Malinowski first quoted the Kiriwina man, anthropologists have generally applied a model of spheres of exchange to understand how money enters into gift economies like Auhelawa. Paul Bohannan (1955) developed a formal version of this model to understand why certain kinds of transactions of items were frowned upon among the Tiv of Nigeria. In this model, buying and selling with money, and money earning itself, falls in one sphere, usually the lowest, while transactions of money for prestige items like heirlooms are often prohibited as a transgression of spheres.[1] In later developments of this model, scholars argued that money earned in the market sphere could be converted into a gift, which could be exchanged in other spheres (Gregory 1980; Carsten 1989; Toren 1989). For example, PNG Highlands coffee farmers can earn hundreds or thousands annually (West 2012). Bridewealth, the gift given by a man's family to his wife's parents and clan to legitimate marriage, is now primarily a sum of money (e.g. Wardlow 2006, chap. 3; West 2006, 96–97). In this region, many spheres of reciprocal exchange are highly monetized in the sense that money can function as a gift. Yet these spheres are arguably not commoditized by the use of money. That is to say, the exchanges are not, as a rule, reversible. One can receive money to cement a marriage. A groom's family may even say they are buying a woman. But the bride's family would never say they are selling a daughter in order to earn money. When a father sets the price of his daughter's marriage, he limits the number of possible people she can marry. From the woman's parents' perspective, it is not solely a commercial transaction (Wardlow 2006, 124–25; West 2006, 101). In Auhelawa too, if one has not preserved enough of one's harvest, one can buy yam seeds, but to do so is so shameful that one should never speak of it and seek a seller with whom one has no ties at all. Selling yams in marketplaces, while not common, is nonetheless licit. Money flows but not freely, and many kinds of exchange are segregated from monetary transactions. When money flows in transactions of alienable goods, it is only against certain acceptable items.

Yet, as Jane Guyer (2004) argues, the model of spheres of exchange radically oversimplifies commodity systems and gift systems by reducing their relationship to a dichotomy. Based on historical evidence, she concludes that Tiv people have always engaged in a variety of exchanges that combine principles of alienability and inalienability and have used many different kinds of valuables as general media of exchange and finance.

Even without money as capital, Tiv traders could finance many different kinds of enterprise through loans and sales of valuables. Indeed, as C. A. Gregory (1997) points out, the difference between spheres and between systems of exchange was more often than not imposed by colonial authorities who wished to monopolize the power to declare one medium of exchange, coins and notes, to be general and to thus limit the possibility of indigenous economic power mediated by traditional valuables. Auhelawa have been participating in various forms of exchanges with money since their first contacts with Australians, including contracts with labor recruiters and sales of coconuts to copra traders. Also, like the people I met on the road, Auhelawa have also historically ventured far and wide to find trade partners with whom they could buy, borrow, and exchange pigs, many different kinds of foodstuffs, and shell and stone valuables. All these exchanges implicate people in certain kinds of moral relationships with others, including but not limited to reciprocity. If these exchanges do not fall into distinct spheres, and the values of reciprocity and self-interest are intertwined, why then do people heap scorn on women who seek to earn money for their family alongside their gardening? In this chapter I argue that money serves as a site for a particular kind of moral imagination in which people conceive of themselves as a kind of economic actor who is neither bound by the obligations of formal reciprocity nor an anomic, self-interested individual. In this sense a particular ideal conception of money as a medium of alienating value serves as an other against which people define themselves.

In the Marketplace

Auhelawa market trade is similar to informal market trade elsewhere in PNG and the Pacific. Throughout the Pacific people earn money by selling a variety of goods in small markets in addition to their subsistence gardening, cash cropping, and wage labor. For the most part, it is women who conduct these kinds of enterprises, and like other kinds of feminized work it is often ignored and marginalized, even though it is essential to the livelihoods of households (Dewey 2011). Most women sell as a part of and in addition to their responsibilities as wives and mothers to provide for their families. Market trading often takes place in interstitial spaces between distinct social worlds (Benediktsson 2002; Koczberski 2007). Informal markets thus allow buyers and sellers to balance competing economic values (van der Grijp 2003; Cahn 2008).

In the abstract, Auhelawa speak of the market and the garden as opposites. Instead of working hard to quietly produce plenty, selling is the shameful display of one's wealth to generate something that one simply consumes. Hence marketing is akin to "selfish" (*aiduma*) eating of one's own garden, like the secret eating of bwalesi yams before the harvest. Garden management is based on careful budgeting of the harvest; marketing is the spending of garden wealth for one's self. Not only is the person who sells in the market only seeking personal gain, but they are depriving other people of their work. To work hard in the garden is to perform a service for others, either one's family or one's network of kin who receive gifts of yams. Hence people also describe the practices of earning money by selling as wasteful because it means people just *miya'awawa'uhi* (sit around doing nothing) in the market. Auhelawa people say that using up one's time is a kind of selfishness that leads to hunger and poverty. Trade that is apparently motivated by each partner's needs, by contrast, is strenuously distinguished from selling or bartering, as the woman I mention above did when she explained trade with bu'una. That kind of exchange was help between relatives or friends and was based on their ongoing relationship.

Yet in spite of the stigma nearly every household in Auhelawa has one member who regularly earns money through market trade to meet household needs. Women earn most of this money through sales of betel nuts, food, or goods in informal markets. While in the past Auhelawa men earned money through cash cropping and processing of coconut, and today a few men and women earn wages as construction workers or helpers at the Catholic mission, most people's income is very low and they sell to raise money to meet immediate, short-term needs such as school fees, health-care fees, kerosene, and other basic commodities. When they sell, they must manage the way other people see them and their display of their wealth. As a way of making ends meet, selling is particularly deviant. To sell something for money, you have to show people what you have to sell. It violates one of basic measures of one's discipline as a gardener. Gardeners store their harvests and do not speak openly about what they have until the crucial moments where they can show forth what they will give to another. A market trader, in a sense, inverts this by laying a mat down in public and laying out food she has grown or goods she has acquired, then taking the money given in exchange and hiding this in her purse for her own family's needs.

People sell a wide range of things. One common business is to retrade goods bought in bulk in Alotau and transported to the village. For instance, one might buy several liters of kerosene at a filling station in town, store it in one's house, and sell it in 1-liter and 500-milliliter quantities at a markup.[2] Putting labor into creating a product is also popular, especially as a market for women. Women bake flour to make rolls, sweetbread, or, if there is no yeast, damper. If a baker has a sealable plastic container, she will store the product in this to carry her product to church or other events to sell as well as to the regular market in the station. Tobacco is also traded, usually rolled into long cigarettes with strips of newspaper and sold for 20 toea each.[3] Garden food and coconuts are also sold at weekday and Saturday markets in the Catholic mission to the teachers, mission staff, and health workers. The predominant item of trade is, however, betel nut, both in the mission marketplace and in the markets of Alotau. Along with everyone else in Milne Bay Province, Auhelawa are avid consumers of betel, lime (*ahole*), and pepper (*tewa*). Every family plants betel palms and pepper vines for its own consumption and for the purpose of marketing. The market trade in betel is not nearly as intensive as in other parts of the province and country. While only a few people plant a large number of palms for harvest, every village will have several mature and growing betel palms for residents' own consumption and for market sales.

The marketplace itself, as a social space, communicates the kind of exchange that takes place there. Besides Alotau, people mainly sell in marketplaces in the Catholic mission station, and since 2010, in a small roofed shelter in a section of Sowala Village, the site of the United Church, away from the church and pastor's house. The Catholic mission, with its primary school and regional health center, is one of the larger establishments in this area and the main site where residents from the southern part of Normanby Island and islands further south seek services. It is also where the Catholic congregation holds mass or Sunday Bible services. The new market building at Sowala is still quite close to all these facilities. A few hundred meters away is the village of Wadaheya, where one finds a bustling trade store founded by Lorenzo Mesaki. People pass through this section of Auhelawa nearly every day on their way to the church, health center, school, or stores. It is as urbanized as a rural place can be, not in the sense of density (although it is noticeably denser) but in the sense of free, individual movements of many people. The markets and stations form a distinct social world where people work for money, worship, and go to school. People sell here, then, not for merely practical reasons, but because they can, at least provisionally, assert a boundary across which they can trade with people who have wages to spend. At the same time, they are firmly embedded in the social fabric of kinship. St. Peter's Catholic Church and Sowala also sit right alongside the homes of three different susu. It should also be noted that most of the Catholic mission staff and the United pastors, ministers, and their families (with the exception of the Italian priest and Melanesian Catholic nuns) all have some kind of tie of kinship or affinity with people from Auhelawa. During 2006 the market in Mwademwadewa was a chief topic of gossip and moral debate. For instance, many people remarked that it was shameful that marketing now takes place every day except Sunday when in the past markets occurred on two days a week. Interest in gossip about market trading was rivalled only by gossip about the birth rate, and both topics were related as signs of social and moral decline. As far as I know, relocating the market to Sowala has not changed this.

Even coming to the market is charged because by doing so the seller is absenting herself from the home and garden where she would be doing other things for her husband, children, and coresidents. Although one can assume that a market seller delicately balances these demands, most women come regularly to market. Yet they do so in sight of others who evaluate them by this standard. One of the common items of gossip is that young women spend too much time in the market instead of working in the garden, and that's why they can't feed their small children. When women come down the road from the villages in the morning to the market in Mwademwadewa, and when they enter the market, they adopt a certain manner that sheds light on how they think about this activity and the money they earn. Here I am going to describe the old marketplace in front of St. Peter's Church. The women spaced themselves apart in the gravel yard in front of the church near the houses of Mwademwadewa residents, sitting with friends from the same village or other relatives.

They laid their goods out in front of them on the ground, usually on a broad leaf. Then they would often sit back from their market and affect an aloof attitude toward it and anyone looking at it. Buyers and sellers in the market talk with each other sitting in groups away from the goods for sale. Teachers and nurses, many of whom have multiple ties of kinship to market sellers, spend their breaks in the market in this way, and when they want to chew a betel nut, they slide a coin onto the leaf and scoop up a nut without a word. Sellers write the price of goods on a small torn square of cardboard or place small pebbles on or near the goods they are selling to indicate the price, each pebble representing a *siling* (shilling, or today a 20-toea coin). Yet often this is unnecessary because many goods have conventional prices. Individual betel nuts and individual sticks of tobacco, for instance, are 20 toea. Transactions are thus straightforward. When a person buys something, they may just wordlessly hand over the coins and gather what they want.

This is not to say that prices are absolutely fixed by convention. For instance, a bun is usually 20 toea but can vary in size, and bigger buns can sell for 30 toea. Sellers gossip about others' prices, but only somewhat. I rarely observed anyone directly challenge someone's price. However, one instance where prices were discussed openly is telling. During a major regional church gathering, where women and men had gathered in one of the largest markets I had ever attended, a man stood up and addressed the market as a whole saying that prices were too high and people should remember that they were selling to villagers like themselves and should be reasonable. As is typical for this kind of criticism, no one was mentioned directly, but everyone received an appeal based on their commonalities. It was only implied that people should not seek to be too eager to make money by selling but should toe the line. As social contexts, then, marketplaces like this and at Mwademwadewa are distinct from yet conjoined with the social domain defined by kinship and its ethics. And while the location for market activity has changed now, I argue that this picture still sheds light on how one performs the role of market trader. In Sowala, for instance, people now gather together under the roof of the shelter on benches. Based on my observations of this market and many other marketplaces elsewhere in Alotau, East Cape, and other parts of Normanby, the same kind of detached decorum of market sales occurs. Above all, there is little to no direct communication about the items for sale, including and especially haggling. The rules of the transaction are built into the environment as much as possible.

One sees the same basic logic at work when selling takes place outside the market. In these instances, the interaction between buyer and seller takes place in the midst of daily life yet as a separate strand. People sell goods out of their homes, such as kerosene, cell batteries, manufactured cigarettes, and occasionally beer. The modes of exchange have to be signaled. For instance, if one had a drum of kerosene for sale, single batteries from a carton, or even a pig, one would probably post a sign on the road near one's village and write KERO VEGIMWANE or KERO MAKET (Kerosene Sale, Kerosene Market) and the price per unit. Often word spreads that a particular person is selling a certain item at a certain price. In each case, customers come to the village and ask for the seller. My adoptive mother Lucy was a very active market seller, often selling cigarettes (*sadua*) she and the family rolled. She kept a small supply in her *bilum* (Highlands-style string bag) at all times in case any young men wanted to buy a stick from her.[4] It was very common for customers, almost always young men, to come after sunset when the family was sitting by the lamp talking. They usually approached quite hesitantly saying, "Is there tobacco?" or simply "I have come to buy [*gimwala*]." She would ask how many they wanted, and they would reply with a number, exchange the coins for the sticks, and leave. During large gatherings outside the market—for instance, at mortuary feasts, village court sittings, and after-church gatherings—men would approach her asking for "my tobacco" (*agu sadua*). She would produce a small cup or plastic bag (for a while, zipper bags that arrived in care packages from the United States) containing rolled sticks and coins from her bilum. The buyer would give the coins, receive the sticks, and leave. She would deposit the coins into the container and return it to her bilum. Lucy was considered by everyone to be a very effective seller, but her practice was common. Many women also brought buns, tobacco, and betel nuts with them to big events for the purpose of selling to anyone who asked. Men and women would usually also have a personal supply of betel nut, pepper, and lime in their handbasket or bag (*peha*), which could be any kind of personal bag. These kinds of personal items are readily shared among people who have some tie of bilateral kinship. It would be hard to sell to people with whom one would normally share these things. However, very few women smoke tobacco even though they sell it regularly, and so they would not share tobacco with men or women. This is why Lucy and other women can gimwala tobacco to men, then immediately turn around and share betel ingredients with the same or similar people. By being a nonsmoking woman, she has withdrawn from one sphere of generous sociality, and this makes it possible for her to assert a relationship of buyer and seller in the moment. Keeping coins and tobacco sticks together in a separate bag within her bilum is more than merely a convenience. It is a communicative device that labels the transaction of tobacco as gimwala in the sense of an exception to the norms of everyday sociality.

While these individual market sales can be easily marked as exceptions, larger enterprises must find another way to signal to their customers that their commercial transaction is not purely selfish or anonymous. One way is to insist that the transaction has its own rules which are neither the reciprocal sharing among relatives nor the anonymous transactions of gimwala. Sellers and business owners allow customers to buy with a promise to pay later, called a *buka* (credit, from the English "book"). For some, it is essential to their business.[5] For instance, my adoptive father, Francis, ran a trade store in our village. When he launched the business in 2000 on his retirement from teaching, he planned to sell mainly to the teachers in the mission. He would allow teachers to book until they received paychecks, and then they would sign over their checks to him to settle their debts. To pay for orders, Francis needed to function as an informal bank for his main customers, secured mostly by his trust and close ties to the teaching staff. Smaller sellers also allow people to buka purchases if they expect repayment, but they fear that they cannot trust everyone, especially those without wages. Many people say that buyers should not ask to buka because they will ruin the seller's business by *bukave'ovi* (credit-finish, or credit everything) the goods for sale without paying. Yet sellers say that they give credit because people persuade them to trust them, or that they have to allow people to buka because they don't want people to get angry with them. In the eyes of these sellers, one has to make a careful judgment about a customer's reliability when one decides to offer them a buka. Kin can pressure each other. Wage-earners, though better able to pay, may leave for a new job without settling their account. A woman who asks to buka flour for baking, however, is more trustworthy since she will be selling what she bakes immediately. Indeed some store owners regularly sold flour as a buka to women who baked for marketing. The trust between a buyer and a seller comes, then, primarily from the personal qualities and history of the buyer rather than the seller's prior relationship to that person.

While people had a clear normative theory of how buka should work, the ways trade store owners manage debts they are owed is particularly revealing of how buka works in practice. It is very common for a store to display a sign that says "No credit" in either English or Auhelawa. Yet many people still ask for credit and in most cases receive it. Business owners say that they would feel ashamed to deny someone credit or afraid that the customer would gossip about them. Instead they record the debt in an account book under the customer's name. Over time, as many people accumulate large unpaid debts, and the store's cash flow dwindles, the owner may add up the debts and post a sign listing everyone's name and what they owe. As people pay off their debts, their names are crossed out on the sign. In many cases, people pay in installments, and the total on the sign is amended with each payment. Store owners thus avoid direct confrontation with their customers and instead use indirect, though public, means to collect. Notably, while debtors definitely dislike being named in this public manner, and would dispute the amount or the payments recorded, no one ever questioned the right of the store owner to do this. It was assumed that by crediting a purchase, the debtor was accepting this responsibility. Although the argument against buka may sound like it is grounded in an ethic of rational self-interest, and may in fact reinforce that value, it only indirectly serves that purpose. By complaining that customers will bukave'ovi the seller's goods, they align taking credit with selfish, heedless consumption of the harvest and the store. They bring the customer into the same moral framework as themselves as sellers, which is based on the discipline of enao. Furthermore, to enforce limits on credit, sellers have to rely on shaming their customers in the eyes of others for violating social norms. This, I suggest, is the same shame to which people are susceptible as sellers as well. They would be shamed if they haggled over prices or tried to ask for too much money because this would look like gimwala in its most selfish form. Thus sellers tolerate buka because it recruits their customers to the same project of moral cash earning, or the enao of money. As many store owners lamented to me about their debtors, "We help them, but they cannot help us." Ideally, however, buka is not supposed to be help in the sense of reciprocal assistance. Rather in this lament and in the indirect request for repayment, sellers present themselves and their debtors as if they were similarly tied to each other in such a cycle of exchange on which the debtors have reneged. When they give buka and when they later shame people into paying back buka, sellers thus make their cash earning less like gimwala in the self of amoral, self-interested accumulation.

In most households of Auhelawa, one member will also travel at least once a year to Alotau for the purposes of selling betel nut and some garden food. One might think that if someone is taking a day's journey to town, this is a major enterprise. In some sense, it is, but Auhelawa very rarely speak of marketing in town as though it were a business. People will say about a woman or a man who travel to town, *Bada ispin* (She is just going for a spin [fun trip].). Even the sellers themselves say the same, quite drolly. In fact, marketing in Alotau is doubly odious for most people because it combines extreme discomfort with idleness, which Auhelawa think is wasteful. There are only a few places in town where people can sit down and display their goods for sale. The main market near the center of town is a large open-air roofed structure. There is also a gated area near the main wharf outside of the town center. This concrete wharf is privately owned by Nako Fisheries, which permits people to sell there. Nako workers also lock the gate at night and open a shed for people to spread their sleeping mats and sleep for the night. Many Auhelawa sell here because they also sleep here, especially if they have no relatives who can accommodate them in town for that night. If they cannot find a space for a stall inside the Nako market, then they sell off the road on the foreshore nearby as many other people do from all over the province. Auhelawa people tend to sit among other Auhelawa in an informal grouping of Duau (Normanby Island) sellers. Other travelers set up stalls among their wantoks (Melanesian Pidgin for people of the same rural place) as well. They spend most of the day here, both socializing with the people around them and selling to people who stop by. As in Mwademwadewa, the transactions are done quickly and wordlessly. Prices in town can be higher than at home, but they are likewise fixed by consensus, not competition. To earn money, sellers must wait for the goods to move. They must also avoid spending the money as it comes in. They abstain from buying food, subsisting on a basket of garden food they have carried with them.

They then spend that money on school fees, a 10-kilogram bag of rice, or children's clothing, leaving them with 20 kina to return to Auhelawa by passenger boat. In my household survey in 2006, I asked detailed questions about the most recent trip that people took to Alotau and usually received this very stereotyped account with few if any variations, suggesting that it represents what they perceive to be a norm.

People's actual practices may be quite different, but I came to realize that, even if they did, people did not entirely see themselves as individual agents in the marketplace. For instance, after church at Sowala one Sunday, a middle-aged married man with children told me he was going to Alotau to sell betel nut. I asked him when he was coming back. In my fieldnotes, I wrote: "P. is going to town to market next week because he has recently heard that the market is *hegoya* (soft, meaning easy). He explained that this means that in about a week, he'll be back. But he couldn't say when. [He said] '*Maket iloina*' (The market rules). When the betel nut finishes, he'll come back."[6] Other people confirmed that the market in town was soft and betel nuts were selling quickly. This was at a time of year when the annual crop of nuts was slowly turning to seed and becoming unchewable. Green betel nuts, which my informant still had, were much desired. Yet although this man thought he could be back in a week, he did not tell me that this was something he planned to do. When he said that the market made the rule (*loina*), he used a word that one uses to describe what elders do for socially inferior juniors and, metaphorically, what tradition, church, and government do for people as a group. In his words, then, he was exercising a choice to sell betel nut at this moment, but he did not see himself as having absolute choice or even much opportunity to maximize his earning. This self-presentation then gives one a key with which to understand the way people responded to my questions about their own marketing. Going to Alotau should mean breaking even, not getting rich. One leaves normal social life, submits oneself to certain market forces, suffers the attendant privations patiently, grabs a piece of the still-remote world of commodities, and comes back home.

Earmarks

One night in 2006, I sat with Francis telling stories by the kerosene lamp. Lucy had gone to Mwademwadewa for a women's fellowship meeting.

After I went to bed, Kolbe, a young man who was my cross-cousin, came quietly into village to talk to Francis. He asked to borrow Lucy's copy of *Buki Wari*, the old Methodist hymn book. Introduced by the Methodist missions in the early 20th century, it featured songs written in or freely translated into Dobu, the Methodist Bible language, set to the melodies of English hymns. The United Church used many of the hymns in their Sunday services, but many other people, including Catholics, had copies because people sang some of the older songs at Christmas. Men liked to sing other hymns from the book at *hilauwa*, all-night wakes held before a burial. Kolbe was planning on attending one such hilauwa for a recent death and wanted to rehearse with some friends. Francis went into his and Lucy's house and fetched the book from her things. A bit later, Kolbe came back and called for Francis. He gave him back Lucy's hymnal and said that they did not want to borrow it. When he got to his friends' house and sat down to practice, he said, he opened up the hymnal and found a stack of 20 and 50 kina notes, at least K300 in all, wedged in between the pages. He wanted to bring the book back quickly and show the money to Francis, saying that he did not want Lucy to think they were trying to steal her money. Some of it was from rent I paid Francis and Lucy every month. Another 50-kina note was Malaki's; Lucy was holding on to it for him. The rest was from her sale of rolled tobacco sticks and baked buns, her two favorite items to sell. This was, in effect, Lucy's bank. A lot of people in Auhelawa also keep their money tucked away in a secret place like this, in an old medicine bottle, a coin purse, or the hidden pocket of a pandanus basket. Not even Francis knew where Lucy kept her money. His money was in our village trade store's cash box. Lucy always liked having her own money from her own market sales and kept this money separate from Francis's store income.[7]

    Across all the different kinds of market trade, sellers manage the way their activity is perceived by others through various kinds of earmarking just like this. In many communities that rely on both subsistence production and market trade, money is often classified according to how it is earned: for instance, Malagasy sapphire miners call their wages "hot money" (Walsh 2003) and Luo farmers of Kenya say that money earned from selling inherited land is "bitter" (Shipton 1989; see also Toren 1989). These terms indicate what kinds of purposes this money can and cannot be used for legitimately. In her social history of money in the United States, Viviana Zelizer (1994) argues that Americans also attribute social meaning to money as a gift and do not treat all money as the same fungible currency. Money from different sources and money intended for specific purposes is often earmarked with envelopes, cards, and notes to convey an affective, personal meaning in the transaction. In fact, a woman's classification of her harvest into seeds and according to her paula (jobs, obligations) is itself a comprehensive system of earmarking, with very little food left that is not reserved for some specific use. In a similar way Auhelawa earmark some of what they produce—garden food, betel nut and its associated pepper, or tobacco—and separate it from the dominant morality rooted in gardening. They sell in designated market places outside the villages. They place signs on the road advertising what they have to sell, and they store the coins they receive in exchange in a separate pocket or container within their baskets, separating the money they earn from the other personal possessions they carry and share with other people. Although Auhelawa do not elaborately construct the indexical relation between money and its origins, in a sense, when they apply the terms *gimwala* and "market," they earmark money and goods as alienable.

Yet if goods in the market are earmarked in this way, people's performance of these transactions also suggests that they earmark them a second time over, separating them from an imagined sphere of purely alienable values. They sell in the marketplace, yet in the marketplace sellers seem aloof to selling. When they post a sign on the road, they curiously make a public written declaration yet avoid the stigma of talking openly about selling. Instead they announce to people what is for sale before they meet them face to face. By permitting someone to buka, to pay later, they make it clear that they trust the person and place their transaction in a moral context, albeit not one of reciprocity. Instead, by telling people that they have a buka, the seller also reminds the buyer that the seller is trying to husband the money from sales and in a sense makes the buyer co-responsible for the seller's success. While these forms of selling are not governed by the ethic of garden work, neither are they the kind of selfishness suggested by the term *gimwala*. By positioning themselves in opposition to gimwala, people create a doubly negative space of economic activity. They can earn money without being subject to the norms of enao yet also without negating these norms and becoming individuals.

When they trade in markets, people perform the displacement of their own agency as individuals. For them, earning money comes through patient waiting, not overt avarice or competition. While they seek to exchange their produce for money, their choices of time, place, and manner for these exchanges positions them in relation to norms of hard work and discipline that also characterize garden work and distance them from the specter of selfishness. In the study of societies on the fringes of market economies like Auhelawa, many make the argument that sellers seek to signal that they are not acting as self-interested individuals. Sellers of betel nut and vegetables in the PNG Highlands, for example, give preferential treatment to customers they know and offer gifts to establish trust with new customers (Benediktsson 2002; Sharp 2013). In Auhelawa, however, sellers position themselves in a doubly negative space. They conduct their gimwala as if it were the socially oriented practice of gardening. At the same time, they use the idea of buka to make their customers morally responsible for their profitability. By tagging items as buka to be repaid rather than gifts, people signal that their market should not be wasted. The buka is in a sense an exception that proves the rule of the market. By permitting people to pay later, people indicate that the norm is to pay immediately (Miller 1998, 40). They conduct their gimwala as if self-interested accumulation is itself moral. Buka and other Auhelawa forms of cash exchange show that earmarking of value need not only take anonymous currency and embed it in separate spheres of value. The seller's metacommunicative practices also make it possible to imagine an informal marketplace as a moral activity. This suggests not merely that people's informal cash earning is restricted by dominant moral norms, but rather that people's performance of the morality of their accumulation is a creative process whereby they can imagine a new way of being.

Besides individual sales it is also common for several individuals to form an ad hoc coalition to acquire money. Coalitions represent yet another way to occupy the doubly negative space and avoid doing gimwala. Another venture by Lucy illustrates a common pattern. In May 2006, Lorenzo's cargo boat the M.V. *Wadaheya* was chartered by an expatriate-owned marine export company based in Alotau for a trip to the remote eastern islands of the province to buy sea cucumbers from local divers. On its way "out east," *Wadaheya* stopped at Kurada. Lucy took the opportunity to give the boat hands, all Kurada-born men, a big bag of betel nut for them to sell to the people on outer islands on her behalf. While Normanby Island villages have plenty of land to plant betel palms, many people on small islands and atolls cannot produce enough for themselves. I heard many stories of people who traveled to Kiriwina (Trobriand Islands) or other remote places in the region and quickly sold bags of soft betel nuts to the residents. Yet the distance and difficulty of travel prevents most people from earning money this way. Lucy makes use of a series of direct and indirect relationships, each defined by different kinds of transactions, to sell her betel nuts. First, she puts her cargo on M.V. *Wadaheya*, a cargo boat operated by Lucy's patrilateral cross-cousin Lorenzo on behalf of his susu. Normally *Wadaheya* travels between Alotau and Normanby transporting cargo for Lorenzo's store and carry paying passengers. Second, Lucy asks Lorenzo's employees, who were also various kinsmen of his and Lucy's, to sell the betel nuts on her behalf. Lucy attaches herself through kinship ties to another enterprise. Many others also recruited collaborators through informal ties to enable them to acquire cash outside normal contexts. It was common for one woman to hold a purse full of money or a bag of betel nuts that she sold on another's behalf. Some of the most prominent coalitions for earning money form around fundraising projects for voluntary groups, clubs, and in particular church congregations. One very popular and widespread kind of fundraising takes place in a public event. Here not only do people distinguish their own market trade from the specter of gimwala, they further distinguish themselves from the traditional norms of the moral economy through a parody of the gift.

Pot-to-Pot

In 2004, as the fiftieth anniversary of the Catholic mission drew near, the Catholic parish committee prepared to hold a major feast in honor of the mission and its founders on the parish's feast day on July 29. As date got closer, people came to the market nearly every day. Both Catholic and United families were raising money they could contribute to the feast. I was relatively new to Kurada, and so I did not know at the time that this was a much larger version of the kind of annual offering made by the congregations in Kurada to their respective churches. I would later learn that fundraising was a common avenue for individual market activity because it made otherwise individual acts of gimwala appear as if they were unselfish work for one's church congregation. It was another example of how traders displaced their own role as an individual economic actor. Each of the Catholic families in Kurada belong to one of several gospel sharing groups named in honor of a saint. In 2004, these were relatively new structures meant to organize lay participation. Each group met each week to read the Bible and pray together. Each took a turn leading the liturgy, preparing music and prayers for either the Sunday Mass or the Sunday Bible service held when a priest was not available. The groups had also been given a fundraising goal, as had the smaller communities of the parish outside Kurada. The United Church at Sowala also formed a group of its own to raise money it could present to the parish committee as a contribution to the feast. Each group would bring a certain number of pigs and baskets of yams as a contribution to the feast as well. The commemorative feast would in this way involve everyone in the community in a roughly equal way. Still, although they were raising money in the market as part of their own contribution, most people did not simply hand over their contribution directly. The money they raised passed through many hands first, through several public fundraising events staged by pairs of gospel sharing groups. In the years since, I have attended many of these events. They are one of the most popular ways to raise a moderately large sum of money for a public purpose in a hurry. Regionally, they are known as basket-to-basket, or *tanatana*. Auhelawa preferred their own local version, pot-to-pot, or *potpot*.

As the names suggest, basket-to-basket and pot-to-pot are events centering on exchange. At the event, two groups come together and pairs of people from opposed sides walk before the assembled crowd, meet in the middle, exchange gifts, and then each place a certain amount of money into a till for each side. At the end, the sums for each side are counted and announced to the crowd, followed by a grand total. This total is then usually given to one of the groups, the hosts of the event, who use it for their group's purposes. The event is followed up with a similar event at a later date which is hosted by the opposing side, which then receives the sum total raised. In some ways it resembles many kinds of reciprocal exchanges among Auhelawa including and especially bwabwale.[8] Yet in other ways the events have the feel of a friendly competition and informal party and resemble the sports matches between community teams held most Saturdays. As we shall see, *potpot* plays on and parodies ceremonial exchange. It denigrates the idea of respectful obligations and instead celebrates the sum total of money raised.

What follows is a thumbnail sketch of a pot-to-pot synthesizing many such events. When I first went to a pot-to-pot, I asked many questions about the rules. Having only just arrived on my first field research project, I remember being acutely aware of a need to find a liturgy or script that people would follow. My hosts served as willing informants, telling what they cooked and why but often with a bemused expression. Many pointed out to me that what I was seeing was not kastam (custom, or a traditional institution or practice, like bwabwale). Kastam was serious; this was just fun. They didn't know who they would be exchanging with. It didn't seem to matter. As one woman said to me, "It's anything to please our friends, to make them happy." In fact, in many of these events the members of one group would be issued a scrap of paper with a number. The other group's members would also receive a scrap of paper with one of the same numbers. Numbers were then called in order or drawn at random. No one knew who would be matched with whom. Unexpected pairings, such as

Figure 4. Representatives of each side count the donations at the pot-to-pot held at Wadaheya village on August 31, 2004

cross-cousins or other relatives, often got howls of laughter. Just as often, both groups simply read from their membership lists in order. For something that people spent so much time preparing, I was surprised at how disorganized it all seemed and struggled to make sense of it.

What was more or less consistent was the pageantry of the event. Both groups tried as much as possible to put on a show for the other side. An event always consisted of hosts and visitors. The hosts would choose a village where they could stage a meeting of the two sides. The visitors would mass at a neighboring village prior to the appointed time. As they slowly assembled, they would festoon their pots and baskets with garlands of frangipani and hibiscus flowers, wreaths and streamers of folded and woven pandanus and coconut palms. Humble coconut palm baskets became colorful packages adorned with betel pepper and tobacco sticks. Pots—already filled with large 'wateya and halutu and often chicken, dog, and sometimes pig, cooked in a creamy coconut milk broth—were layered with bright red flowers and deep green leaves. These are, it should be said, not merely lavish decorations but also colors and forms closely associated with churches and their many celebrations. The host village would also be bedecked with palm streamers and bunting. Branches of betel nuts would be hung from the beams of houses in easy reach of attendees. When all was ready, the visitors would form a line on the road outside the host village while the hosts would form a receiving line alongside the same path. While singing a light, festive English chorus, the visitors would process into the village and shake hands and hug their hosts one by one. Then the leaders would move off to one side while the two groups would seat themselves as two more or less separate galleries of spectators. The leaders would usually set up a table or a mat in front the groups as a stage. Here people would come one by one to exchange their gifts and place their contributions into their group's bowl—all under the watchful eye of the leaders of each group, who emceed the event, calling out names boisterously one after the other. The presentation of one's gift was another chance for a performance. For instance, in one pot-to-pot Simon Peter's brother Philip and his wife, Noeline (my sister's namesake), had built a miniature bier across two long branches. Such a device is usually built from bamboo as a vehicle for carrying a large fatted pig into a village as a bwabwale gift. Instead of a pig, Philip placed his ornately decorated pot of yams and meat. When I caught sight of it, he flashed me a wicked grin.

"I masterminded it!" he exclaimed. In the same way, people presented their gifts in such an ostentatiously generous way that everyone roared with laughter and the recipient cringed in mock horror. When it was Philip's turn to present his gift, he was joined by several of his friends, who carried the pot to the front while he marched in front of them beating a PVC pipe that he had fashioned into a fake kundu drum. In this way he staged a miniature feast procession to present his satirical bwabwale. Others dumped baby powder on one another or smeared fragrant coconut oil on their partners. Two women once came to the event dressed as men and clowned around in front of everyone before handing over their presents. Whenever two people exchanged, they usually shook hands exaggeratedly and often hugged. Nearly every exchange resulted in squeals, cheers, and applause. Then they would drop their contribution, which could be anything from 2 to 10 or 20 kina, in the bowls and quickly returned to their seats with their gifts.

While I knew that each event was supposed to be reciprocated, often the return match was postponed indefinitely or canceled. In the one such event I attended, no one reciprocated the gifts they had received. In fact, due to weather the pots were simply exchanged en masse, with each person simply taking a random pot from the other group. When push came to shove, the reciprocal cycle between groups also seemed to give way. It was common for groups to decide to take their own members' contributions, rather than pool them. People were wary that they could not rely on a balanced exchange between sides. When, for instance, the Wadaheya susu and its natuleiya held a pot-to-pot to raise money for a public memorial, they chose as a partner a community organization from East Cape, which was raising money for a new classroom. On the day of the first event Wadaheya hosted people from East Cape. The contribution was marked at 10 kina per person. Auhelawa people complained that the pots were paltry compared to what they had prepared for their guests. In the end, the groups decided not to pool the contributions, although they did repeat the event a year later. In general, pot-to-pot did not provide a mechanism for large-scale informal financing of public projects, as its design might imply. It usually turned into a very elaborate way for a group to pass the hat among its own members and did not rely on partnership with another group as such. Moreover, while people seemed to eagerly anticipate these events, and it seemed like the default choice for fundraising, people also complained about how often they happened and the trivial purposes for which they were staged. One man once said to me he thought the whole thing was a bit silly. There's no place you can eat chicken for 2 kina, he said. People were just out for a good time, and it was all a waste. It was criticism much along the same lines as people's criticism of women at the market, except the criticism was of the gifts and to an extent the pretense of reciprocity, not the donations.

In market sales, traders frame the value of money in opposition to gimwala, equating it with a harvest. In pot-to-pot, the moral value of the money given is defined in opposition to the gifts of pots. The gifts of pots are obvious parodies of reciprocity, and so the freely given money looks quite sincere by contrast. We can think of the money in terms of the earmarking people do with many of their economic resources. First, as we have seen, the harvest is earmarked, with the best food allocated to the moral purpose of transmission to children as seed and others as gifts. Marketing mirrors this practice. People set aside their money from marketing by placing it in a secret bank, a pocket yam house for money. They segregate the goods they wish to sell, like betel nuts and tobacco sticks, by placing them inside a container, producing a boundary at the site of the container across which they will engage in the exchange of alienable values instead of free sharing. Thus earmarking can work to embed value in relationships and disembed value as well. It can work to impose qualitative values on fungible resources, embedding certain otherwise economic goods in the context of a moral economy, and it can also be used to create an exception to the norm of mutuality. Pot-to-pot exchanges are also a kind of earmarking. The money contributed to the collective goal is given alongside a parody of competitive generosity. In that sense, the game of giving for pleasure and to acquire a treat in return is also a bit of deviance, much like a buka, which serves to distinguish the money as a selfless voluntary contribution.

One could even speak of a genre of such fundraising events found among voluntary groups in many different societies. Church rummage sales ask people to donate unwanted clothes and goods for sale in a marketplace with the proceeds going to the church. Similarly bake sales ask people to prepare food for sale at usually very steep prices, with the revenue going to a public, charitable purpose. These events are always done with a certain amount of self-consciousness. They consist of sales of goods for cash, but the transactions are not based on the self-interest of either party. Rather, goods are donated, and the money spent is recognized as a freewill donation to the host of the event, usually a community-based organization or public institution. Each transaction in such an event itself implicitly says to both parties and the assembled participants that the transaction is not a purchase, and that both buyer and seller are in fact donating something to the host of the event.[9] It is in the same spirit that people come to pot-to-pot. And so the moral imagination enabled by money comes, in a sense, full circle. The fundraising people do to prepare for the pot-to-pot is another example of the displacement of agency. When people sell to earn money, they can present themselves as raising money on behalf of a group. When they come together as a one group opposed to another for an exchange, they mock their own competitive generosity, making this into a tit-for-tat exchange in which each side seeks to swap pots and eat fine foods and sweet meat rather than create a lasting partnership. The money pooled together then is elevated as a higher moral purpose than the outward transmission of one's garden food. What was once transvalued from petty hoarding to a harvest reaped through patience and diligence is once again transvalued as the opposite of another kind of selfishness, a show of strength of a group and the voluntary commitment of its members to a public purpose. Individualism of a new kind, that of the voluntary donor, is realized as a value in its own right.

Money and Moral Imagination

We can see that although Auhelawa attach a stigma of selfishness to a certain uses of money, this is not in itself a sign that transactions are embedded in distinct spheres or that people strictly classify certain kinds of transactions as gifts as opposed to purchases. Not only is petty trading common and commodity consumption integral to daily life, but people also find ways to reframe the money they accumulate as moral. The image of selfish gimwala is, in this sense, a vehicle for moral imagination, much in the same way that witchcraft is an other that represents the opposite of moral practice for Kaguru people of Tanzania (Beidelman 1986). The opposite of immoral gimwala is the diligent enao one practices in the garden and in the yam house. The private enclosure of the yam house provides a model for thinking about earning money in unselfish ways. So it is that people store money in small purses and containers, tucking them away in hiding places and otherwise presenting themselves as being empty-handed. This form of money, in the context of the other kinds of communicative devices associated with sales, allows people to imagine the money as a harvest, and hence themselves as a moral gardener as opposed to a hasty, greedy trader.

And yet I conclude that in mapping yam houses onto purses people are not in fact subordinating money to the logic of reciprocity. The money earned through market trade is not, for the most part, given as a gift alongside yams or in any way forms a cycle of reciprocity in any of the main institutional venues for this kind of exchange. It can, however, be used for the family's own expenses and given to voluntary organizations and churches. In this sense, we must be careful to distinguish the conceptual mapping between yams and money from the domestication of foreign wealth. Yam houses are icons of a gardener's capacity to participate in exchange. They are also sites where people do another kind of earmarking when they sort and rank the food they harvest into different categories. In this management of the harvest, which is itself as much a part of enao as regular care for plants, a gardener separates the yield into unequal halves, setting aside the 'wateya mohili (king-size *Dioscorea alata*) for outward transmission, and then recursively divides the lesser part, setting aside seeds for each child, setting aside halutu ai'aina (large, starchy tubers of *Dioscorea esculenta*) for guests and other members of the family, setting aside the lesser 'wateya and halutu for later in the season, and first eating the yabayaba (immature, worthless yams and other secondary crops). In market trade, people also perform a similar kind of earmarking of their alienable wealth, setting aside betel nuts and money intended for market and separating them from the sphere of daily sharing. Thus one's market container or purse represents iconically one's accumulated wealth and indexes one's own status as a market trader, and it also serves as a site for recursive earmarking—but it is the inverse of the hierarchy of earmarking that one sees in yam houses themselves. In the yam house one sets aside the best yams to be given as gifts in feasts and allocates seed yams in separate piles as icons of one's matrilineal descendants. Unearmarked tubers remain as one's own household food supply. In one's peha, a portion of one's personal possessions are earmarked as goods for sale, and the remaining possessions are available to be shared within a sphere of everyday generalized exchange. Likewise, when people consent to buka transactions, they also mark the transaction as deviant and thus conversely signal that cash sales are normal and expected. Gardeners fear that sloppy management will lead them to *aive'ovi* (eat-finish) their harvest and lead to *vahali* (hunger). Market traders say that if they are too permissive, then buyers will bukave'ovi (credit-finish) the stock and wipe out the seller's money. Thus it is the formal process of dividing and ranking yams that is mapped onto the otherwise fungible resource of money, yet toward the end of imagining a store of value that is both moral, because of the care placed in amassing it, yet distinct from reciprocity. The money purse is modeled on the yam house, but it is also its mirror image. Or one could say that if pot-to-pot is a parody of reciprocity in feasting, then the resemblance of money and purses is also a kind of serious play on the value of yams. What women do in seeing money in the lens of yams is to create the possibility of an inversion of value that is not also a negation of value and thus imagine an alternative kind of value in money.

As we see in the next chapter, this rhyming relationship between money and yams, neither identity nor opposition, also allows money itself to serve as a novel method for reflexive sociality. Churches are a site for an alternative kind of belonging, based not on perduring connections and obligations but on a fellowship among individual believers. Yet this kind of new society is plagued by the impossibility of knowing what people really believe. To solve the problem of how individual belief relates to collective action, people again turn to money as a mediating symbol. The funds raised in the market and events like pot-to-pot often help individuals contribute to the church's annual freewill offering, which becomes another site where people can measure both the strength of individuals' belief and the collective strength of their congregation. This kind of reflexive sociality draws on the same poetic resonance of harvests, yet subverts the morality of the garden in favor of a new way of life.

5

ONE MIND

What Was the Great Change?

Even prior to the official declaration of a Protectorate of British New Guinea in 1884, Australian mission bodies had sent missionaries to southeastern New Guinea. After this region formally came under colonial control, other churches sent missions as well. Although they worked independently of each other, the colonial state and missions coordinated on a number of matters and saw themselves as equally contributing to a project of transformation of indigenous societies into peaceful, law-abiding subjects of the British Empire. The Australasian Wesleyan Methodist Missionary Society sent the minister and missionary, William Bromilow to establish a mission on Dobu Island, off the northern tip of Normanby Island, in 1891 (Bromilow 1892, xlv). Bromilow quickly posted Polynesian teachers and Australian ministers in communities across the islands of the eastern end of New Guinea, soon sending a Samoan teacher to Auhelawa in 1902.[1] As with the other mission bodies, the administrator of the colony, William Macgregor, worked closely with Methodists and supported their work. Writing about these early days, the general secretary of the Methodist mission, George Brown, tells a story of a trip with Macgregor to Dobu to see the mission as it had developed under Bromilow. Brown writes that Macgregor asked him

> what was the great change I noticed in the appearance of the people since [we] first landed. I mentioned several things. [Macgregor] replied: "No that is not it at all. Don't you see the people have quite a different expression on their faces now? The change is not a matter of dress, or even of manner, but an entirely different appearance and expression." I had often noted this, and we missionaries had often talked of it. As the people are brought under the influence of Christian teaching there is not only a softening of their facial expression, but also the signs of intelligent interest, which were certainly absent before. (Brown 1908, 501–2)

This was in fact the kind of change that many of the Methodist missionaries themselves said they sought. They did not want people to simply join their church but to experience a genuine inner and sustained conversion, expressing itself as a new attitude and a new life.

When I lived in Auhelawa over a century later, everyone professed to be a Christian, although they belonged to either the Roman Catholic Church, the United Church of Papua New Guinea (formed from a union of Protestant denominations, including the Methodists), or one of the smaller fellowships of Pentecostals, which had been spreading through the region in recent years. My tortured explanations of my own irreligion were merely read as a lack of interest. As Francis reasoned, since I was baptized a Catholic, I was still a member of that church, and he and other Auhelawa should treat me as such. Nonetheless I was welcomed in all the congregations of Auhelawa as an observer and fellow Christian. And so on a typical Sunday I attended two church services, first with Catholics in Mwademwadewa, and a few hours later, with the Uniteds at Sowala.

In either church station on a typical Sunday morning, people slowly trickled into the yard outside the church building, found a place to sit and talk with others. This long liminal period could last for some time. There was no reason for being on time since it seemed like services always started late. Many people arrived only halfway through. Sitting with

Figure 5. Francis Pade after *tapwalolo* at St. Peter's Catholic Church in Mwademwadewa Village in 2006

church members who lived nearby, especially at Sowala, I would hear people gossip and complain about their fellow members. Why couldn't they be faster in the morning? Why do people come only one at a time? The resident pastor, his wife, or a deacon, would beat the village slit-gong drum to announce the time. And yet, in spite of this, services would usually start only after a large group finally arrived. On one Sunday, a United woman rose at the end of the service to announce upcoming celebrations of Easter Week. She took the opportunity to remind people that they really ought to be on time, saying, "When you see people on the road, you know it's already time to move." For her and others, lateness was essentially noncooperation by individuals who refused to attend and refused to support the church. In these situations, people usually say that others have "a different idea." Ideally, a congregation should have "one mind" (*nuwatuwu ehebo*), a phrase not only used to evaluate the quality of Sunday services but as a way to talk about prayer, worship, and the congregation itself. *Tapwalolo*, a word people use for all these things, and Christianity itself, is based on a group that comes together as one mind. Those who came late detracted from the worship of the early. Moreover, it seemed to evoke a specter of insincerity in their church overall. Even when a large number of people appear for worship, Auhelawa say that most of them are merely "worshipping falsely" (*tapwalolo oya'oyama*). There is no way to be a Christian in Auhelawa without tapwalolo, and yet even tapwalolo is no guarantee that one's worship is real.

One could say that the message of individual salvation brought by Brown and Bromilow is now being worked out in the terms of the same moral discourse that Auhelawa derive from gardening. People either give themselves generously to others, or they hold themselves back selfishly. Christianity is thus primarily a collective and social phenomenon. Subordination to the group is the measure by which Auhelawa understand the nature of individual faith. Yet if Christianity is collective in nature, it is a different kind of unity from what one sees in the cycles of reciprocity between susu, and even to an extent the kind of union that grounds membership in a susu. Christianity is, for Auhelawa, a universal faith that all members choose freely. People come to church because of their *atemuyamuya* (love) of God, and this leads them to "give from the heart" (*atetalam*) to their congregation. The one mind of the congregation in tapwalolo is not simply the weight of obligation to the group. It is, specifically, a union based on a fundamental sameness among members as individuals. This unity is subjectively felt and outwardly expressed in the form of not only timeliness but also good preparation, coordination, and a correctly executed liturgy.

For some scholars (e.g., Kahn 1983), this kind of situation suggests that Western missionaries had only a superficial influence on converted societies in PNG, and most Melanesians are only nominally Christian. They may agree that a few families here and there have become Christians in a significant way, but most come to church only rarely or for special occasions, and this indicates that most people remain unchanged in spite of over a hundred years of Christian presence.[2] My own experiences in Auhelawa leads me to question this view. When I first arrived, it was important for people to decide what family I would live with and thus to which susu I would belong. It was just as important for them to know what church I belonged to. More generally, not only were church activities of one sort or another always going on, but every public event, whether bwabwale or a meeting of village court, would start with tapwalolo. It was not merely the civic religion of the village either. Like kinship, Christianity was all-encompassing of social existence and to an extent possessed totemic significance. Auhelawa were definitely Christians, but they were also practicing Christianity and thinking about this practice in a distinctly Auhelawa way. At every tapwalolo, everyone participated reverently, treating their own cooperation as sacred in itself. If ever I appeared to be lost while the congregation rose to sing a hymn, someone standing next to me would quickly lean over with the hymn book, pointing to the words in Dobu that they must have known I did not and could not understand. Furthermore, the standard people hold for true participation and authentic worship—that is, one mind—is actually quite hard to achieve. In practice, they believe that they regularly fail to achieve it. Auhelawa question their own collective faith just as much as secular Western anthropologists. Auhelawa also believe there are limits to looking for signs of their salvation in their collective activities. Even an apparently devout congregation can consist of individuals who worship falsely. In this sense, the "one mind" frame is always incomplete.

In recent years, Christianity has become an object of more sustained ethnographic description in an effort to examine exactly this ambiguity. The Auhelawa concern with collective aspects of Christianity are, for many, an instance of people transforming a foreign cosmology and theology into terms that resonate with their own cultural schemata (Barker 1990; Chowning 1990; Macintyre 1990; Thune 1990; Burt 1994; Heekeren 2004; Scott 2005; Monnerie 2010). For others, Christianity, as a product of and often medium for distinctly Western cultural constructs of individualism, presents converts with a situation of incommensurability, and hence their religious practice ruptures the fabric of social relationships (Robbins 2004, 2007; Robbins, Schieffelin, and Vilaça 2014). The evidence for the former claim of continuity comes mainly from cases like Auhelawa where a mission church has grown slowly since the colonial era. John Barker has suggested that in these kinds of communities Christianity is not experienced as a cultural rupture, but that instead mission Christianity forms part of a "neotraditional complex" (2012, 68; see also McDougall 2003, 2009; Weichart 2010). With few exceptions (e.g., Mosko 2010), evidence for the latter claim of rupture is often based on cases of recent religious revivals brought by charismatic churches (Jorgensen 2005; Eves 2011). It may be, then, that observers are talking past one another. What I show in this chapter is that while in one sense Auhelawa Christians are working out the idea of faith in collective terms, in doing so, they are not necessarily reducing Christian ideas to indigenous categories. Rather, I show that congregations and collective worship are yet another site where people collaborate in a process of reflexive sociality. In the medium of their collective worship, they enact Christian subjectivity and Christian sociality as an inversion of the morality of the garden and an alternative form of belonging based on intimacy. What missionaries presented as an individual choice to leave one's social group is realized today as another kind of group that exists alongside the secular world of gardens and markets. The rules of this group, the Christian congregation, are in some ways still to be decided. In their Christian practices, we see that Auhelawa are attempting to reflexively account for their own relationship to Christianity in the same way that anthropologists do.

The Mission and the Villages

Bromilow's early annual reports on his work in Dobu show that he thought about conversion much in the same way as his colleague Brown did, as an private, inner change reflected in one's public demeanor and behavior. Bromilow writes that he examined every single person who sought membership in the church through baptism with great care, assuming that only a few would ever really be able to withstand the temptations of sin. In these reports, the first stations are described as isolated refuges for missionaries, teachers, and their wives. Bromilow and other missionaries write that these would also be places where candidates for baptism would be separated from the influence of heathen Dobu culture and exposed to the influence of a Christian lifestyle as an alternative. In their writing, mission and village stood as shorthands for both alternative choices and separate worlds. They drew, in that sense, on two of the most widespread tropes of Christianity, the choice between the way of life and the way of death of the Didache, on the one hand, and Augustine's City of God, on the other. Bromilow and other missionary correspondents talked about the mission station as a light that shone outward to the villages in the darkness and spoke of the villages as "the enemy's camp" (1896, lxiv). Candidates were described as resisting the firm opposition of their families, and when they failed, it was because they succumbed to a life of sin that was all around them.

In many instances, the missionary authors take solace in this. They know their road is a hard one, and so their slow progress is simply proof that they are on the right path. In one of his reports, though, Bromilow slips a bit, saying, "One by one do candidates for Church membership come in—but, oh, for a great ingathering" (1895, lix). In every report, missionaries listed the numbers of people they counted at their services, the number of students attending the mission school, the numbers of places from where they preached, the numbers of congregations they had founded, and the number of baptisms. So in spite of their desire for an inner change of individuals, Bromilow and his team also aimed for a wholesale social change too. This was the harvest they had come to New Guinea to gather, and they took every opportunity to remind their audience of donors in Australian churches that the laborers were few indeed.[3] Even as they made peace with indigenous institutions of feasting, mourning, and exchange, they fought against very basic elements of social reproduction, labeling them vaguely "immorality" but making clear from the context that they meant premarital sex and serial marriage (e.g. Bromilow 1897, lxvi). In a report on the first full year at the mission

Figure 6. The path leading up to Hegahegai Point, the original site of the Methodist mission at Bunama

at Bunama, Ambrose Fletcher writes about the waifs, orphans, and students to whom he and his wife ministered: "To win them from heathenism a settlement is indispensable" (1901, xcv). Indeed, Bromilow and his wife also wrote frequently about the budding Christian community of boarding students, orphans, and candidates, including several women who married Fijian teachers. Even though conversion was individual, missionaries fantasized about making their station into a replacement for indigenous social structures. In his memoir of the Dobu mission, for instance, Bromilow alternates between stories of individuals who choose to reject their old life (e.g., 1929, 108–9) and stories of the growth of the mission, which by the end of his tenure was a substantial industrial plantation and boarding school (e.g., 1929, epilogue). Thus Bromilow concludes that Dobu, and by extension New Guinea, has been transformed inside and out.

Light and Darkness

Missionary work was oriented, then, by dichotomous oppositions between Christian and heathen, mission and village, and white and black. These were all brought into alignment with each other by a discourse of light and darkness. The metaphor of light and darkness mediated the contradictions in their own ways of thinking about conversion as both individual and collective. In many ways, Auhelawa today rely on the same kind of metaphor to manage similar contradictions. In their own telling of colonialism, missionaries "brought the light" (*masele hi'avalai*). Before Bromilow and his teachers reached Auhelawa, people lived in a time of darkness (*guguyou yana hauga*) and a time of war (*aleha yana hauga*) dominated by constant attacks by neighbors who captured and cannibalized their victims (Schram 2016). According to Auhelawa oral history, a Samoan man named Pati came to Alogawa Village in 1902.[4] He met a man named Maleko, who befriended him and, according to one story, protected him from threats from fellow Auhelawa. Eventually, Pati was given unoccupied land at Sowala Point to erect a church, and today this is the home of the Ekalesiya Sowala (Sowala congregation) of the Bunama circuit. In 1954, Christopher Duduwega, who had been working as a carpenter at the Roman Catholic mission on Sideia Island, invited Australian missionaries to start a mission in his village of Mwademwadewa, which is today the home of St. Peter's Catholic Mission, Kurada and its parish church, primary school, and health center (in neighboring Eli'awa Village).

There is a well-known story in which Pati first attempts to institute tapwalolo. As a historical anecdote, it highlights what Auhelawa regard as essential to tapwalolo and what kind of change Christianity entailed. As was told to me, Maleko explained the proceedings and led the congregation while the pastor Pati read and preached:

> In those times, [Maleko] was worshipping (*itatapwalolo*). A group came in with their lime, and they went up. When they picked up their lime, he went down to them and said, "Hey, forget it! . . . He talks, he preaches, and we(incl.) listen." So, some of the old men said, "Ah, some of us(excl.), we(excl.) are chewing betel nut and some of you(pl.) are talking. And that's how it is. Some are chewing betel nut and also some are talking." That's how it was, those old people then.[5]

The story is funny to Auhelawa because it captures a deep misunderstanding between the onlookers and Maleko in wordplay on the pronouns they use. Maleko says that while the missionary preaches, "we(incl.) listen" (*ta-benalei*), including himself and the onlookers. They, however, address Maleko as part of a plural second person, saying "you(pl.) are talking" (*am-aubabada*) and refer to themselves as an exclusive we, saying "we(excl.) are chewing betel nut" (*a-louhaba*). The inclusive-exclusive switch sets up a contrast between ways of reading the same situation. It resonates iconically with the contrast between the reverent attention of the congregation and the disrespectful attitude of the onlookers, who thought it was acceptable to chew betel nut during tapwalolo. These two perspectives also correspond to the difference between the preconversion and present generations. The teller says that the onlookers were "those old people then," making them stand for all nonconverts and aligning himself in the present with Maleko's congregation. He implies that he and everyone today knows what makes tapwalolo different from talking and would know how to act when a tapwalolo was going on. The onlookers, unchurched and ignorant, mistake a sacred ritual for mere talk. The story thus presents in a narrative form the Auhelawa Christian tropes of light versus darkness, the old people versus the new people, and tradition versus tapwalolo. As a historical memory of evangelization, the story identifies conversion with the separation from the indigenous society and the joining together in a collective body to do something new. To be a Christian, one must participate in tapwalolo with other Christians.

The story of Pati also sounds like the kinds of stories that Bromilow and his fellow ministers wrote in their reports. The story captures a dual division that is similar in some ways to the dichotomy of mission and village. Yet in this local telling of the meeting of Christian and heathen, it is the heathen who refuses. Christianity is the unmarked identity—one chooses to be *non*-Christian. This makes sense when one considers the role of tapwalolo in the flow of daily life today. As mentioned, nearly all public events are opened and closed with prayer offered by a leader on behalf of the assembled group. Whenever more than two people eat together, and usually at all regular meals, the food is blessed with a tapwalolo. And every week people attend Sunday services, also classed as tapwalolo, in their church, as well as evening devotions. Minimally, a tapwalolo is a simply a prayer by a congregation to God. For this, there are only two roles that are needed, a leader and the congregation. The leader initiates and directs the tapwalolo, and the other participants act collectively under his or her leadership. God is also posited as an unseen addressee of the prayer. The leader begins by announcing the beginning of tapwalolo, optionally remarking on the occasion for the tapwalolo and the purpose of the worship. The congregation turns its attention to the leader. She or he then says:

ta-tapwalolo
we(incl.)-worship
Let's worship.

or

ta-pwagogo na ta-awanoi
we(incl.)-bow.head and we(incl.)-pray
We bow our heads and we pray.[6]

The leader and the congregation then bow their heads and close their eyes. The leader prays in a full voice while the congregation listens. At the end of the prayer, the leader cues the congregation to say "Amen" in unison with him or her.

While it is only the leader who speaks during this minimal form of tapwalolo, everyone is also thought to be participating silently. In the Sunday liturgy of the United Church, leaders of tapwalolo will often explicitly mention to the congregation what they should do while he or she prays. This comment is typical:

> teina hauga yada awa'au'augelu yaubada ba'idada
> **This time is our(incl.) friendly talk with God.**
> maidoida tapwagogo
> **Let's all bow our heads.**
> na yau alinagu mwala'ina ainaiena yada awa'au'augelu yaubada ainai ya'atai
> **And I will say our friendly talk to God in a big voice.**
> na omiu nuwamiyena hinage amsapot
> **And all of you also support in your minds.**
> tapwagogo na ta'awanoi
> **We bow our heads and we pray.**[7]

As this comment suggests, the prayer is supposed to engage the minds as well as the bodies of the listeners, even though they are not speaking. Prayer leaders use phrases such as "in our(incl.) heart" (*atedaiyena*) or "in your(pl.) minds" (*nuwamiyena*) to qualify the kind of prayer listeners give by listening to the leader's spoken prayer. They tell listeners to give their mental "support" (*tubwe, sapot*), which the listeners register by their silence, bowed heads, closed eyes, and reverent demeanor from the beginning to the end of the event. When a tapwalolo is initiated, everyone breaks off from whatever they are doing, falls silent, and attends to the leader, shifting their position if necessary toward him or her. They cannot get up and walk out, and walking into the space around the leader and his or her congregation is frowned upon. Thus there is no role for a passive audience in tapwalolo; everyone is either leading or following.

Tapwalolo is thus implicitly a statement by a collective speaker to an imagined addressee. This is further reinforced by the use of the metaphor of one mind for the congregation at worship. If every single person is not fully engaged with the tapwalolo, then people would say that there are "many different minds" (*nuwatuwu vagadi vagadi*) instead of one, or that certain people have a "different mind" (*nuwatuwu udoina*), an expression meaning that an individual is obstinate or aloof to the concerns of the group. People talk about having one mind in other, nonreligious contexts, to mean agreement among people to do something and hence an absence of conflict, argument, and bad feelings. One mind means that cooperative work will go smoothly because everyone will help achieve a common aim. Individual unwillingness and noncooperation are the main obstacles to having one mind. When work doesn't go well, this is because individuals still have different thoughts and have not subordinated their own minds to the mind of the group. Similarly, in tapwalolo people form themselves into one mind by signaling that they are setting aside individual concerns and participating in a collective action. They cease talking, turn toward the leader, and bow their heads, all of which are read as signs that the leader's prayer is in fact the prayer of the congregation as a whole. The concept of "one mind" is how participants can be assured that what they do is part of an authentic Christian belief.

Tapwalolo in the Sowala United Church

Now I shift to an analysis of the practice of formal Sunday services among Ekalesiya Sowala, a congregation within the Bunama circuit of the United Church of Papua New Guinea based at Sowala Village. This congregation derives from the church established by the Methodist mission. Ekalesiya Sowala members explicitly and implicitly position their practices in relation to a frame of one mind and many minds in several different ways. The United service requires the faithful repetition of prescribed liturgical forms and heavy orchestration by leaders of the congregation's participation. Music and prayer are good places to see this kind of regimentation. Ekalesiya Sowala place these forms in the frame of one mind and thereby read the successful execution of a rote pattern as a sign of unity and thus true worship.

All the music sung during tapwalolo are hymns from one of a few hymnals from the mission era. The most frequently used is the *Buki Wari* (*Song Book*), which is a collection of English Methodist hymns translated into Dobu, many by William Bromilow himself. Dobu is also the language into which Bromilow first translated the Bible, and the hymns partake of

Figure 7. Opa Haimanu leaves the Sowala United Church after Sunday *tapwalolo* on November 12, 2006

the same stilted variety of Dobu he used in translation. In recent times, youths of the church have wanted to introduce English and Pidgin choruses into the worship. This has been somewhat controversial among older church members, who say that only mission-era hymns should be used because these were composed as "prayers to God," whereas modern guitar music is frivolous entertainment. The congregation has accepted a compromise. Guitars can be played during the preliminary period while the congregation enters the church to wait for the beginning of the service. Younger male members of the congregation play, usually accompanied by young women playing the tambourine and singing along. These songs are aimed mainly at children. They are light, simple, and repetitive, like English children's songs. Many are accompanied by dancing and movement. Some adults who are in the habit of arriving early to the service also enter and sing along with their own children. As the congregation continues to arrive, more enter and join in. Finally, the pastor and leaders of the service appear at the door of the church building and pause, which signals that the service should begin. When they appear, the singers will then set aside their guitars and begin singing the slow, penitent hymn "Yeisu u da tooro"

("Jesus, you must stand," to the tune of "Jesus, Stand among Us," an 1855 hymn). The rest of the congregation joins them in this hymn, and the pastor and leaders slowly process from the door to the lectern in front of the congregation. So in this way, Ekalesiya Sowala makes use of guitar music while also communicating that it is not part of proper tapwalolo.

Hymns are also sung at the intervals of the different elements of the service: after the invocation prayer, the Bible reading, the sermon, and during the exit from the church. For each song, the leader will stand at the lectern and announce the song by its number in *Buki Wari*, and then read the first line. Usually he or she will repeat this number several times as members page through the hymnals. Many people, however, know all the hymns well enough that they only need to hear the number and the first line to be able to recall the words. The leader then says, "We stand and someone whose voice is able, please start our song," or "We stand, and we sing our song." The songs are sung in four-part choral harmony without accompaniment. Congregation members strive to sing their parts well and to harmonize with the group. Anyone having any familiarity with English Protestant hymns would immediately identify the melodies of most of these songs. I often found myself imagining the sound of a pipe organ playing along with us. It is worth noting that these songs also sound very traditional to Auhelawa. For one, they are all sung in Dobu, a language that is familiar to most but definitely better known by the older generation as the language of the mission-era church. Younger people are more fluent in English than Dobu and prefer to read the Bible in English. Also, the songs have lyrics that were written to teach the basic doctrines of the church.

On rare occasions, the leader of a Ekalesiya Sowala service would combine the congregation's singing of a traditional hymn with a prayer on behalf of the group, making the ensemble of voices into an icon of the tapwalolo as one mind. The leader of tapwalolo prays the invocation over the voices of the congregation as it sings the processional hymn. In a church that denies itself the use of instrumental accompaniment, this has the effect of heightening the experience. It not only marks off the performance from other singing but also highlights the leader's words. The leader can take this opportunity to explicitly frame the moment as "one mind." In one such instance, backed by the unison of voices, the leader closed her eyes, held her outstretched palm over the congregation, and prayed that God would send his spirit among them. Then she said:

> yaubada mehe'uhi nuwana nuwatuwu vagadi himiyamiya ahubena
>   teina ainai
> **God, there is fear, [and] perhaps, many different thoughts on this day.**
> avaivehuludi yeisu keriso yehamwena
> **We(excl.) remove them in your name, Jesus Christ.**
> uvaidi mwauwahiyeidi
> **Take them and set them aside.**[8]

Her prayer amplified the meaning of the Dobuan lyrics of the hymn: Jesus, stand among us. She continued to pray that God's spirit would guide the congregation in their lives, but also in "work of the growth of the congregation" (*yama ekalesiya ana ini'ini yana paipaihowa*). Her reference to the *ekalesiya* (congregation) has special resonance in that moment because the people who make up that entity were joined in creating a model of what that kind of group should be—that is, many voices singing as one, while one voice prays as many, and in that prayer, God removing the individual minds and replacing them with His mind. A picture of the group coming together, coming to God, hearing God, and being one in thought is projected onto the group several times over, guiding the action of participants in the process.

At many points of the service, especially in the confines of the concrete church building in Sowala, at the appointed time for tapwalolo, the proceedings also form what Richard Parmentier (1994) calls a diagrammatic icon of the group that people imagine themselves to be as Christians, a congregation with one mind. This kind of group is capable of the collective action of tapwalolo because the individual members submit themselves to the collective purpose, and the present members strive to replicate the forms of the past, creating continuity with the mission era. Here it may appear that the communal form of the congregation grounds Auhelawa Methodists' identity at the expense of individual agency. An example of how speakers elicit this perception of the congregation in the event of worship comes from a sermon by a woman of Buitowolo named Loise. Introduced by another church member, she rose, bowed her head, closed her eyes, and prayed on behalf of the group:

tapwagogo na ta'awanoi
We(incl.) bow our heads and pray.
yaubada ano'oweigo na atupuweigo na awasawasaigo mahana'alapwahi
    teina ainai
God, we(excl.) praise you many times over on this midday.[9]
yaubada ahubena teina wau alaoma yam walo habi benalei
God, on this day, we(excl.) come here to hear your word.
na yaubada ya'awa'awanoi ahubena teina ainai tomowa ehebo
    hilaoma'o mulitai abo yam walo mayawahina ya'aiyauya
    ehebo aidiyai
**And, God, on this day I pray that every single person who has
    come here, and to each and every of whom your living word
    I will share,**
yaubada ya'awa'awanoi alimwai ta yaluyaluwa tabuna ainaiena owa atedi
    u'abiyemaselei yo nuwadi u'abiyemaselei
**God, I pray to you that through your Holy Spirit, you cause their hearts to
    understand, and cause their minds to understand.**
hava dova yam yaluyaluwa tabuna ainai—yam aiyauya aliguwena—
    ya'aiyauya aidiyai yaubada owa u'abiyemaseleidi aidiyai
**God, explain to them what I share with them through your Holy Spirit—
    what you have shared with me.**
ta walodine hiya hivaidi
And they take this word.
ta hauga maidoina yadi miyamiya aidiyai ihaguidi yadi miyamiya bale'u
    teina ainai
And every day it helps them live their lives on this earth.
teina yama awanoi ihae alimwai natum yeisu keriso yehana vehabana
This our prayer goes to you in the name of your son Jesus Christ.
[Amen]

There are three things I want to highlight in Loise's prayer. First, she explicitly names this event as "hearing God's word." By this, Loise meant not only the Bible reading which the group was about to hear, but also her own sermon (*guguya*), which would focus on explaining the Bible passage and applying it to contemporary lives. In Loise's prayer, the event is objectified and lifted out of the interaction between herself and other participants in tapwalolo. It exists as something people can "take" (*vai*) with them. The message exists independently of herself and is unchanged as it passes from her to her audience. At the end of her sermon, Loise wraps up her sermon with many of the same images from her opening prayer. She says:

buku ana walone ainaiena yalauvahili
The words of the book from which I read
...
ta walodine tavaidi ta iya walodine imugaiyegita
And [now] we take its words and its words lead us.

This leads to the second observation I want to make. In her opening prayer, Loise says that she will "share" (*aiyauya*) knowledge that the Holy Spirit has "shared" (*aiyauya*) with her. At the end, she says "I shouldn't preach while you all listen to it" (*Nige mata yaguguya na ambenalei*). This distinction is made in many sermons by other church members. To say that one is giving a guguya is to say that one has the moral authority to preach and lecture. It is a word used generally as a term for a kind of advice or instruction by a senior relative to young people of a susu. Thus while it is conventional name that Auhelawa would use for Loise's talk, it is also an awkward metaphor for how Auhelawa themselves conceptualize their Christian worship. This is not to say that they confound or confuse the authentic meaning of the English word "sermon." Rather it is because they understand the hierarchy of moral prestige the translation implies that they reject it in favor of *aiyauya* (which is equivalent to the English word "sharing" and is arguably just as awkward a calque). So we come to the third observation. In this framework, Loise prays that God opens the hearts (*ate*) and minds (*nuwa*) of the people listening so that they understand (*nuwamasele*) it. In her setting of the scene, each individual listener is now participating through his or her inner thoughts. She frames the sharing of God's words, through her, to everyone, as in fact part of a communion of the group with God at a cognitive level. Arguably, whenever Auhelawa talk about Christianity, they draw on this kind of discourse. Their basic words for Christian belief include the root *nuwa*, which means "mind," e.g. *nuwamasele* (understand, mind-light), *nuwabu'i* (convert, mind-revolve).

Thus in Loise's framing of her sermon, she and the audience are one as a congregation, united in their minds, and drawn together in their active, emotional, and intellectual engagement with God's word. In this light, it is interesting to note how Loise then organized her talk. Throughout her fifteen-minute presentation, she made it clear how she was moving through the required segments of a conventional sermon. First she says that she will be speaking on "what the Holy Spirit has revealed to me." She then says that she is speaking on a Bible reading that follows from a series of stories about the death and resurrection of Jesus, ending on Ascension Day. (This week's reading was story of the Emmaus Road in the Gospel of Luke [chapter 24], in which two apostles encounter the resurrected Jesus but mistake him until they break bread together.) She then announced this passage by chapter and verse, twice, as speakers usually do in church, and paused while people turned to the page in their own Bibles. She then began to read the passage in Dobu from a relatively recent translation of the New Testament in this well-known mission language. She then freely retold this story in Auhelawa. At the end of her telling, she announced that she was now moving on to "our(inc.) verse." In United Church liturgies, every service has a theme, reading, and verse from that reading, which is meant to be the main point of the reading. Loise, like many preachers, followed these as requirements, referring to them as independent facts about her sermon. In other sermons, speakers refer to these as "this plan" or "this paper" as if they were assigned to them, which in fact they are. This and Loise's clear announcement of the required turns in her sermon all serve to distance herself from her own message. In fact, Loise had an original message. Picking up on a word in the Dobu reading, *itamatatau*, she translated this in Auhelawa as *itadi'wa* (mistake, or overlook). She then went on to say that Christians often itadi'wa the good intentions of other people and reject them. Indeed, she said, "the spirit of God lives in them [also]." Instead of mistaking this and rejecting people, she said, all Christians should take these people, teach them, and help them to see God, so that all people could come together as "one group" and work for the church.

Auhelawa conceptualize Christianity as a subjective belief, but the Uniteds of Auhelawa claim a Christian identity through being part of a conventionalized, regimented, and normative order that is called "one mind" but does not purely consist of their own subjective choice to commit to it. At the same time, Uniteds believe that the true embodiment of one mind in a successful tapwalolo is actually very hard to achieve. What may appear to be mere routine was, for them, something that needed a lot of commitment and effort to do well. In my many visits to their services, I noticed that attendance fluctuated unpredictably even when the weather was fine and the roads good. Services never started on time because not enough of the congregation had arrived. The individuals designated to lead the different segments of the service would often bail out at the last minute, leaving the work with one or two people. It was not uncommon for the leader to apologize tearfully for a lack of preparation before proceeding. In actuality, even though a United tapwalolo is very repetitive, what the participants would count as an actual replication of the ideal form was the exception and not the rule. Because it was so important to displace individual authorial agency by perfectly replicating the traditional form, every little breakdown in individuals' execution made it seem like the entire collective action could not be fully achieved. Moreover, in the frame of one mind these failures were always read as symptoms of weak conviction and insincerity, because tapwalolo is conceptualized as collective thought through collective action. I could not help but wonder why people set for themselves a bar that was so hard to meet. The Sowala United Church usually has only the assistance of a local pastor and his wife and for long stretches was run entirely by the congregation. Yet the normal pattern in this church was to oscillate between bland (*toma*) services and fiery exhortation for everyone to pull together and work harder for the church. In that sense, a kind of collective self-doubt is built into the practice of tapwalolo, especially the larger and more formal tapwalolo of Sunday. The collective actor often cannot be brought into being in spite of enormous effort to elicit it. The practice of tapwalolo conjures the possibility of its failure by an incapacity to control what lies beyond it.

Mulolo

Perhaps the most successful use of the concept of "one mind" to connect collective action to individual belief is the annual freewill offering called mulolo. In both the United Church and the local Roman Catholic diocese, these are given in cash on a single day as part of a large public event. In each church's event, the congregation collectively attempts to reach a fundraising goal that represents their congregation's commitment to their church. Many trips to the market and many potpot events over several weeks lead up to this big day. Through the pooling of money, people give a material form to their own commitment as individuals and as members of a congregation with one mind.

Annual fundraising events were part of the work of Australian Methodist missionaries from the very beginning of their efforts. William Bromilow describes the first meeting in 1899 as follows: "Each village pastor led a band into the church with songs of praise, and the gifts of money or native articles were laid in front of the rostrum in the true spirit of giving. Giving in its true sense has not hitherto been known amongst this people, and we recognize that only the Spirit of God could have influenced our members to join so heartily in these contributions to God's work" (1900, lxxix).

As Bromilow explains here, the amount given was not as significant as the fact that people gave it without an expectation of a return, or as he says, "in the true spirit of giving." Bromilow and his fellow missionaries were somewhat aware that indigenous institutions of feasting were based on reciprocity, and so free will offerings were, for them, also evidence of a choice by donors not to apply this maxim to their dealings with missionaries.[10] Ultimately, Bromilow hoped that the mission would become "self-supporting" through these kinds of donations, and much like the "great ingathering" for which he prayed, a self-supporting mission would be a sign of an authentic conversion of its individual members.[11] In this respect, it is important that the missionaries collected money, directly or indirectly, from the converts because money can be counted, much like the number of churches and number of baptisms or, for that matter, the number of donors to the missionary society whose names were listed in the back of every annual report. Like these annual statistics, every annual meeting served as yet another opportunity to mark the mission's progress toward bringing people into a fold in which their membership was based on an autonomous choice and conversely toward ending the heathen social order based on reciprocity. The more self-supporting the mission was, the less influence heathen social structure had.

Much in the same way that attendance at Sunday services is understood in terms of one mind, Auhelawa understand freewill offerings as proof of their own Christian faith, and they understand their often meager results as a sign of their failure. As in Bromilow's day, the donations in a mulolo entail no obligation to be returned. Unlike a gift of bwabwale, which is either a vaga (debt) or a maiha (repayment), the gift to the church is an expression of love for the church. As people explained to me, mulolo is the word in Tubetube language for *velau*, which can be a gift of betel nut among friends, an embrace, or a handshake. In choosing to think of their donations as velau, Auhelawa are not saying that they are as insignificant as shared betel nut. Rather, like Bromilow they are making the same kind of distinction between Christian and traditional exchanges. They are choosing not to think of them in terms of reciprocity, a value that we have seen structures how people conceptualize many of their important relationships and orients their own economic behavior. Christian giving is done for another kind of moral reason, one's love for the church. In this sense, the gift resembles the reverent attention given in worship, done with an open heart and mind turned to God. By separating the donations from reciprocity, it makes it possible to think of them as forming a sum. In the lens of one mind, this sum is a representation of the group which gives it. Creating a "self-supporting" church, though desirable, is not really the goal anymore. Rather mulolo contributions are, like Sunday services, a space in which people apply the lens of one mind and realize themselves as Christians through their group membership.

The United Church congregation at Sowala Village usually holds its Offering Day in May. The Catholic community holds an event that is modeled on the local Methodist tradition on the feast day of its patron saint, Peter, on June 29. The two mulolo I observed in 2006 were both held on Sundays after the main service of the congregation. What I describe is a basic outline of the event based on my observations of both cases. After the Sunday service, a group of men put a table in front of the assembled congregation. They would run the event and would collect, count, and record the contributions. They put a bowl and notebook on the table. Behind them, they propped up a chalkboard to face the congregation. On the chalkboard and in the notebook, they made up a balance sheet listing in columns the name of the lay groups that had members in the congregation, contributions, and a running total. Sowala differed from the Catholics in that Sowala's contributions were tallied by village while the Catholics tallied the contributions by the ten base communities (locally known as Gospel sharing groups or small Christian communities and composed of several adjacent villages) of the local congregation.

The congregation sat at a distance facing the table, leaving space for people to proceed upward to present their gifts.

One person at the table called up each group to the table one at a time. The group would mass in front of the table at several yards remove holding in their hands their bills and coins. The group sang a church hymn or chorus while processing slowly toward the table. They stood directly in front of the table and completed their song, thrusting their money gifts forward into the bowl all at once. As the song finished and the group started to back away, other people came up from the sides and behind individually to drop in small coins on top of what had been given. The men at the front then rapidly dumped the money from the dish to count and sort the bills and coins into stacks. When they had worked out the total given in the name of one group, it was recorded on the balance sheets and added to the running total. The total given by the group and the running were then announced from the table to applause from the audience.

The contribution of additional money in support of a group making a presentation demonstrates an important aspect of the mulolo as gift. Despite their spontaneous appearance, these supportive gifts of coins were planned by individuals in advance. Many came up from the sidelines during pauses in the action to change bills and coins into smaller denominations, which they then could parcel out among various other groups with whom they had some tie. The money each group presented was not purely their own contribution but at least in a token way involved the support of others to whom they were related. When I asked one participant, a Catholic, from my village why I saw him drop a few 20-toea coins in the dish for another village at Sowala, he said, "If it's our father's village, then we have to put something." Many of the people who gave these small gifts in other groups' names were similarly the patrilateral or affinal kin of the group. It seems to point to a more general pattern of action in all domains of Auhelawa life. No person stands alone or acts alone. Rather all action involves at some level facilitation and support by others and is done with others in mind. One sees this in the support people give to another person's bwabwale gift, or when people sell market goods in cooperation with or on behalf of another. At least on the sidelines, one could see evidence that a group's offering was not simply a voluntary sacrifice but also implicated them as a group and as individuals in networks of help and sharing from their kin.

At the same time, these gifts that top up a group's presentation also have a bit of the same air of parody that the decorations in pot-to-pot have. In both cases, people's help is never strictly embedded in kinship. People are encouraged to give supporting gifts to other groups as well, as if these supporting gifts were themselves velau. In the Sowala mulolo, one of the men behind the table would usually shout out some epithet at the group while they sang, meant to remind the audience of some distinctive talent of the group that they shared with others. For instance, for a village that had a lot of sago palms, he said "Our(incl. edible) sago!" or "Our(incl.) roof thatch!" The items he called out at different times were varied and consisted not only of natural tree products, which villages usually share with other associated groups, but commodity foods (for villages with stores or who were active in marketing), a school, and a boat. This was meant to remind the audience what their fellow congregation members had done for them and to encourage them to give supporting gifts. While many people took care to make these sorts of gifts, they were clearly subordinated to the main purpose of standing with the group. They were made with trivial amounts of money, itself only a part of the total amount an individual was prepared to give. Some people asked to change notes so they could give several coins to several different groups. It seemed to be more important to stand with the group than to actually make a significant contribution to their total. This was underscored by one incident during the Sowala mulolo. As one woman's group moved toward the table to present their gift, she plucked off a few betel nuts and sticks of tobacco she had tied onto the leaves of a decorated palm frond and flung them into the audience, saying, "This is to help you!" Her light sarcasm provoked laughter from the audience, and a few stood up to join with her group and give a few coins.

At each event, after every group had presented their offering, the announcer called two more items from the list, each one serving as a last chance for anyone to add to the mulolo. First he called out for gifts "in memory of those who had died." A few more people came up individually to drop in some more coins, none making any remarks about the person they were remembering. Then the announcer called for gifts in *saukwaiya*, a Dobu word explained as "where you look around for any last coins you've been holding in your pocket." A few more came to drop in some coins into the dish. At Sowala, when saukwaiya was called, a chorus struck up one final, spirited song accompanied by a guitar. A few people came up to drop a few coins. The song continued, and indeed got louder. A few more came. A few even threw coins from their seats. After a bit more time and a few more coins appeared, the song ended, and the people at the table began the count. Then the grand total was announced to the audience, who applauded. In the end, these gifts from the sidelines are really more of a sideshow. They don't constitute a gift in themselves to the group standing, or if they do, it is only a velau. In the last act of mulolo, people stage a playful little final request for yet more money which, it could be said, pokes fun at the whole event. In saukwaiya, the request for coins one hides, people present mulolo as an earnest, yet rather insistent, demand which is met reluctantly and grudgingly one coin at a time. Thus supporting gifts and extra contributions are presented as if they too were, despite appearances, really responses to a demand for velau, and not in any real sense part of an ongoing relationship.

Finally, after the total has been announced, various members of the congregation rise to give thank-you speeches (*walo velau*). Here one sees people explicitly specifying the value of the money raised and linking this to a particular quality of the congregation. In the speeches the money was referred to as the total, the result, the limit of the strength (the maximum possible effort) of the congregation, a gift (*velau*) to God, and a gift (*velau*) to the church. The purpose of the money was described as the development (*abi'abi*) and growth (*ini*) of the church. In many of the speeches and prayers, the Gospel story of the widow's offering was frequently cited. This was the reading and topic of the sermon in the service beforehand as well. In this story, Jesus says to the widow who gave all that she had as an offering that he would bless her gift many times over. In a prayer of sanctification of the money, the speaker cited this story when he prayed that God would bless (*velau*) what the congregation had given by making the church grow and develop. Here it is important to note that, like any exchange, one can assume a great deal of indeterminacy of the actual value for the parties involved. Mulolo gifts are no more free gifts than Maussian gifts are always mechanically reciprocated. At least, each of those possibilities is subject to contestation in every actual instance. What I wish to highlight is not, however, the intentions of the actors but the role that mulolo as a ritual plays in framing actions in terms of a certain discourse of value. One sees this discourse in the speeches and prayers at the end of the event. They suppress alternative readings of the value of the gift and emphasize the symbolic quality of the quantitative value raised.

One also sees this discourse in the way people talked about the event at Sowala beforehand. Members of the church talked about what they hoped to achieve in an almost purely numerical idiom. The circuit administration had assigned to the Sowala congregation the goal of raising K3,600. Each congregation in the circuit was given a different goal, and congregation members at Sowala took this as a judgment about their strength as a group, both their numerical strength and the individual commitment of the members. For instance, once while talking to members of the Sowala congregation about their mulolo goal, I asked the new pastor how much his home congregation usually raised. He was born on the small island of Skelton, in the Engineer group, which lies near enormous reefs from which people collect beche-de-mer for sale. He sheepishly admitted, "Sometimes we reach K30,000 or K40,000." Someone pointed out to me that communities endowed with an abundance of marketable resources, like beche-de-mer or trochus shells, were expected to raise much more. Although Sowala could not hope to raise so much money, the Sowala members marveled at the fact that their neighboring congregations with relatively few resources could completely provide for themselves through donations, paying not only the salaries of the pastors and ministers but for the upkeep of their concrete and iron church building and staff houses.

To plan for their goal, Sowala set a target contribution of K36 per head, apparently based on an assumption about the number of church members. Each family would contribute based on the number of church members they had. After the event, many people said they were disappointed that the congregation could not reach K1,000. (They raised K959.30.) Others praised the few groups who raised over K100. The number served not so much as a measurement as a symbol of a quality of the group. It is worth noting that although they wanted to raise as much as possible, thresholds of value matter too. If they could not raise their assigned goal of K3,600, then they wanted to at least break K1,000, of which each group should give K100. Multiples of 100 seem to symbolize completeness more than quantity per se (see also Guyer 2004, 53–60). In this way, a congregation comes into being through gifts of charity, as a distinct, autonomous social entity. The group is the sum of individual velau, not the articulation of interdependencies of help and debt.

Mulolo is, I argue, an extension of the process of making use of money to define an alternative sphere of value which is neither the atomistic, anomic field of the market nor the encompassing complementary dualism of reciprocity. In the previous chapter, I argued that people defined their own money earning through market trade in opposition to an ideal concept of monetary transactions as purely self-interested haggling. By thinking of their profits from trade as like a harvest of yams that comes from diligent, patient work, they made it possible to distinguish their own market trade from this negative horizon. Rather than thinking of themselves as self-interested actors who consume heedlessly, they regard money earning as a site for self-denial and through this realization of themselves as moral. Mulolo takes part in the same logic at the level of a collective. Through donations, people realize their congregation as a collective actor that also reaps a monetary harvest in the mulolo event. The ideology of one mind also adds another additional layer of theological significance. Much as a well-orchestrated service is never simply a sign of good planning but also evidence of a collective Christian spirit, so too is mulolo not simply an instrument of value but a sign of the strength of the group's faith. The value of the sum was defined by its existence as something shared among the group as a pool of resources they all owned collectively.

And yet the 2006 Sowala mulolo, much like a typical Methodist tapwalolo, cannot help but raise doubts in people's minds about that reading as well. The circuit had instructed Sowala's congregation to aim for K3,600. In the end, and in spite of their best efforts, they did not even raise K1,000. While some voiced the possibility that each congregation's sum really could only reflect the economic opportunities in their community, just as many if not more said that people should have tried harder and given more. In the relatively low result, people saw signs that some among them were participating insincerely or obstinately refusing to give at all. If only everyone would come together as one mind, then they would reap even more.

The Limits of One Mind

The problem the churches face is that, by definition, the harmony they call "one mind" must come from the willing participation of individual minds beyond group control. By insisting that established rituals and money gifts are the only reliable media for enacting unity, they anticipate their own failure to draw every single person out of his or her essentially private existence. A mistake or a poor performance is automatically treated as a symptom of a deeper instability. Failure to reach a fundraising target means that some individuals are personally less committed to the church than others. Auhelawa talk about this unknown and uncontrolled externality as tapwalolo oya'oyama. The phrase denotes a range of different things. The word *oyama* means trick or lie, which can be an innocent joke by a child or a calculated deception. When reduplicated and used to modify a verb, it means "falsely" or "dishonestly." One informant, an elder member of the United Church, used the phrase to describe a range of different things. He said that in the early colonial period, many people "did not know tapwalolo" and so did not go to church. Even in areas like Auhelawa where a missionary was present, people went to church but only tapwalolo oya'oyama, because they were secretly performing *poison* (homicidal sorcery) on members of the congregation. He also said that today, people were *tautapwalolo oya'oyama* (false Christians, or false members of the congregation). He explained that even though they went to church, inside (*hola*) themselves they only wanted money. They go to church, but they don't listen to the preacher. They hear, but when the word of God is spoken, they are thinking only about what they want. In church meetings, they argue and don't work. They don't respect the Sabbath. He also gave some examples of people who went to church but were known to have bad, immoral ways. The mind of individuals is the source, then, of insincere worship and what threatens the possibility of one mind among the group. The design of tapwalolo posits the minds of individuals as essentially different, distinct and intrinsically unknowable, and thus establishes its own limit of efficacy as reliable evidence for true subjective commitment.

So it would seem that members of Ekalesiya Sowala today are, in fact, dealing with the same kind of contradiction in the conception of Christianity that faced the first Methodist missionaries. The missionaries relied on a metaphor of light and darkness to mediate the tension between individual conversion and authentic subjective commitment, on the one hand, and a new community that could replace the old order, on the other. No amount of social development could ever truly demonstrate a person's change of heart. Similarly, no tapwalolo can ever fully demonstrate that the congregation is really communicating with God, because that communication is taking place in the minds of the participants and not in the words of the speaker. Ekalesiya Sowala uses the concept of "one mind" as a way to establish the connection between doing Christian things and being a Christian. Yet this connection can never be fully established, because by definition it is the private minds of individuals that must become part of the congregation's one mind. In that sense, although Auhelawa Christians seem to rely on a ritual that has been practiced for generations, they have the same kind of suspicions of ritual efficacy that recently converted Christians do and seek to find a new ground for reading outer behaviors as sincere belief, as these Christians do as well (see also Robbins 2001; Keane 2007). The framing of worship in terms of one mind is not an alternative conception of what it means to be Christian; it is another way of trying to understand what should count as sincere individual belief as the defining feature of the Christian person.

The informant who explained tapwalolo oya'oyama to me went on to say that many new churches were now appearing which he said was a sign of the end times, as prophesied in the Bible. These people also practiced tapwalolo oya'oyama. He said that these new churches were different from the Methodist and London Missionary Society churches. These churches chased away (*heusili*) and opened (*ho'e*) the darkness. The new churches did not do anything. "They think they're chasing demons, but they're just acting proud and showing off," he said. There were only a handful of Pentecostals among Auhelawa during the time of my fieldwork, but they had been growing in number and influence throughout the region. According to many, Pentecostals were *parapita oya'oyama* (false prophets). Catholics, by contrast, attract hardly any suspicion at all. Auhelawa Catholics in fact only practice Mass about once a month. Their regular weekly Sunday service, led by the catechist and lay members, centers on a Bible reading and sermon, much like the plain, reformed worship of the Ekalesiya Sowala.

Arguably, Pentecostals, more than Catholics or any other church, present a genuinely different idea of what tapwalolo is and means, and thereby attract a disproportionate level of attention. Pentecostals here, as in many parts of PNG and the world, practice what is called block worship in which participants weave back and forth among English choruses, guitars, collective prayer, and a cacophony of individual spoken prayers, without any clear transitions or obvious coordination at all. Even many people who are not drawn to Pentecostalism see this kind of worship as authentic, enthusiastic, and joyful and may wish to borrow elements of it for their own services. Still others do not always feel comfortable with it, and some think of it as ostentatious if not subversive and morally dangerous (see also Webb 2011). Yet even though Auhelawa say that Pentecostalism is very different, I think it would be a mistake to treat it as a rival movement competing with older and more institutionalized churches. This is the standard metanarrative in which this kind of situation is usually placed (e.g., Ernst 2012). Indeed, Pentecostals, Methodists, and Catholics often come together as a congregation to do tapwalolo outside their usual Sunday services. Pentecostal ways of prayer and worship find their way into United Church celebrations as valid expressions, though like the guitar choruses, usually only around the edges. The contrast between these two forms is as variations on tapwalolo, not as rivals. Any variation of tapwalolo has to find a way to reconcile the inner and outer aspects of a person's religious identity, and for Auhelawa, Methodist and Pentecostal worship are each incomplete attempts to do this.

Metaphors Auhelawa Christians Live By

I end this chapter by returning to the broader question of conversion. Today, all Auhelawa people not only claim to be Christian but are also active in contributing in one way or another to a specific Christian congregation as a distinct kind of community. In this respect, they differ from another, earlier account of a United church congregation elsewhere in Normanby described by Carl Thune (1990). Thune worked in Loboda, which is a Duau-speaking community that was one of the first places outside Dobu where Bromilow sent his missionaries. As in Dobu and Auhelawa, people use the term *guguya* as a translation of English word "sermon" to denote the same kind of biblical exegesis in a Sunday service (Thune 1990, 118). Loboda people also classify the authoritative speech of male elders as guguya, and so Loboda Christians understand this to be what preachers do in church. Christians in Loboda makes the foreign ideas and practices of Western Christianity conform to indigenous idioms of relationships. Yet Loboda preachers are not lineage elders, and so Thune concludes Christianity is regarded with skepticism. Can the same thing be said of Auhelawa Christianity?

Auhelawa Christianity is and always has been practiced through translations from a foreign language into Auhelawa. The congregation has one mind, much like any cooperative group. Offerings to the church are velau (or mulolo), much like small gifts to friends, and soliciting gifts is voiced in terms of help, like the mutual assistance of kin. So it would seem that Thune's argument could easily be applied to Auhelawa. As I have shown in this chapter, something more is going on when Auhelawa people frame their worship as the collective action of a congregation. In Auhelawa, the translatedness of Christianity is always present in every Christian practice. By translatedness I mean that when Auhelawa make use of Christian discursive practices, they also reflexively position their own local translations of Christianity in relation to other translations of Christianity (Handman 2015). Loise, for instance, explicitly rejects guguya as a label for her talk and in her prayer labels what she is saying as *aiyauya* (sharing). In maintaining this gap between languages, Loise and United church members use vernacular metaphors to add layers of meaning to new situations and thus create new ideas.

Considering culturalist approaches to Christianity like Thune's and others, Jon Bialecki (2012) argues that they effectively assert a null hypothesis: where Christianity is encountered, no one really converts. Christianity is always perceived as a variant of some existing category. More generally, culturalists conclude that there is no essence to Christianity across space and time, only diverse appropriations of Christian practices into various particular cultural schemata. If so, and because anthropologists generally agree that cultures are powerful forces, those who want to argue that Christianity is a distinct culture must surmount a rather high hurdle. Indeed, when one considers Christianity across time and space, it presents a special kind of problem of analysis. Whenever one engages with Christianity as a lived social practice, one immediately must recognize two things. First, Christian theology, cosmology, ethics, and practice all assume in some way that Christians are individuals capable of choice and hence personal conversion. Second, Christianity has always operated across cultures and is itself culturally diverse in its expression and its significance as a social identity. Christians are taught to think of themselves in relation to a singular subjective truth, but there are many ways to be Christian, and Christianity sits in a different relation to other social institutions in every context one finds it.

The debate among anthropologists of Christianity thus far has basically been over which of these sides of the same coin to emphasize. There are several examples in PNG alone where conversion to Christianity led to the repudiation of traditional institutions and the adoption of a new subjectivity (Tuzin 1997; Robbins 2004; Jebens 2005; Jorgensen 2005). Yet, as much as Christian individualism seems to remake lives and worlds, especially of recent converts, these transformations always seem to be incomplete. Christian individualism needs an other, much in the same way that gimwala serves as an outer horizon of morality for market traders. For this reason, Simon Coleman argues that Christianity is a "part-culture" that comes to life in the negation of the mundane world (2006, 3). Through this relation to an other, Christian individualism can be expressed and thus shared among fellow Christians. Coleman wants to emphasize the importance of individual subjectivity, and he argues that the Christian part-culture typically depicts alternative forms of sociality as traditions in the sense of an inherited past that constrains individuals' agency in the present. Because a negative identity cannot be experienced directly, Christians define themselves as the inverse of and successor to society. Their individuality, that is to say their ascetic refusal of normal social life, can only be experienced, communicated, and thus realized in inverting what they are not. Rather than dragging one's feet on the road, good Christians come early to church (and gossip about everyone not present). Rather than each occupying a "different mind," good Christians voluntarily come together on Sunday as one mind (even though solitary activities are normally oriented to the benefit of others). Taking the inverse stance toward normal sociality is not, however, the only way in which Christian social identities take shape. Other observers have noted that Christians realize themselves as such by cultivating a sense of their own inner experiences. Joel Robbins (2001), for instance, notes that Urapmin Pentecostals indicate their devotion in prayer by shutting their eyes tight and by making public confessions in a marked singular first-person voice, sometimes in the presence of those who made them angry and caused them to sin. Bambi Schieffelin (2007) describes how Kaluli Christians have modified their use of evidential markers in speech to index that their claims to knowledge are personal. Similarly, Auhelawa people, while generally preferring to frame worship as one mind by using a plural first-person voice, make use of a wide range of bodily idioms to denote inner states and their connection to sincere expressions. Participation in church activities is a gift from the heart. Conversion to Christianity is *nuwamasele* (*nuwa* [mind] + *masele* [light]) or a *nuwabui* (*nuwa* + *bui* [turn over]). As Robbins notes, this cultivation of one's inner conviction itself makes use of and extends vernacular ethnopsychology. Urapmin and many other Melanesian peoples usually place a great deal of emphasis on the "opacity of others' minds," assuming for instance that because mental experience is private, that others' intentions are fundamentally unknowable (Robbins 2008). If we consider the possibility that Christianity is a culture, a distinct way of thinking and feeling that challenges prevailing patterns of life, then Christians must figure out what the individual and social dimensions of their own form of Christianity have to do with each other.

In Auhelawa, people create a conceptual blend to think through what it means for them to be individually and collectively Christian. A conceptual blend is how Gilles Fauconnier and Mark Turner (2002) describe the cognitive process of formulating new concepts through metaphor.[12] One example they offer comes from a newspaper account of a new speed record by a catamaran traveling from San Francisco to Boston in 1993. The sailors aimed to beat a previous record by a clipper in 1853. In the story, the reporter describes the catamaran's position midvoyage by saying that "barely maintaining a 4.5 day lead over the ghost of the clipper Northern Light" (quoted in Fauconnier and Turner 2002, 64) That is to say, at the time of observation the catamaran was at a point in its trip that the clipper did not reach until four and a half days later in its voyage. The image of a catamaran several days' journey ahead of a boat from the nineteenth century, though unreal, is also immediately comprehensible. This image is a conceptual blend created by merging two mental representations of distinct real-world events. Through it, the relative greater speed of the modern boat can be conceptualized. In Fauconnier and Turner's model of conceptual blending, the clipper's voyage exists in a "mental space" with certain features (2002, 41). The catamaran's voyage likewise exists in its own mental space. These mental constructs share one feature in common, the course of the two boats. On this basis, a third unreal space can be imagined in which the two boats are racing on one course, and the lead of one boat over the other can be calculated. Fauconnier and Turner go on to argue that this kind of process of merging distinct mental spaces and "running the blend," or performing calculations in the merged space, pervade all forms of reasoning and are central to learning of all forms (2002, 44).

Let's consider the statement *A Christian congregation is one mind* as such a conceptual metaphor. In one mental space is the idea of collective Christian worship, what Auhelawa call tapwalolo. In whatever form it takes, tapwalolo consists of an assembled group who attend to and are directed by a leader. Members coordinate their actions with others in the audience. Ideally, they come together in the same place at the same time. They face the same direction toward the leader. The group serves as an audience to the leader's words; each member individually concentrates on the words of the leader. The second mental space contains the idea of a group with one mind, a cooperative group like a party building a house. They come together in the same space and time, and each person has the same purpose in being there. In the blended space, actions of tapwalolo are construed as being work toward a common goal. There are many ways in which other kinds of one-mind groups are not like groups in tapwalolo. For instance, most people in tapwalolo are not interacting with one another or the leader, although there is a minimal differentiation of their roles. Also, unlike one-mind work groups, tapwalolo does not have a definite outcome, like a successfully completed project. Rather, it is a sequence of events repeated each time anyone worships. These can be set aside in the blending of spaces. The common feature they possess, coming together in a shared space and time, allows one to construct a new idea of a congregation as a body of people whose participation contributes toward a goal. In this blended space, it becomes possible to think about tapwalolo as something that counts as Christian worship and part of actually being a devout Christian. In this way, seeing the congregation as one mind creates a normative standard against which actual participation in worship can be measured. At the same time, running the blend in order to assess the status of Christian belief has limits. Although a one-mind group has a shared purpose and thus posits the same mental state in each participant, there is still no way to know directly whether each participant in tapwalolo actually shares the same purpose, or even has the same beliefs. In tapwalolo, all should "support" the leader through concentration, but if this support is not really there among some, there is no way to know. So, this conceptual blend does not completely resolve the question of what counts as truly being Christian. It must be replaced by something else, and for Auhelawa mulolo offers a new metaphor for the congregation as a Christian community. Mulolo is also framed as the actions of one mind, and yet it merges the money gifts with the construct of tapwalolo to perform a new calculation. Although these gifts are also called hagu (help) and velau (free gift), which might suggest that they are reduced to indigenous categories of value, not all aspects of hagu and velau are taken up in the blended space. Only their difference from vaga, gifts which must be reciprocated exactly, matters because this means they are forms of atetalam (gifts from the heart). The collected sum of money then becomes another icon of the Christian congregation but only in the blended space created in mulolo.

Auhelawa Christianity as a social identity emerges from this process of creating new metaphors with which to see Auhelawa Christian practices. Given this, I want to make a more general point. Ethnography has generally shifted its frame of reference to conjunctures of cultures, and one dominant approach has been to examine the ways in which local cultural categories serve as a schema for locating foreign ideas and practices. Christianity is itself an inherently global, and hence multicultural, phenomenon, making it a perfect example of the kinds of problems anthropologists wish to solve now. The culturalist approach to Christianity is particularly relevant in this light. However, what I argue in this chapter is that making metaphors to translate foreign ideas into locally recognized categories is itself a social practice, consisting of many of the same processes of creating and circulating knowledge about society that I have described in previous chapters. Also, and similar to these forms of reflexive sociality, translating Christianity into one metaphorical frame is always partial. One frame may help realize a particular idea of Christianity in one situation but still leave unanswered questions in other situations, and so it must be replaced by a new frame.

The reason why, I conclude, is general and not particular to Pacific cultures or their historical experience with Christianity. An individual, subjective commitment can only go so far to generate a viable social order. If one's religious self is something that can only be experienced through inward asceticism, then for this to become a social identity it needs to be transformed into something that can be communicated and so establish a believer as a member of a group of co-believers. Thus even if one is individually drawn out of one's previous social existence, one needs to establish a code, and thus a norm, for being outside a system of norms. Even where an autonomous self is ideologically valued, a total rationalization of codes of communication, as Max Weber imagined, is never fully possible—whether in collective ritual, codes of conduct, or a personal confession—because communication always presumes a shared context for interpretation that precedes it (Tomlinson and Engelke 2006).

All forms of Christianity are defined by both the failure to produce a permanent social order out of individual commitment and the continual effort to produce this order anew. In this respect, local forms of Christianity are not adaptations of foreign ideas to specific cultural context; they are extensions of Christianity itself or further attempts to communicate the charisma of its prophecy, none of which is ever fully satisfactory, and thus all of which necessarily give way to new forms. It is not merely in the Pacific where one sees social innovation in Christianity. Many US Pentecostals increasingly doubt whether they can really be Christians as individuals and seek relationships as a ground for their subjectivity (Bielo 2012). Similarly, in neoliberal, urban Zambia, Pentecostals proclaim a prosperity gospel not for its visions of individual success but for its capacity to realize gift-giving relationships that have become untenable in the wake of economic decline (Haynes 2012). These cases suggest that in their effort to establish themselves, Christian religious expressions do not always disrupt the social order but innovate it by producing new kinds of sociality (Robbins 2009). As Kenelm Burridge writes: "Christianity is a missionary and troublesome faith. Because it seeks new and more universal moralities it cannot rest on a single achievement. It has an innate capacity, which is also instructional, to transform itself. And the means of its self-transformation is largely through generalized individuality [of each community]" (1978, 29).

Thus when Bromilow prayed for a "great ingathering" and when Auhelawa attempt to persuade their fellow congregants to pull together to support tapwalolo, they are both in their own ways reaching for a material object and environment that can serve as metaphor and model of the kind of social order that they see Christianity as being. Metaphors of a temporal threshold or binary opposition of light and darkness serve the same purpose. In materializing and externalizing what they imagine as subjective, they are not thus reducing their subjective experiences to the material language they happen to adopt. Rather, this particular social apparatus always proves to be provisional and tentative. It offers people a means by which to approximate the uniqueness of Christian individualism but ultimately proves to be an other against which to define this individualism. In that sense, the cultural significance of the movement of Christianity is not that it spreads a cultural logic of individualism, or that it is appropriated into diverse social institutions, but that wherever it goes the charisma of individual salvation forces people to react to its impossibility with a variety of innovative, creative, new forms that are neither heathen nor Christian, neither traditional nor modern.

6

THE WEIGHT OF TRADITION, THE CHILDREN OF LIGHT

Into Custom

The first time I attended a mortuary feast, a man explained the proceedings to me by saying "When someone dies, we go into custom." During my fieldwork, I attended several of these kinds of events held to mourn a death and came to understand what he meant. When the natuleiya of a susu hear of a death in that susu, for instance, they go the village to see the body. As soon as they appear in the village, they begin to wail and sob. The village owners embrace them and wail as well. In their keening voice, each speaks to the spirit of the deceased. The visitors cry out, "My father, I remember you!" and the hosts cry out, "My mother's brother, your child is here." Both groups cry, but the tears of each index their different relationships to the deceased and thus make complementary opposition the basis of their relationship. In this way, death interrupts normal life and the flow of normal social relationships, because mourning interpellates everyone into positions based on how they are related through kinship to the deceased. The protocols of mourning are not just rules to be followed. They are means by which people elicit from one another a relational, interdependent personhood predicated on an encompassing order of kinship.

Still, not all deaths are mourned in this way. I also attended many feasts in which the susu of the deceased declared that they would not receive bwabwale, nor would any food be forbidden to visitors. Instead, all would eat a common meal together. This kind of feast was called masele (light), and as the name suggests, it is explicitly aligned with Christianity as an alternative to bwabwale as tradition. Indeed, masele is supposed to negate all the things that separate susu during mourning. As one retired United Church pastor from Auhelawa explained to me, now that all Auhelawa are Christians, they should simply "sit, cook, eat, full stop." A masele feast requires none of the crying, prohibitions, and reciprocal exchange of bwabwale. It calls on people to be fellow Christians, much as Sunday services are an expression of one mind. In contemporary practice, then, whenever someone dies, everyone has to mourn, but the susu of the deceased also has to position itself with respect to a history of mourning. Would they "go into custom," or negate tradition altogether? During feasts, I never knew what approach the susu of the deceased would take. My Alogawa hosts and other informants would provide me with their own accounts of what was happening and whether or not the actions of others should be counted as kastam (custom, tradition) or masele.[1] Yet even within one event, people's judgments on the meaning of these acts conflicted.

In general, Auhelawa people thought that bwabwale, as a form of kastam, was on the decline. Feast gifts, they noted, were smaller now, and people were reluctant to take on new debts in bwabwale for fear that they could not reciprocate them later. This too was linked to the perceived decline of yam harvests, and people's greater selfishness. Mortuary taboos, particularly for widows of deceased men, had largely ceased. Instead of wearing dirty clothes and abstaining from washing for a year, widows and other mourners were released from these prohibitions quickly after the burial. Other kinds of respect could be shown through work and gifts. Many desired a mix (mikisi) of bwabwale and masele, and indeed, many mortuary feasts already looked like a hybrid of both patterns. It might seem reasonable, then, to conclude that a new norm is emerging, and the mourner is now simultaneously implicated in a network of kinship relations and a community of fellow Christians. In this chapter, I challenge this interpretation. It is not that the rituals of mourning or the ideas underlying them are changing. Rather, the ways that people read others' acts of mourning are multiplying. No act of mourning has one single, definite meaning unless people agree on one interpretive context for it. In spite of people's statements, bwabwale, masele, and mikisi are not simply choices made by the susu of the deceased. These are terms by which people attempt to establish what kind of people mourners should be and what kind of relationships they should have. These terms are based implicitly on a temporal order which presumes that there is a linear movement from the past to the future, and hence that the present is a time of change. When we examine mourning events in detail, we see not so much empirical change as the use of a historical discourse as a means to organize and coordinate the different possible meanings that people now find in rituals of mourning. Indeed, although contemporary Christian mourning represents change itself, in practice it can never fully break away from kastam as its alternative.

Auhelawa Mourning

Elements of Auhelawa mourning have already been discussed at length, but here I bring all of this together in light of the ways that Auhelawa perceive historical change. Any traditional mortuary feast is, at heart, an encounter between sides, the owners of the feast who receive gifts and the visitors who give them.[2] The susu of the deceased serve as hosts for all the events related to mourning and burial and the subsequent feasts and exchanges held in honor of the dead. As recipients of bwabwale gifts, they are called *tonibwabwale* (owners of the bwabwale). Their bu'una of various kinds can also join with them to support their work as galiyauna (sextons) and will be "people who eat the bwabwale" (*bwabwale tau'ai*). On the opposite side, people who attend the feast to give gifts are visitors and would not traditionally eat from their own gifts. Within this group of visitors, particular people will be principal mourners because of their specific tie to the deceased. The spouse of a deceased person and the children of a deceased man will be expected to attend every event related to this death and will be expected to display all the signs of respect to the owners, including several onerous taboos on self-care, hygiene, and diet. For other people, because of many overlapping ties of bu'una, namesaking, and other relationships, it is conceivable that they could potentially be on either side. All have to orient themselves to the event of death and proceed as either an owner or visitor.

When one is close to death, one is taken to one's natal village. News travels fast, and yet during this time, everyone avoids making direct reference to the death, instead saying that they have heard about an asiyebwa at a particular place. Rather than saying someone has died (*mwalowoi*), one says "Ana hauga i'ovi" (his/her time is over). This initial period, called malahilili, is observed by a generalized respect for the susu of the deceased. Public events are canceled, and people are reluctant to be seen at the markets, in the gardens, or at church. When death comes, the susu erects a small shelter in their village where affines, natuleiya (children of men of the susu) and tubuni (children of natuleiya) can come to dou (wail) over the body. Mourners from other susu are supposed to show their grief for the deceased to the deceased's susu. They do so through signs of respect (ve'ahihi), including dou, as well as abstaining from washing, wearing nice clothes, and eating fine foods. The social network of the deceased is split in two. Indeed, arguably this is contained within the term ve'ahihi itself. The word is related to *ve'a* (part) and *oive'aha* (to sort out into separate groups, or to organize). Among the various people who mourn, there are two sides, which should not mix. If, for instance, a natuleiya were to enter the magai of the susu, which is already forbidden, someone might ask rhetorically, "Hava ana oive'aha?" (Which side does he or she belong to?). Respect is, then, not merely a prescribed ritual act of grief. In the eyes of the owners, everyone's actions immediately place one on either one side or the other of a social divide created by the death. Acts of respect are a method by which the mourner makes him- or herself an object for the observation of the deceased's susu and establishes their complementarity and interdependence.

After the death, the owners will hold a feast called aemehelino (crying) in which visitors come to the owners' village to mourn again. As soon as they appear in sight of the owners, visitors will begin to dou, joined by the owners. One's dou is addressed to the deceased. In each dou, owners and visitors call out to the deceased by the appropriate kin term. The owners who dou with the visitors do this as well. Each will *douta'eta'e* (cry-talk), speaking to the deceased in exaggerated syllables and melodic tones, uttering short phrases such as "I cared for you," "You watched over me," and "Your time is over and I am sad." Each speaks to be overheard by the other side. The kin term and the feelings and deeds they describe index their differential relationship to the deceased, and hence the complementary opposition between the owners and the visitors. As people explained to me, the spirit of the deceased is still present during this and all the feasts of mourning and memorial to come, as are all the spirits of the owner susu. The spirits are watching the mourning performed for them, and listening to the dou addressed to them.

The spirit of the deceased is farewelled at an all-night wake called hilauwa, which means to stay awake. Over the course of the night, owners host visitors and anyone else who comes to the owners' village to mourn. Here too the respective sides of mourning are indexed by people's actions but in a different way: natuleiya, tubuni, and others sing for the owners while the owners quietly sit near the body of the deceased. In 2006, I attended one hilauwa held in the village of Gogosuluwa. I was accompanied by other people from Alogawa and nearby villages. We stopped in a village adjacent to Gogosuluwa at the house of unmarried men of this susu to wait for other people to arrive. When we finally came to Gogosuluwa, a large crowd had already assembled under one of the larger village houses around the coffin of the deceased man. The owners had spread a large tarpaulin over a bamboo frame to create a covered space for people to sit and tied large bunches of betel nut and pepper to the frame for their guests. A young man sat near the coffin on a chair while everyone else sat on mats on the ground. The people of the village remained on the edges. Some worked in the kitchen to prepare food for the singing visitors. Others sat in a small group, and a few occasionally left the area to cry and dou by themselves. The visitors sat together in small clusters, huddled near the white light of Coleman lanterns. We sang church hymns from the early days of the Methodist missions, written in songbooks in Dobu and Tubetube languages. While Sowala members used these songbooks in Sunday services, these particular songs were rarely sung, nor were these sung at village Christmas Eve celebrations either. As people later explained to me, people chose songs about death and the promise of heaven. The singing was practically continuous. One small choir would sing, slowly and soulfully, and then after a few songs, another group of visitors would take up a song while the first group rested.

The owners and visitors played distinct roles. At midnight, Tagelani, a man who was a bu'una of the owners, appeared before the crowd dressed in Sunday clothes. He called everyone together for a tapwalolo. Everyone turned to face him and he gave a prayer of thanks to God for his plan for people, and his protection.[3] The songs we sang tonight were, Tagelani said, God's songs, and songs of praise to God, and he prayed that we all would hear and understand them. We returned to singing. After a few more hours of singing, the owners served us some food, boiled rice and tea, prepared in a hurry without coconut milk. As dawn broke, Tagelani appeared again in Sunday clothes. He was joined this time by Elobi, a woman who was a visitor to the village. The two led everyone in a devotional service, a United Church practice. Owners and visitors came together once again as a congregation, and Tagelani and Elobi prayed on our behalf and led us in a hymn. Tagelani read a passage from Paul's second letter to the Corinthians. Elobi explained the passage by saying that Paul said we would all meet God when we died, and that he was preparing a place for us in heaven, and we would be made new again. She reminded everyone to examine their lives to prepare for this day. After this, the sun rising behind a steel gray sky, the hilauwa ended. A man of Gogosuluwa pulled back the shroud covering the open casket and whispered to the deceased. He then pulled the shroud aside. The owners immediately began to wail. The visitors quickly and quietly got up and left the village. Later, I asked others what this man was saying and was told that normally one says to the deceased, "Get up and go to Bwebweso," the mountain home of the dead. Even in the midst of the dual division of owners and visitors there were hints that another framing of people's relationships was possible. This potential frame was based on the one mind of a congregation at *tapwalolo* in which all present were alike as individual participants.

After *hilauwa*, the owners begin to prepare for burial. The next feast, called *welowelolo* or *ipa'ipatu*, comes in the following days, if not the very next day.[4] The galiyauna begin to dig a grave in the susu cemetery. In the owner's village, visitors bring food and wail again beside the body of the deceased with the owners. Owners serve food to the visiting mourners, and in turn the visitors cook for the owners the gifts they have brought.

When the grave has been prepared, the owners go to the magai to watch as the coffin is lowered into the ground by the galiyauna. At this feast, the owners also release the mourners from some of the mourning taboos they have observed since the death, such as those against eating good food, washing and combing their hair, or walking on the road in front of the owners' villages and magai. Starting with this feast, each time the mourners return to the owners' village to offer bwabwale gifts, the owners also release them from mourning taboos. In the feasts I observed, release from a taboo was often accomplished very quickly by an owner coming before a group of the mourners and washing one of each of their hands with a wet cloth and placing a flower in each of their hair. Mourners still wail with the owners on their arrival, but the owners now console them by whispering in their ear that they do not have to mourn anymore. The owners say, "Be strong and we go," or something similar. Being permitted to cease wailing, or being released from any mortuary taboo, makes the mourners *bayau* (free). Specifically the weight (*vitai*) of mourning is lifted from them, and they no longer struggle under it. In this sense, too, kastam is itself conceptualized as a weight, an obstacle, or a burden. Indeed, one person said that the owners sometimes whisper to mourners, "Don't think about kastam anymore."

Here I want to note that Christianity enters into the traditional forms of mourning in ambiguous ways. Many forms of mourning include Christian ideas and practices as a supplement to or substitute for ritual acts of mourning. So, for instance, the only songs that are sung during hilauwa are Christian hymns, although the fact that they are only used at these times makes them feel special and important. In the past, people told me that mourners would recite magical spells (*oba*) continuously. Hymns are considered to be perfectly equivalent to this. In the same way, the cooked food that is served for attendees to eat, though it is not necessarily shared, is blessed with a Christian prayer, as if it were a common meal. At the same time, Christian prayer and worship is also inserted into the traditional sequence at various points as an exclusive self-contained activity. During the hilauwa I observed, Tagelani and Elobi read Bible passages about and preached on the promise of life after death. At the end of the event, the owners farewelled the deceased's spirit on its journey to Bwebweso. In the same way, at other burial feasts, both mourners and owners step aside from their activities to participate in a tapwalolo, and in some cases they bring the coffin to St. Peter's Church for a funeral Mass led by the parish priest at Mwademwadewa and then return to the exchange of bwabwale and the release of mourners from their taboos. One could arguably conclude that there is no contradiction here. Both tapwalolo and traditional feasting mark the end of a period of mourning and return mourners to normal life. And yet feasting is meant to release mourners from the weight of their obligations, and tapwalolo at times appears simply to banish this concern altogether.

Indeed, while Christian practices are always present in every act of mourning in some way, people generally conceptualize Christian mourning and traditional mourning as alternatives. At hilauwa or aemehelino, the owners meet to decide among themselves whether they will observe one or the other. They then announce the decision (*loina*) to the attendees: either bwabwale or masele or some combination of the two. The visitors should respect this decision as the rule for the following events. If it is to be bwabwale, then they will bring gifts. Sometimes, the owners will say that they will accept certain kinds of gifts from certain classes of relative. If it is to be masele, however, then visitors and owners will bring food, and all the food will be shared. And since no gifts are given or received, then no debts are incurred, and there will be no obligation placed on the owners to attend future feasts at the visitors' villages. Yet in spite of this, the decision of the owners to practice masele is never uncontroversial. The owners clearly anticipate this reaction in what they announce to the group. They explicitly refer to the Christian era and ask for "all of you and all of us(ex.)" to come together and eat together. In one case, the son of a deceased woman pointed to his shirt and said, "You see that I am wearing clean clothes." He then went on to say that he wanted sports to be played on Saturday, because that is what people normally do. Even though everyone told me that the owners have the power to do this, I was always surprised by how much discussion there was about this supposedly closed decision. Reactions could range from murmuring from the crowd to explicit objections from individual visitors. Mostly visitors would stand and say that if the owners had decided, then they would respect the rule. It underlined that even though the owners claimed authority to make rules, the visitors had to acknowledge this authority for it to be effective.

In many cases, what happened was that neither party could ever come to a complete agreement about what they were doing together.

In the next section, I examine two cases of mourning that are ambiguously situated between bwabwale and masele in this way. In most people's minds, these are a mix of both kinds of mourning, and as such they may suggest the possibility of an emerging alternative form of mourning. In fact, in both cases people set out to perform mourning in one way and ultimately mourned in another. In each case, people were diverted from their initial plan in different ways also. For that reason, I argue that it is better to examine these cases as genuinely indeterminate in their meaning as symbols and in their efficacy as symbolic mediations of people's social relationships. They insist on people performing their roles neither as kin of different susu nor as fellow Christians, and although people conceptualize them in terms of historical time, they are neither traditional nor antitraditional. They do not express a specific social form through a stable symbolic language of one culture or another. Rather, in both of these cases, some people attempt to change the frame of the whole ensemble of actors, living and dead, from one alternative mode to another. It is not simply that individuals each have different subjective interpretations of the meaning of what they are doing. Rather people attempt to elicit a particular meaning—traditional ritual or Christian negation of tradition—from acts of giving and mourning and thus draw other attendees into specific kinds of relationship. Ultimately, to posit one kind of relationship based on one mind, people end up also having to elicit another relationship based on their ties of kinship to the deceased person and the obligations to each other that arise from those ties. Following this presentation, I move to consider what the indeterminacy of ritual symbolism might suggest for ongoing debates about personhood in anthropology right now.

A Little Bit of Custom

In actual cases of mourning, simply choosing to do masele is not sufficient for staging a feast, and many acts of mourning are read by people as being both bwabwale and masele. I argue that the apparent mixing of masele and bwabwale does not indicate that people compromise between the values of complementarity and unity. Rather, in attempting to constitute a social field as a mechanical unity and to displace alternative readings, people have to draw on the method of bwabwale to elicit a complementary dual division. Masele needs to draw bwabwale into itself in order to be a complete frame for casting people as a unity. I first present an example of the limits of the choice of masele to completely frame the social field as a mechanical unity. I then present an example of how people were able to accomplish mechanical unity through masele feasting by first drawing a bwabwale relationship into it.

The first example shows that one can never simply choose to hold a masele feast. This example comes from the death of Lorenzo's mother, Adrina, on a Friday in August 2004. Her adult children, led by her eldest son, convened to discuss what kind of celebration they wanted to have. Lorenzo, her eldest son, was an active member of the local Catholic parish and lived with her in the matrilineage's village, where he managed a large trade store. Not only was he wealthy by local standards, but he, his siblings, and most of his children were all active in the church and highly educated. Although he did participate in mortuary exchanges on other occasions, he usually talked to me about bwabwale and other traditional institutions as relics of the preconversion era. He, his business, and his lifestyle all seemed to many like a concrete example of the modernity that Auhelawa associate with the church era, for good or ill. When his mother died, the other members of his matrilineage, their natuleiya, and the children of natuleiya came to the village to wail. Eventually, Lorenzo appeared in the village and said that later that day, there would be a tapwalolo at St. Peter's Church, then his lineage would bury his mother, and they would all eat together. Then on Monday they would have another small meal. He said that he wanted the sports league to play on Saturday and for women to come to the marketplace in the Catholic mission. Normally these events would be canceled out of respect for the asiyebwa. In this way, it was strongly implied to everyone that there would be no bwabwale, because the deceased's children and matrilineal descendants did not want to have one.

It had been only three short months since Lorenzo brought me to his village and then to Alogawa, where Lorenzo's cross-cousin Lucy adopted me. Looking back on my fieldnotes from this time, I can see that I was attempting to read this new situation as a kind of bwabwale, albeit one that was being modified. The people from Wadaheya and Alogawa who were explaining everything to me were also encouraging me to see the event in this way. They highlighted the aspects of the proceedings that were components of a bwabwale sequence. For instance, onlookers pointed out that the deceased woman's son's children, who lived with him and in a neighboring village, were being quiet and respectful because they were natuleiya. I noticed that their matrilateral cousins, susu mates of the deceased, were working as the grave diggers and thus became forbidden to everyone else because they had touched the corpse and dug the earth of the magai. When I asked permission to enter the cemetery during the digging, the galiyauna permitted it, but one also quipped, "Don't touch the ground, or Lucy will chase you!" It wasn't as though any of these commentators had a particular interest in either what was done, what it symbolized, or how I read it. Rather, they seemed to be able to situate everyone's actions in a discourse of bwabwale, and particularly its link to kastam in the sense of a code of rules, despite the explicit decision for masele.[5] Many actions of individual participants seemed to index bwabwale too. After the burial, during the supposedly common meal, these workers ate separately. Also, some elements of the mourning seemed to evoke the idea of bwabwale, but only very subtly. Before the meal, some of the natuleiya and affines were seated in a row. A host of the feast went to each one with a bowl of water and a cloth, daubing water onto their hands, making a gesture of washing them before they were invited to share food with the hosts. In this way, mourners were ceremonially released from a traditional taboo on self-cleaning less than twenty-four hours after having undertaken it. Nonetheless, it was also clear that some elements of the mourning would not fit into the bwabwale frame but instead needed to be read in the frame of masele. For instance, all the attendees to the feast also went to the church for a funeral Mass officiated by the parish priest. More important, it was announced that there were not going to be exchanges of food, without which there is no relationship of complementarity.

On Monday, I attended the second meal in the woman's village. Many of the same people who came to dou on Friday returned and began to cook the food that they would share with the hosts. After a few hours, I heard a conch being blown somewhere down the road. A conch is a traditional way of announcing the arrival of group coming to a feast with gifts.

The Weight of Tradition, the Children of Light 179

A large group of men from another matrilineage who were natuleiya to the hosts appeared, bearing a pig and baskets of yams. Several were carrying a long, slender tree trunk to which they had tied long ceremonial yams to the stumps of its branches. Suddenly the crowd started buzzing around as the visitors quickly entered, planted the yam pole in the central clearing of the village, and started to pile their gifts around it. I asked the woman's son, who up until now was firmly directing the activities, what was happening, and he said half-jokingly, "I don't know. I'm a bit scared!" Later a member of this group told me that his matrilineal uncle had told him to take a pig and yams to the hosts. When they appeared, he said, "everything changed"; the party was no longer masele, because the visiting mourners were forcing the hosts to accept a bwabwale gift. While it is not clear that merely giving a gift in a certain style or with a certain intention is sufficient to compel everyone to participate in a bwabwale, it is clear that neither is the choice not to participate. While at the outset, the hosts of the feast insisted that what was going to happen should be read from the perspective of masele and not bwabwale, several things seemed to break the frame. Many things could be framed through the lens of bwabwale as a sequence, as my informants suggested to me when they gave themselves the task of explicating others' actions. Neither reading then could claim to represent a consensus. While many people put forward explicit statements or conspicuous displays as attempts to guide people's reading of the events, none was firmly taken up by all until the visiting group barged onto the scene with a large ceremonial gift. As a gift, it was both an act and a statement about itself as an act. The donors loudly and forcefully gave the gift in a way that overrode any possible alternative perception of how it related to other acts of mourning. The gift was not merely forced upon the recipients, but as a type of gift it was able to achieve a consensus in the way that ritual acts of unity—the tapwalolo and sharing of food—could not.

It is not enough then to simply choose to mourn in masele over bwabwale. Lorenzo announced his and his susu's desire for masele, but at some level he and others recognized that this required the cooperation of others. In many ways, bwabwale was always present as a potential and could be brought out through how one perceived the proceedings. In some ways, people recognize this when they voice their own desire for masele mourning. The death of the father is a crucial moment in any

Auhelawa person's biography, because it is in the mourning of a father that one has the first opportunity to transform one's relationships to one's father's susu. It is a commonplace of Auhelawa discourse about death that a father's dying wish for his children must be honored by all. For instance, natuleiya often claim the right to occupy villages and make use of garden sites based on the word of the father. In talk about this relationship, people say that a father also often refuses kastam (bwabwale), meaning that when he dies he does not want his children to mourn and give bwabwale gifts to his susu. In one example, a man's children returned from their salaried jobs in Port Moresby on Father's Day with a new bed, linens, clothes, and a big *bagi* shell necklace for their aging father, as well as clothes for the father's sisters.[6] He said to his children that when he died, they should not perform any acts of mourning, because they had already done so by giving Father's Day presents. Similarly, when one of Lucy's brothers died, she cited his wish for masele as why she chose to refuse to host any bwabwale exchanges and instead insisted on welcoming his children to her village for a common meal. In that case, however, months later, Lucy's brother's children approached her and asked permission to bring her a gift to release them from the taboo on walking the road in front of their father's village, Alogawa. She eventually accepted but continued to insist that these children, as natuleiya, had no special obligations to her or Alogawa susu.[7]

If Wadaheya susu could not firmly establish masele, then the next example illustrates how people can do so when they align bwabwale with masele, instead of oppose them. In this example, the intention to do masele is ultimately attributed not to a decision of the hosts but to the decision of the spirit of a deceased man. In January 2006, Francis's sisters' children, all residing in Tupwagidu Village, planned to hold a memorial feast for several members of the lineage who had died over the years, including Francis's brother, who was a United Church pastor. The event which this feast would celebrate was the placement of cement headstones over the graves of those being memorialized. This kind of event and its associated feast are usually called *sementi*, and it is considered to be the final act of mourning, coming a year or more after someone has died. Even though the name and the purpose of the event are new, the feast is not necessarily masele. A sementi echoes a now defunct generational feast called *so'i* on Normanby Island, which is held to memorialize several deaths of a lineage. A sementi is generally no bigger than a feast held when one person dies. It can involve either bwabwale exchanges or masele commensality. In this case, the men of the lineage planned to enter the cemetery and erect the memorials, while in the village several groups of natuleiya, including myself and my siblings, would cook for everyone. After the work was completed, hosts and guests would all eat together in the village. When I first arrived, I asked what kinds of gifts people would be bringing, and one of the hosts scoffed and said, "This is only *teibolo* [table]," that is, the food would be given to all freely, like food served to a congregation from a missionary's table. No food was bwabwale, and nothing was to be exchanged. Later I asked another owner about this, and he furtively agreed that they had chosen masele, but they might take some gifts from visitors after all. He said that there was a disagreement but did not elaborate.

Toward the end of the day, the workers came back into the village from the cemetery. They had not been able to finish their work pouring the cement base for the headstone for my father's brother. The timber frame they had constructed to mold the cement was too long for the grave, even though they had carefully measured it. They had to start over tomorrow. I walked home to my village and planned on coming early the next morning. The next day, when I arrived in the hosts' village, there was hardly anyone there. It looked like everyone had dropped their preparations for the feasts and left behind the baskets of food and pigs. I asked someone waiting behind where everyone was, and he said that they had all gone to the lineage's cemetery. Feeling a little foolish, I rushed down the road toward the cemetery, which was several villages away, and at the top of a hill. About halfway up the steep, muddy path to the cemetery, I practically collided with a pastor of the United Church, smartly dressed in his church's uniform of black trousers, white shirt, and black tie and carrying a leatherbound Bible. By the time I got to the top, visitors and hosts of the feast were turning to head down the path. Whatever happened was already over. I went back with the group to the village where we would hold the feast. Later I found out what had happened. The day before, while the workers were still in the cemetery, some visitors and hosts had argued over whether visitors could give gifts in honor of their dead magai relative to the hosts. The workers unexpectedly found that the frame did not fit. Everyone agreed that the spirit of one of the deceased being honored was offended by the argument and caused the problem with the frame. Whenever there is work in a lineage cemetery, the spirits of the lineage dead hover nearby and watch over it to ensure that they are properly respected. This particular deceased person was in fact a United Church pastor and had said before he died that his children should not perform bwabwale for him but only remember him with masele. His supernatural action was meant to be a warning to his descendants to honor him with a real masele feast and not to argue over gifts and debts. So, the next morning, the hosts and guests all went together into the hosts' cemetery to have a tapwalolo. They prayed to their deceased ancestor to ask for forgiveness, and "to ask him to ask God to forgive them." The work continued in the cemetery and was eventually finished. At the end of the day, the owners and visitors cooked and ate together.

The Location of the Person in Masele and Bwabwale

Through masele and bwabwale, people frame acts of mourning in relationship to specific ideas about agency. Each presupposes a kind of person who performs them, and insofar as each ritual also serves as an effective performance, it instantiates a particular social order composed of these persons. Based on the alignment of mutual avoidance and balanced reciprocity, bwabwale presupposes that each person is defined relationally. The complementarity of the respect relationship means that both mourners and owners are mutually implicated in each other's capacity to act, their social standing, and indeed their being. Each individual, as Marilyn Strathern argues, is a "social microcosm" (1988, 13), a dividual person. Rather than being autonomous individual entities who combine to form larger wholes, a dividual person comes into being as a result of these perduring cycles. This position suggests that respect, rather than being simply a script for self-presentation or an acquired habitus is a precondition for one's recognition as an agent. It is only through having one's ritual acts perceived by others, and one's gifts received by others, that one comes into being at all. Yet masele is predicated on the grounds of oneness and unity. Perhaps this is why masele seems so hard to carry out in real life. Although people can imagine themselves as individuals, they only know this individuality as the negation of their being as kin.

This sense of a dividual person has become a very influential way of for anthropologists to think about different social orders. Yet, quite contrary to the way scholars apply it now, Strathern's argument about the Melanesian dividual was always a thought experiment about what social theory would be if it started from an alternative understanding of persons. Rather than being a positive claim, it was supposed to force anthropologists to confront the ontological biases that prevented them from more universal explanations. Reflecting on this divergence helps us understand how the apparent mixing of ritual forms in Auhelawa is better understood as the merger and confusion of epistemic frames.

The dividual has many parents besides Strathern, including especially McKim Marriott. For Marriott, Hindu society conceptualizes persons as dividuals. By this he means that the society makes no distinction between mind and body—that is, the substance of the person's being and the codes with which it communicates itself to others. Stated more positively, when dividuals interact, they absorb and transmit parts of themselves, which are "coded substances" (Marriott 1976, 111). In asserting this, Marriott claimed that the concepts of Western social science could never explain the patterns of Hindu society, because these concepts were themselves based on a dualism of code and substance or subject and object. Many different approaches to social analysis assumed a dichotomy of individual and society. Thus Marriott said all Western social science resulted in distorted models of other cultures. A complete model of society can only be based on "the pervasive indigenous assumptions" of that society (Marriott 1976, 109). This was not meant merely to separate Hindu society from the project of social theory but to break new ground. As one commentator noted at the time, there are always two targets Marriott has in mind when he talks about dividuals. One is to create a social science of and for India. The other and more general goal is to rethink social science as a collection of "alternatives" (Marriott 1992): to divest social science in the West of its own implicit ontological commitment to dualism (Larson 1990). The dividual is not, in this second and more general sense meant to replace the individual in models of non-Western societies. It is at best a provisional suspension of the individual-society dichotomy to create an opening for a new method to emerge.

Like Marriott's ethnoscience, Strathern's conception of a dividual person is meant both as a critique and as a step toward a new method. She launches into her inquiry by saying, "Scholars trained in the Western tradition cannot really expect to find others solving the metaphysical problems of Western thought" (Strathern 1988, 3), by which she means principally those that follow from the conceptual opposition between individual and society (1988, 12). This metaphysics of society does not exist in Melanesia, and so Melanesia is a privileged place for rethinking social theory. As she says, the Melanesian person is as much a dividual as an individual. Citing Marriott for the term, she says that a dividual person is a social microcosm composed of many parts and capable of taking on new parts and removing others in different situations. In that respect, the flow of social interaction and relation makes persons, rather than do unitary persons make the relationships between them. Like Marriott's argument, this is meant to reveal the implicit dualism—of subject and object, mind and body, and individual and society—in the axioms of social explanation by pointing to a negative case (Strathern 1988, 11). Yet like Marriott, Strathern also wishes to move beyond mere negation of Western theory and let a new mode of explanation arise from the abeyance of Western dualism. Western observers obscure the images that people hold of themselves and their social life, so we must suspend the individual-society dichotomy, not to replace it with some specific alternative but instead to let the images present in people's discourses inform understanding, a method she calls exegesis.

The concept of a dividual rapidly achieved a wide reach in anthropology and other social sciences. At first, no one saw it as being a merely middle-range theory of Hindu or Melanesian society. Instead, scholars invoked it in a challenge to the universalism of the individual subject (Miller 1984; Ewing 1990; Kulick 1993; Weiner 1993; Escobar 1994; Knauft 1994; Turner 1995; Strauss 1997; Boddy 1998; Harvey 1998). The dividual allowed people to imagine an alternative kind of self which was not defined by essential attributes but produced by its interactions with its social environment and defined by its relational qualities. What Westerners had taken as givens of the human subject, not simply a unitary self but also an essential gender and integral body, could be argued to be composite, situational, and plural.

The antiessentialist interpretation of the dividual, however, has never been the only reading of the concept. Another prevalent interpretation has concluded that Melanesians and Hindus are fundamentally different because of their cultural conceptualization of themselves as selves or as persons. What Marriott and Strathern pose as a provisional negation of individual personhood has for some always been read as a substantive empirical claim about Melanesian societies (Mosko 1989, 1992; Foster 1990; Hirsch 1994). In some ways, this essentialistic reading harkens to a long-standing debate about whether societies define the self as either sociocentric or egocentric (Hollan 1992; Spiro 1993). In this light, many other scholars have argued that other non-Western societies define persons as dividuals. These scholars tend to associate the dividual person with Marcel Mauss's (1985) concept of a premodern *personnage* or with the total social fact of reciprocity, and thus they are inclined to see dividuals in every society besides the modern West. Associated with gift economies and kinship in this way, dividual and individual act as proxies for the traditional and the (Western) modern (Piot 1992; Rowlands 1993; Carrier 1994; Busby 1997; LiPuma 1998; Verdery 1998; Niehaus 2002; Uzendoski 2004; Rival 2005; Hess 2006; Daswani 2011; Werbner 2011; see also Coleman 2011). These are not concerned with the goal of moving toward an ethnoscience that derives from the forms taken by actions themselves. Instead, for them alternative conceptions of personhood demonstrate the power of collective representations to shape individual experiences and conceptions of self in profoundly different if not incommensurate ways.

Strathern herself emphasized that her intent was not to analyze Melanesian social forms but to highlight how Melanesians might analyze their own forms. As James Weiner says, building on this point, "What Strathern compares is not Melanesian and Western social relations as such but the contrastive ways of eliciting them or making them visible in each case" (1993, 291; see also Kulick 1993; Rumsey 2000). It is not necessary to see dividuals and individuals as incompatible and incommensurate ways of being. Nor should one see them as the essential traits of different kinds of cultures. Indeed, if one seriously entertains the possibility of being a dividual, then culture in the classical sense of a Durkheimian collective consciousness itself becomes suspect. It is too often forgotten that dividual and individual are alternative possible ways for actors to see social life. As models and modes of interacting, each provides alternative ways of eliciting a certain social form from the actions of others. In that respect, the difference between these modes is grounded in an underlying universality: making relationships depends on a reflexive account of social life. Social process consists both of performing symbolic actions and eliciting meaning from these actions through perception. To apply this view in an ethnographic analysis, one needs to return to ethnomethodology as the chief source for both Strathern and Marriott's ideas. This principle in turn suggests an approach that focuses on communication in social processes.

Ritual is a mode of symbolic communication and, in particular, a way that people constitute their world, their relationships, and hence themselves as actors in a particular form. Bwabwale—involving dou, avoidance, and reciprocal exchange—symbolizes and, through its practice, produces a persisting, mutual interdependence or dividual persons. To argue this way is to reduce the dividual person to the status of a particular cultural construct within the culture of Auhelawa, and in so doing, to set up Auhelawa as a premodern alter to Western culture and its individual person. Moreover, this particular reading of Strathern's concept includes a specific set of assumptions about the nature of symbolic meaning itself. Many theories of meaning presume that language or any communication carries the intentions of a speaker in a coded form. This turns on the assumption of a communicating subject who is an autonomous mind and speaks first in a private inner language, then utters or performs an equivalent statement in symbolic language. Alessandro Duranti (1988) challenges this assumption in J. L. Austin's (1975 [1962]) speech-act theory by saying that Samoans, for one, do not hold the same folk theory that a speaker has to intend to perform a certain act in order for its performance to be effective. Thus even unintended utterances can still be binding because how they are received is what makes them effective. From the perspective of Marriott and Strathern, the assumption that meaning is an intention, and that social actions carry individuals' intentions in symbolic forms, partakes of the dualism of Western metaphysics, splitting meaning into thought and action.

There is, however, another way to conceptualize the meaning of ritual symbols. Here Strathern's original thought experiment is especially helpful. What if, she might say, people's individual intention did not count in communication? Where would we look, then, for the efficacy of ritual symbols as communication and performance? It would lie solely in the reading another actor gave of events; that is to say, the meaning is something an other perceives (Strathern 1988, 272). To communicate, then, is to make oneself available to be read in this way. I argued above that this is effectively what acts of respect amount to. One behaves in ways that one's father's susu can read as one complementary difference to themselves and thus as the basis for establishing interdependence through reciprocity. One's symbolic performance of one's status as a natuleiya is possible only insofar as one obtains the recognition of the father's susu as an audience. In the same way, people construct their co-membership in a susu through the symbol of having one blood, but they also extend the boundaries of this category to nongenealogical bu'una when both recognize the formal congruence between symbol and group. In this way, it is more useful to assume that meaning is a perception, not because this corresponds to a specific local cultural theory of agency or subjecthood, but because it gives room to see how the recipients of actions participate in making it what it is.

In this reading, dividual and individual are not distinct types of person, each associated with specific cultural values or institutions, like reciprocity and contract. To reduce the thought experiment to a positive claim of this kind is, in fact, to smuggle back in the very hierarchy of norm and practice, or group and individual that Strathern wanted to question. Indeed, I think it is important to remember that, even when Strathern first discusses the dividual person in the context of the typical Melanesian society, she says that the Melanesian person is as much dividual as individual (1988, 13). Both persons exist as potentials to be read into specific situations, and one reading always haunts the other. While people may profess and enshrine in their institutions an ethos predicated on dividual being, and this mode of being may be dominant, individualism, as its negation, still exists as a possible alternative reading and is incipient in every pattern of action, although often denied and excluded (LiPuma 1998; see also Wardlow 2006, 20, 227). Another way of saying this is that the scene of communication, or any kind of symbolic interaction, includes within it a representation of itself in one or another set of terms. It is not the projection of abstract concepts, rules, and norms onto events but, in Roy Wagner's terms, a fractal image. A particular shape has to be elicited through a process of communication and perception, rather than intentionally imposed by an actor. If meaning is elicited through perception, then we can look at the cases of attempts at masele in a new light as a merger of epistemic frames in which multiple persons potentially exist, but none is ever firmly established.

The concept of bwabwale and masele are themselves contained within the scene of mourning itself. Signs such as tangled hair and dirty clothes, for instance, not only serve to index the person's role as a mourner but comment on the other actors and objects in this sense. In the same way, clean, neat clothes and Bibles also elicit a reading of an assembled group as a congregation, based on the model of the congregation that forms in any other tapwalolo. In this sense, in mourning people not only act but also deploy specific objects that serve to frame the actions, objects, and actors around them.

As accounts or frames, though, bwabwale and masele can be applied to similar kinds of objects, and so people's acts of mourning become hard to decipher, and no one single framing of a social event of mourning ever dominates. Both masele and bwabwale depend on manipulating objects—pigs, graves, food, tears—in ways that anticipate another person with whom one mourns. They both use pigs and food, among other things, to signify this mourning with others. Yet each imagines a different relationship among the people, their gifts, and one another. A person can attempt to elicit from others a particular kind of relationship, either complementarity or unity. Yet it is not enough to simply intend to communicate a particular relationship in a particular symbolic form. There needs to be a "reciprocal recognition" between people about what kinds of acts will count as what kind of relationship (Gregory 1997, 23). In some cases, this is clear-cut. For instance in the midst of mourning with dou and ve'ahihi, when someone appears to lead a tapwalolo, people reconfigure themselves with respect to the tapwalolo and displace division with unity for a time. Similarly, when someone is being buried, people reconfigure themselves with respect to their different relationships to the cemetery as a magai and constitute themselves as divided. Even when hosts and guests in a feast eat together, the guests would never enter the hosts' magai or have contact with the gravediggers, who are bwabwale. In this sense, any act of contemporary mourning involves switching from one mode to the other. The two modes remain distinct because they are carefully distinguished by the objects and actions specific to them.

Yet as the two cases discussed above suggest, people also mourn in ways that are ambivalent. At these moments, in spite of one's intentions, one's actions are not recognized for what they are by the other. And so the events take on a disorderly quality. It is hard for people to provide coherent accounts of the unfolding of the event, and they struggle to fix the meaning of people's actions, as well as the type of person who serves as an agent for these actions.

As a method for accounting for the meaning of mourning, bwabwale is often more stable. People can provide a complete, normative account of bwabwale in a discursive form and so set up clear lines for what should and should not count as constituting relationships of division. Although people have a clear, normative understanding of tapwalolo and can account for people's actions as signs of their worship, they do not have a similarly explicit, discursive formulation of masele as a distinct alternative. The most prevalent way of defining masele discursively is by posing it as the negation of all the characteristics of bwabwale (Schram 2007). As such, masele is easily transvalued as teibolo, an unrestricted giveaway. The command to mourn without showing respect or giving gifts seems hard for people to fully accept, because no positive alternative is given. Masele can easily sound like the old Nichols and May skit about the $65 funeral.[8] In the skit, Mike Nichols plays a grieving relative seeking to plan a basic funeral for the lowest possible price. Elaine May, the funeral director, tells him that a basic funeral costs only $65 and then asks him if he'd like to buy the extras: a coffin, hearse, burial plot, and so on. Outraged and bewildered, he asks what he's buying for $65. The response: We have two men who take your dearly departed away "and do God knows what." Because a masele is defined by the negation of customary procedures, it always runs the risk that other mourners will expect something else and see it as an absence of mourning, rather than an alternative to mourning.

If the simple decision to abstain from bwabwale is not sufficient to constitute people as a unity, then as one sees in the second example, people can draw on the method of bwabwale to elicit the form of unity. The people involved in mourning could not achieve a reciprocal recognition that the food between them was to be shared, and so they argued. When something unexpected happened, though, they collectively attributed it to the agency of the deceased. They posited the continuing presence of their relationships to the deceased after death, then chose to reconfigure themselves with respect to this person to whom they all had some connection of kinship, but of different kinds. They allowed themselves to be bound in a relationship of division between matrilineages in order to accept that they should become a unity. To frame their mourning as masele, they have to first frame it as bwabwale. To a lesser extent, the token gestures of washing mourners to release them from taboos quickly seems to do the same thing. Their masele meal can be defined as both a negation and a fulfillment of the alternative. In that case, the sharing of food was ultimately overturned when another group of people brought a gift that was presented in a way that strongly compelled the reading of bwabwale because of the form of its presentation. Once the frame for their gift had been established by the conch and the tall planted pole, no one could deny that the gift was part of a reciprocal exchange.

I began this analysis by rejecting the assumption that constructs such as bwabwale and masele are symbolic representations of people's relationships, which people could intentionally project onto situations. Instead, I adopted the working assumption that the meaning of people's action was brought out through others' perception of it and so could be analyzed only in the relationships between action and its reception. Harold Garfinkel's ethnomethodology influences my way of thinking about this relationship (1967; Garfinkel and Rawls 2002). For Garfinkel, human action does not have to be intentionally motivated to be socially effective. He assumes instead that all action is, as he would say, inherently accountable (Garfinkel 1988). When people act, they do so in a way that makes it available for people to notice, observe, report on, comment on, and give an account of what it is and what it counts as or stands for. In this sense, action contributes to the making of social order not because it follows a rule in an abstract sense, but because it is taken up by a flow of other actions that ratify it, extend its effects, and link a sequence of actions to an account of "what is going on." Accounts of social formations and processes are not just given by observers such as anthropologists. In fact, we live in a world that is saturated with many ongoing accounting regimes, and indeed, we all participate in a distributed process of accounting for what is happening while it is happening. Bwabwale and masele are two alternative methods Auhelawa people use to account for what people's mourning accomplishes and what kinds of relationships people have with others who mourn. When people mourn in certain ways, they make their mourning available to be accounted by these methods. Depending on what methods of accounting people use, they posit different kinds of persons and create the grounds for different kinds of relationships. Given this set of assumptions, one would not assume that constructs of the person such as dividual and individual should typify whole complexes of social forms and values in an absolute sense. Rather, in this view, any social situation is inherently multiple, and it is only when an account of "what is going on" develops through people's interactions that a particular social form emerges.

A Brief History of Death

Now I'd like to set aside the question of how bwabwale and masele are related and look more broadly at the question of how mortuary practice has changed in Auhelawa. Written historical evidence and the memories and oral traditions of Auhelawa indicate that observance of death has in fact changed substantially. Not only have burial sites and practices changed, but the kinds of exchanges between sides in a feast are now generally much smaller, and periods of mourning in which natuleiya and affines observe taboos are much shorter, if they are observed at all. Throughout this region, where scholars have long observed that mortuary feasting and exchange are central social institutions, a shift toward more relaxed practices seems to be the trend. For instance, Martha Macintyre (1989, 134) observes that on Tubetube, many of the taboos and mourning rituals of the traditional sequence of events after death have been stopped, but that people still make traditional exchanges of food, and these exchanges still played the same role in solidifying kin groups. Susanne Kuehling reports that the traditional mourning taboos on Dobu Island have been "significantly relaxed" and many lineages perform an "alternative feast" in which no mourning taboos are imposed and lineages take a "short-cut" by holding an exchange between owners and visitors a few days after the burial (2005, 244). She writes, "A quick feast is in line with 'modern ways' . . . [The contemporary form of this feast] now serves Christian ideals by limiting mourning restrictions" (Kuehling 2005, 245).

Yet more than any specific change in people's empirical patterns of behavior, it seems as if people are now highly conscious of the layers of history. Even though they bury the dead in cemeteries, they still remember the caves used as shrines for preceding generations. At any event of mourning I attended, people told me that something of what they were doing was kastam, even if people still ate together or prayed together too. The historical lens was always available for people even though they might want to define themselves in opposition to it. In keeping this memory, it also becomes possible to foresee a future in which there is no kastam, no mourning, and only a small party, as people say, a common meal after the burial. It is only in this light that contemporary practice appears as a mix of old and new, rather than a substitute for traditional forms or an adaptation. In this sense, even when people choose to practice bwabwale, this bwabwale is defined in relation to a past tradition just as masele is defined in opposition to tradition. Indeed in 2004, when the man at the first feast I attended told me, "When someone dies, we go into kastam," I rather boldly (or stupidly) asked, "Some people in PNG have renounced all of their kastam. Does anyone here want to do that?" Unfazed, my interlocutor said, "The hosts of this feast talked about what to do, and this issue came up. The dead man made bwabwale to different susu. People have to pay back the bwabwale he made while he was alive."[9] Years later, after I understood how Auhelawa see these events, I finally understood what he meant.

So what we see is that not only have there been empirical changes to the practice of mourning, some imposed by colonial government and some developed locally, but all mourning practice is now positioned in some way in a historical discourse of kastam and masele. This historical discourse is neither merely nostalgia nor the adoption of a modernist narrative of progress. This new temporal framing seems to come into mourning only because of another kind of innovation. The owners of the bwabwale also have the power to rule on what kind of ceremony they want to hold. As in the other cases in this chapter, the man who labeled bwabwale as kastam for me also seemed to mention that the owners had a debate about how much kastam should apply. Because owners now must make this rule, then it becomes possible to conceptualize masele and bwabwale as choices.

One could then argue that the owner susu occupies a space which offers them choice, agency, and thus a space for creative innovation of tradition. And yet the act of making a rule itself partakes of the logic of bwabwale and would itself not be possible without bwabwale as a framework for relationships between susu. The owners, as the susu of the deceased, exclude the other kin of the deceased from the decision. It is, in that sense, an extension of the boundaries that arise during asiyebwa. In death, the susu comes together in the form of a corporate group, as represented by their magai. Their ruling, as a decision they impose on outsiders, is a symbol of their oppositional relationship to this group as well. At the same time, in making this decision, the owners implicitly recognize that it must also be accepted, and so they announce it to people during the public events of mourning such as hilauwa and aemehelino. Thus their assertion of either tradition or its negation is itself premised on the complementary relationship among different susu. A susu cannot simply bury a dead member on its own.[10] Thus even when someone professes an intention to negate tradition with masele, in saying this, they presuppose the existence of a social universe organized in terms of the basic dualistic logic of kinship, and that this presupposition is shared by their audience. If anything has really changed in the Auhelawa history of mourning, it is that this temporal discourse provides another site at which people can establish a mutual recognition of their relationship as kin of different susu. What usually happens is that visitors in one way or another undermine this mutual recognition in favor of one based on the roles of giver and receiver.

Another could thus conclude that even though owner susu attempt to assert the right to choose between traditional rules and their Christian negation, in actuality they do not exist as an autonomous being that can exercise this agency, because their assertion of choice is predicated on their mutual interdependence of themselves, natuleiya, and other kin. In the above statement, the speaker seems to suggest that the dead man himself, by virtue of his biography of exchange, made the choice for them. Although some people may have wanted to choose how many and what kinds of exchanges they would take on, they were compelled by the cycle initiated by those that came before. One could argue that the social forms and relationships constituted through mourning, whether they take the form of self-consciously traditional or Christian patterns, are nonetheless fundamentally—some might say ontologically—distinct. Whatever variation on the forms of mourning that takes place, in this view, the order that people enact is irreducibly part of kinship sociality and its ethos, including principally the norm of reciprocity.

It does need to be said that simply because people declare their allegiance to Christianity over tradition this does not mean that they can ever escape the fact of their intrinsically social being. Christians may want to see themselves as individuals, and thus as autonomous agents, but from what we see in this chapter, there is always a limit to this. Thus Christianity and kastam not only alternate but also merge in real situations. I do not think it is helpful, though, to explain this by positing a fundamentally dividual person as the basic unit of all these social forms. Rather, it seems like death itself is a site where competing ideas about persons and relationships converge, and thus a useful venue for reconciling their contradictions.

All societies have to resolve in one way or another the problem of the corpse.[11] When someone dies, society has to have some kind of instituted pattern for disposing of the remains and, in so doing, making way for another to succeed to the positions occupied by the deceased. When someone dies, the intersection between that life and the lives of those left behind comes to a close. Rupert Stasch argues that Korowai (West Papua) parents think about their relationship to their children as consisting primarily of moments of "intertemporality," an intersection of otherwise discrete lives (2009, 141). It is, on the one hand, a prized moment of connection yet, on the other, by definition a necessarily finite coexistence. In their bond with their children, parents see their own mortality and eventual replacement by the next generation. Thus in any society, although in different ways, the problem of the corpse is the problem of how to recognize the end of intertemporality with the past. In Auhelawa, one way people recognize the end of intertemporality is to recall a father's dying wish, which is fulfilled after the father dies, and hence changes the children's relationship to the father's susu. Thus the father's life, having ended, stands as a metaphor for the past, in contrast to the lives of children, who stand for the present. Moreover, in this temporal lens preceding generations stand for actions that they do not and cannot choose. When Korowai explain their own pattern of life, they often say "predecessors did thusly" (Stasch 2009, 145). In the same way, for Auhelawa death elicits a frame in which sociality appears as rules, obligations, and now tradition or kastam.

This is not to say that mortuary complexes, as collective rituals, determine people's historical consciousness absolutely. As I argued in chapter 1, the existence of social groups based on unilineal descent does not inevitably lead to a social construct of time as static or episodic. Still, the process of resolving the problem of the corpse does facilitate particular kinds of temporal consciousness. Thus at the very same point where people have to mark the transition of a person from the status of living to dead, from kin to ancestor, they can also project onto that same boundary a historical sequence, "the old men of the past" as opposed to "we the new people." Masele and bwabwale as alternatives thus at some level are not opposed but mutually implicated. In bwabwale mourning, owners end the dou of visitors by whispering to them that they can stop thinking about kastam. Their mourning is over, and thus tradition is positioned on the horizon of the past. In the second case as well, we see that masele became a consensus only when people could anchor it in the past, and in the agency of a deceased person's spirit, rather than the agency of the living in the present. When people could imagine that masele was the choice of the deceased's spirit, then they could take it on as a rule for their mourning. In that moment when they prayed to the deceased, promising to give up their dispute over exchanges, they were both carrying forward the traditions of the past and marking a rupture with those traditions.

The events at Tupwagidu, in the end, seem to represent a new framework for reading ritual symbols and potentially a new type of social institution. It is an example of a process that Alan Rumsey calls "emergent typification" (2006, 64). Rumsey argues that many studies of change in contemporary indigenous societies tend to assume either that intercultural contact and influence inevitably lead to transformation or that all innovations are ultimately driven by and subsumed under a tendency toward continuity. In place of these, he argues that observers look for the sites where people step outside their own sociality and comment on what it is and what it stands for or counts toward. What I would add to this argument is often the emergence of social order is shadowed by its alternative. At some points alternative accounts of order are strongly dissonant and thus encourage people to abruptly shift back and forth between stable states, as when Auhelawa interrupt their performances of ve'ahihi in order to sit down together as one mind in tapwalolo, then switch back. When constituted through the signs of respectful avoidance and collective prayer, division and unity appear to be radically different. Yet these alternative accounts can find unexpected resonances with one another and seem to support one another. We see this when masele draws the logic of bwabwale into itself to constitute people as a unity. The dividual and individual are indeed different kinds of person imagined by two very different accounts of social life, yet that does not mean that can never be merged. In fact, in Auhelawa they exist in a constant dialogue.

Conclusion

Auhelawa people would often tell me that words I was learning in Auhelawa were in fact not the real language of Auhelawa and came from somewhere else: Dobu, Duau, Suau, Pidgin, or English. Once a person corrected me for saying *wasem*, instead of the original Auhelawa word for "wash" (*ladana*). A woman nearby turned and said, "Ama babadao nige hisese'ulu. Se'ulu imahalava na alinamai ibuibui. Ai vauavaumai alinamai amikimikis" (Our old people didn't go to school. School arrived and our language changed. We new people are mixing the language). And then, hearing her own use of an English loan word, *mikisi*, she slapped her hand over her mouth in mock horror, and we both laughed.

She wasn't wrong. Most people talk about language and many other aspects of everyday life in historical terms with this word: *mikisi*. Many times they also simply say "Hauga isesens" (The times are changing [sens]) or "Kastam i'o'ovi" (Tradition is ending). Auhelawa interpretations of linguistic change rest on an Auhelawa theory of history. It may not be one that is completely unquestioned, and to an extent it does not completely cohere with other knowledge that Auhelawa people produce of themselves. Such is the nature of practical knowledge. Nonetheless, contained in this woman's words, and in many Auhelawa attitudes, is a very firm understanding of how and why societies change, and based on this a very firm conviction that contemporary Auhelawa life is changing. In this book, I have shown where such ideas come from and why they gain currency and authority. They are not drawn from one single source as part of a new master narrative. Rather, we have seen that Auhelawa people draw on diverse elements and employ diverse media for realizing particular accounts of where they and their community sit in world history, and what this means for who they are. Auhelawa people must blend together these different frameworks and work through their contradictions.

For instance, yam houses allow people to see themselves as economic actors because it is in yam houses that women can reconcile two rival conceptions of the household as a social unit and their own dual role as mothers of dependent children and links in a matrilineal chain. The morality of the patient gardener who stores food in a yam house also becomes a way for women to extend their moral agency to include market trade. Yet in borrowing one image as a model of another, new social situation, people do not reduce that new situation to being an instance of an existing category. The metaphor of one's market trade as a yam house for money is tenuous, since market trade is often read by others as being more like gimwala, subsistence trade done out of need. In conducting their actual market trade, women also position themselves against the specter of amoral haggling they see in gimwala.

Similarly, the image of a cooperative group united in purpose allows people to reconcile competing ideas of Christianity as an individual commitment, on the one hand, and as a social identity, on the other. Yet this kind of translation of Christianity throws up new contradictions, requiring people to recruit money as a medium for another kind of metaphor of the same collective self. It is perhaps only when earnings from market trade are donated that money most convincingly appears to be a new kind of harvest, and yet in this context it is only money's function as a unit of account, not as wealth in its own right. Through the numerical sum of money donations, a Christian congregation can finally condense all the social work that goes into voluntary cooperation and turn it into what they believe it should create, one mind.

It is clear that Christianity in particular is something that Auhelawa struggle to account for in their historical stories about themselves. Christianity represents a new historical era. Embracing its singular alterity could potentially rewrite every single story of that Auhelawa tell in terms of an epochal shift from darkness to light. Certainly Methodist missionaries explained their own work in these terms, and they hoped that it would ultimately become true. Yet even if everyone in Auhelawa today says they are a Christian, the idea of Christianity as a new era still poses problems. Because Christianity is a moral system that foregrounds an individual's uniquely private experience of salvation, it gives people no discourse with which they can imagine social relations. The social and individual dimensions of religion remain distinct in every Auhelawa Christian practice.

This is especially true in rituals of death. After generations of colonial rule and mission teaching, Auhelawa regard the central social institution of mortuary feasting ambivalently. Many see the changes to precolonial practices as accommodations with Christianity. Yet they know that exchanges and prohibitions in mortuary feasts still provide salient markers of social identities and relations, and that adherence to the customary protocols of mourning will be read by others as effective performative signs of their relationships to other lineages. Even so, there are some who wish for a new model based on the idea of a Christian congregation to replace kastam (traditional) mourning. Yet these Christian reformers cannot find any way to talk about what a Christian way of mourning would be, or what it would represent, other than as the negation of kastam mourning. It is thus far more common for every collective act of mourning to be described as a mix (*mikisi*) of both tradition and Christianity. Yet on closer inspection, we have seen that this masks a tenuous compromise. These supposedly collective performances of collective order in fact have no single, clear, uncontested script.

Now, in conclusion, I would like to ask what it means for Auhelawa people to frame their contemporary everyday life as a state of historical mikisi. After a century of being incorporated in a global order of nation-states, and after a century of contact with markets and Christianity, the future is still only arriving, the times are changing, and yet no new era has really begun. Furthermore, Auhelawa people question the possibility that they as a community share a set of norms, even with respect to the most important institutional mechanisms of social integration like mortuary ritual. By contrast, the PNG state has historically imagined that traditional local cultures can coexist with a modern, liberal, and multicultural nation. In PNG, everyone is imagined to be from a particular traditional community yet simultaneously part of a modern, developing nation-state. If Auhelawa people believe that their society is neither traditional nor modern, where do they position themselves as political actors in this postcolonial state?

To begin, it helps to look more broadly at the different ways in which postcolonial states have attempted to instill a new consciousness in their citizens. Like all liberal societies, postcolonial nations have trouble reconciling a political order based on individual rights and the fact that members also belong to a variety of particular communities. Citizenship remains a contested concept, especially in a diverse society like PNG, as I show with reference to a recent controversy over its symbols of national identity. This leads me to consider the alternative visions of postcultural belonging that have emerged recently in PNG as a response to the contradictions in its liberal order, and then finally to Auhelawa's own postculturalism as another variant of this recent turn.

Multicultural Citizenship in Postcolonial States

Liberal democratic publics require a particular kind of history. Jürgen Habermas notes that liberal modernity "has to create its normativity out of itself" (2015 [1991], 22). To become modern, a society must reject the past as a source of social order. It must instead define its political community in terms of its own rational norms, and generally see itself as continually perfecting its own order, rather than adhering to an inherited tradition. To do so, it needs to create the sense of a history in which the individual subject is progressively freed from external constraint in favor of voluntary belonging. Differences among members, however, reveal the limits of liberal modernity, especially when these differences are cultural: that is, they derive from one's participation in a distinct institutional system apart from the state and not shared by the majority. As Francesca Merlan (1998) notes, Australian liberal multiculturalism renders cultural differences as legacies that one inherits yet that do not determine all of one's participation in the polity. One can be an Aboriginal citizen of

Australia, but only if one sees oneself as coming from a specific Aboriginal place and community that is defined by a continuity with its past yet is now subsumed within an otherwise rational, liberal order. There is no possibility for an distinctly Aboriginal way of being an Australian citizen, since the only form of Aboriginality that the state recognizes is the personal identity of an individual who is otherwise the same as all other citizens in her adherence to the norms of liberal democracy. In demanding that Aboriginal peoples produce an "innerness out of [their] past," the Australian state erases the particular cultural values and biases that define membership in its political community (Merlan 1998, 233; see also Gershon 2012). It denies that Aboriginality is and can be a lived social practice in the present. If Habermas's concept of modernity is a sui generis normativity, then a modern state is thus both unable to recognize differences among citizens and generally hostile to social connections that are not part of the rational order of politics (Povinelli 2006).

One sees another version of this contradiction in former colonies of the West. As Will Kymlicka (1996) notes, throughout the nineteenth century Western liberal thinkers debated the problem of the rights of minorities within colonial empires. Yet with the decolonization of Western empires after the Second World War, the question of granting special recognition to indigenous or minority communities within a imperial polity virtually disappeared. The autonomy or independence of former colonies was assumed to solve the problem of the minority status of colonized peoples. New nations would no longer be minorities. They would create their own liberal states, which would protect the individual rights of each citizen. In that sense, postcolonial nations faced a special version of the problem of modernity. They had to inherit the political traditions of their former colonizers, yet it was also assumed that they would generate their own normativity as modern societies as well.

For instance, leaders of African independence movements often appealed to the ideas of the African renaissance in literature as a source for distinctively African values that could guide their new nations. Yet these values were not meant to signal a return to or revitalization of tradition. Kwame Nkrumah (1965) in Ghana and Julius Nyerere (1968) in Tanzania, for instance, sought to articulate an African political philosophy in support of their efforts to transform their societies. This transformation would furthermore lead to total political and economic independence from the West. More important, in embracing a generic national culture as the basis for citizenship, new African states more or less avoided the problem of minority rights altogether. Drawing legitimacy from traditional African values did not mean granting autonomy to ethnic or indigenous communities within the new national polity. Independent African nations would seek modernity by generating a very selective form of innerness as the basis for their own sui generis normativity. This innerness would draw on an image of a pan-African culture as depicted in the writings of educated African thinkers. Thus, through a generic cultural citizenship, African leaders would create liberal modernity in which individual citizens could transcend their roots in the past and become genuinely modern subjects, as opposed to mere minorities within a Western empire.

By contrast, when it attained independence in 1975, PNG did not really have the option to create the same kind of cultural citizenship.[1] Even more than African states, PNG is overwhelmingly diverse, and the vast majority of people live in rural communities governed by their own particular social institutions. Like Nkrumah and Nyerere, leaders invoked supposedly pan-Melanesian concepts of justice and cultural styles of art as national symbols (see Foster 2002, 46). For instance, in a series of essays for the PNG *Post-Courier*, Bernard Narokobi (1980) argued for a Melanesian Way that could guide PNG's state. Yet the image of a Melanesian cultural citizen would always be complicated by the fact that there was no one single cultural identity of which all could claim to be a part as citizens, even in the most general and abstract sense. Citizenship in PNG has thus always had to be both liberal and multicultural. While in some ways, Narokobi's idea of broadly shared Melanesian cultural values resembles pan-Africanist thinkers, he also argues that all people of PNG are united in the empirical fact that they each belong to a specific rural place. For Narokobi, customary institutions and rules in each local community were a separate, parallel domain that complemented the Western legal system inherited from the colonial period (Demian 2015). The customary rules of each community may all coincide on a more general level but need not have any substantial connection with any other community in PNG. The content of customary rules in a particular community could be different from other customary rules elsewhere; what was important was that the domain of custom was functionally equivalent to law, and that through their participation in the same kind of system, all PNG citizens could understand and support the rule of law in an independent state. A citizen of PNG is not conceptualized as one who belongs to a pan-Melanesian community and thus shares some bond with all other citizens. Rather, a PNG citizen is one who comes from the same type of community as all the other communities which make up PNG.

For Narokobi, therefore, PNG becomes a liberal and multicultural society through ethnographic citizenship rather than cultural citizenship. To be a citizen of PNG is not to claim a particular identity, but to see oneself as a certain kind of social subject. One's citizenship does not derive from the inheritance of any one specific tradition, imagined or otherwise. Rather, a person becomes a citizen of PNG because she, like others, already belongs to a culture in a village governed by its own traditions. Indeed, and unlike Nkrumah and others, Narokobi's Melanesian Way is relatively free of ideology and presents the independent PNG nation as one in which people of all walks of life participate in political decision making in the same spirit as a village moot. In an earlier essay, he argues that "cooperation, consensus, democracy blossom in small-scale communities. Participation and involvement are most effective in a small community" (Narokobi 1975, 24; quoted in Golub 2014, 167). For Alex Golub, as much as his philosophy celebrates village societies, Narokobi has no nostalgia for a traditional past. Rather he looks to find analogies between indigenous social institutions and Western political theories in order to imagine an "authentically Melanesian form of modernity" (Golub 2014, 167). Golub finds in Narokobi's analysis and creative reinterpretation of the diversity of indigenous Melanesian social forms an example of the same kind of sui generis normativity that Habermas attributes to modernity.

Yet if PNG sheds its dependence on Western institutions by generating its own authentically Melanesian political theory, this theory itself rests on a functionalist theory of village societies as a type of normative order (Golub 2014, 177). To generate its own normativity, PNG had to generate an innerness out of an ethnographic imagination. In a country where most of its people live in rural societies, PNG citizens stand in the public sphere not because they all share common values, but they all are "landowners" of specific places. These rights to their ancestral lands, limited though they may be, give each person an equal stake in the future of the country. Yet to see themselves as citizens of independent PNG in these terms, people must adopt an external, scientific gaze in which their own interests and values are functional components of a social system. While the state nominally recognizes ownership by custom, in practice customary ownership of land is treated specifically as an inalienable right of kin groups which have historically occupied it (Jorgensen 2007, 60; Golub 2014, 176). In the epistemic frame of social science, individuals become customary landowners by virtue of their membership in a particular kind of social order based on some form of kinship system as a structure of groups. Ethnographic citizenship is able to solve the problem of membership in a multicultural liberal society because it recognizes only differences that can be treated as what anthropologists might call cultures. Anthropologists have always debated what they mean by culture, and so this point is something of a disservice to actual anthropologists. Nonetheless, as an ethnographic state, PNG does arguably cede epistemic authority over the nature of difference to a social-scientific paradigm.[2]

The Limits of Postcolonial Liberal Citizenship

Because they recognize only individual subjects, liberal societies deny what Polanyi called the reality of society: that is, people's material dependence on social ties (1947, 115). As such, they always run the risk of eliciting opposition from those that are left behind in their attempt to build a society based on voluntary individual membership. The same is true for cultural citizenship as a liberal project. For instance, in postcolonial Ghana, cultural citizenship has never fully subordinated difference to a liberal order. Nkrumah was deeply suspicious of chiefly societies like the Asante of Ghana, seeing them as a source of opposition to his plans for reform (Kallinen 2016, 111–12). More generally, if a distinctive source of shared values is the basis for political independence of a new nation, then arguably any community can claim that its own distinctive traditional institutions are a warrant for their autonomy from the state. Many postcolonial African states have also had to compete with the associations of regional elites who campaign for control over their own affairs on the basis of their difference from the rest of the nation (Eyoh 1998; Nyamnjoh and Rowlands 1998; Geschiere 2009). When political membership is based on cultural citizenship, minorities can protect themselves only through iterative independence movements.

Ethnographic citizenship, as seen in PNG, grapples with the same contradictions of liberalism. In this case, it is a separatism of the mind, rather than of territory. Since the nature of citizenship itself depends on an ethnographic gaze, political actors seek to claim this epistemic authority for themselves and thus gain the power to determine who can participate in politics. One example can be seen in a recent series of events surrounding the decorations of the national parliament building. The Haus Parliament (Parliament House) in PNG has long been a national icon. It was designed to resemble the sloped roof of a Sepik River region men's cult house, and other buildings and design elements gestured toward other architectural styles of the country (Rosi 1991). In late 2013, Theo Zurenuoc, the relatively new Speaker of Parliament, ordered the removal of an ornately carved lintel over the entrance and a group of carved poles in the foyer (Evara 2013). These two pieces had been commissioned from students of the National Arts School at the time of the building's construction, and were each neotraditional representations of national unity. The lintel consisted of nineteen faces, each carved in a distinct style to represent one of the nineteen provinces of the country. The carved poles synthesized many carving styles and were collectively titled *Bung Wantaim* (Unity).[3] Thus the two pieces embodied the nation's ethnographic citizenship. The country is represented as a juxtaposition and fusion of diverse cultural forms. While the parliament building had often been called the Haus Tambaran (Spirit House) due to its reference to the Sepik region, the parliament hall was flanked by two other buildings styled after meeting houses in other regions, and so together the parliamentary complex also juxtaposed several different cultures. Zurenuoc argued that these symbolic expressions of national unity were flawed, if not dangerous in themselves. He said that the faces were not actually Melanesian in origin, and he believed them to be demonic. After months of controversy over his abrupt destruction of the lintel, Zurenuoc (2014) published a proposal for new decorations. In place of *Bung Wantaim*, he proposed a Unity Pole, a single tall pillar inscribed with the word for unity in each of the country's eight hundred languages, sitting atop a sculpture of the Bible. In place of ethnographic citizenship, Zurenuoc called for Christianity to become the basis for political membership. The former (and first) prime minister, joined by Andrew Moutu, the director of the National Museum and Art Gallery, sued Zurenuoc to prevent further destruction, and eventually the case was heard by the National Court. The court decided that Zurenuoc had a religious motivation for his actions, which violated PNG citizens' basic right to freedom of conscience. Justice David Cannings (2016), the author of the majority opinion, also noted that while Christianity is widely practiced in PNG, it is not universal, and so the state must be impartial with respect to religion, because citizens may choose to practice traditional religion rather than Christianity. In the end, Christian citizenship was rejected as being illiberal, and ethnographic citizenship appeared in a new form, as a quintessentially liberal right to one's culture as a system of belief.

International observers have tended to link Zurenuoc's actions to the politicization of religion throughout the Pacific region (e.g. Eves et al. 2014). Some emphasize Zurenuoc's early statements that the carvings were demonic, and that Parliament was afflicted by demons, saying that his actions reflected increased influence of Pentecostal churches in PNG. Indeed this was not the first time that PNG politicians had pushed for a declaration of PNG as a Christian nation. The previous government had in fact created a national covenant with God and declared a new public holiday called National Repentance Day (Fox 2011). Zurenuoc's supporters also campaigned for local communities to destroy "idols" (that is, their own traditional carvings) in public burnings on the 2015 Repentance Day (National Community Transformation Network ca. 2015). There is undoubtedly an ideological basis for Zurenuoc's opposition to ethnographic citizenship. In his vision, a PNG citizen is not simply a Christian, but also a bourgeois individual who is unfettered by the constraints of tradition. Rather than living a society of customary landowners, PNG citizens live on a "green island of gold, floating on a sea of oil," that is, a country possessed of valuable natural resources as the state's sovereign wealth (Zurenuoc 2015).[4] Citizens enjoy this wealth not as landowners but as beneficiaries of the development it will bring thanks to foreign investment.

While the whole affair and public response does offer evidence for both the politicization of Christianity and possibly an ideological shift, I would like to offer another reading. Zurenuoc's actions are symptomatic of a loss of faith in ethnographic citizenship as a basis for liberal modernity. Since taking office, Zurenuoc had sought to present himself as a new generation of political leader who would replace the Melanesian Way with a shared commitment to universal values of rationality.[5] While *Bung Wantaim* is the product of a collaboration by several carvers trained in distinct regional traditions and synthesizes many different carving styles in one work, the proposed new Unity Pole juxtaposes different vernacular words for the same idea. In that sense, each work embodies very different conceptions of the unity of the PNG nation state. *Bung Wantaim* depicts unity as creative creolization. The Unity Pole uses language as a new metaphor for cultural difference, and in particular, presumes that different languages nonetheless share a universal set of semantic categories, making them perfectly intertranslatable.

Contestations of the state's epistemic authority over difference have also taken a turn that is both darker and harder to analyze in terms of a bourgeois ideology. In recent years, there has been a rise in reports of people who have been murdered after they have been accused of practicing sorcery. With the increasing availability of mobile phones and Internet access in rural PNG, these stories circulate much more rapidly, now also often accompanied by photographs and videos of accused persons being tortured and killed by their accusers. In February 2013, Kepari Leniata, a woman of Mount Hagen, Western Highlands Province, was accused of sorcery after a child died in a local hospital. She was killed in a gruesome public execution, which was filmed and circulated on Facebook. Human rights organizations in and outside the country mobilized to pressure the government to protect accused people from violence. Sorcery-related killings (SRK) became a new watchword in public discourse. By 2014, after a number of highly publicized sorcery murders, Parliament amended the Sorcery Act, a 1971 law which some had interpreted as giving credence to sorcery accusation, since it prohibited sorcery and made it punishable by law. For many observers in PNG, the problem was in fact cultural. They lay the blame equally at the feet of accusers and their community. For instance, after the murder of Leniata, the *Post-Courier*'s editorial board wrote:

> When we hear stories of Papua New Guineans being accused of sorcery and burnt alive in a somewhat public spectacle, we recoil with fear and disgust and ask whether we should indeed be proud of ourselves as a nation of individuals who respect our fellow human beings and believe that justice is

dispensed in a legally constituted court of law and not a kangaroo court chaired by individuals misled by superstition and trickery....

The photographing of yesterday's brutal act by the crowd (including school children), without making moves to stop and condemn the murderers' actions, points to a bigger danger of ordinary Papua New Guineans accepting this callous killing as normal and this methodology of dispensing justice as acceptable. (PNG *Post-Courier* 2013)

According to this view, the problem was not the accusation, or the violence it sparked, but the fact that the community failed to stop it while it was happening. Although the editorialist avoids explicitly stating that the onlookers did not act because they believed in the same "superstitions," it still makes clear that it is their cultural otherness, their sense of what is normal, that is the problem. From the perspective of the national press, PNG's liberal order was threatened by an excess of cultural difference. Some kinds of difference—belief in sorcery, for instance—violate the rights to safety of individuals. If a culture of PNG holds that sorcery is real, then it cannot be part of a multicultural public. More important, this view rests on the epistemic authority of a new kind of expertise. This expert knowledge borrows from anthropological theories of culture but treats individual behavior as a presenting symptom of a disease at the social level. Culture is defined as a set of propositions—beliefs—that individual members acquire from their social environment. Individuals, as vectors of culture so to speak, do not see their own knowledge about the world for what it is. Only an outside observer can do so, and this outsider can assess whether these kinds of difference can come into the public sphere. The editorial goes on to cite reports by Amnesty International and Human Rights Watch on SRKs that linked the issue to endemic levels of violence against women in the whole country, and which they had described as a feature of all cultures in PNG. In the same spirit, the editorialist of the *Post-Courier* suggests that SRKs had become a threat to the rule of law.

This however is not the only epistemic lens that people apply to SRKs. Dan Jorgensen (2014) identifies a set of distinct features of the construct of sorcery that recur in many recent accusations, including the one leading to Leniata's killing. First, accusers and their communities often state that the sorcery itself is imported, from Simbu Province or from Australia, and is more potent than local forms. Second, they assume that this new sorcery can be only be divined and then banished by similarly new, imported techniques. The new sorcery can only be seen by a new kind of a specialist in sorcery, called a *glasman* (PNG Pidgin: diviner), who can see the invisible signs of affliction. This, besides being a kind of terror, is a way of positioning oneself and the accused outside traditional categories. Jorgensen notes that the perpetrators of violence are often marginal young men without a social identity. I would add that by using drugs and shirking normal social roles, such men also perform an antitraditional self. Finally, Jorgensen argues that the sadistic torture of accused is a new and borrowed form as well. Indeed, in a community neighboring Jorgensen's research site, people also claimed that new, foreign sorcery was now the cause of new sicknesses, and they responded in that case with a concerted campaign of violence modeled on a military operation (Wesch 2007). In many recent cases of supernatural panic and accusation, the accusers say that the magic they attack is not related to traditional magic of the past. It comes from another place and spreads from place to place. Jorgensen emphasizes that recent killings are more often in response to this generic national sorcery complex. I would argue that as a delocalized and untraditional phenomenon, it also escapes from kastam as a trope of belonging. By responding to this magic in new ways, the accusers also reject a spatiotemporal framing of difference as empirical and social. They do not see themselves as subjects of culture as it is defined by ethnographic citizenship. SRKs are, then, not an excess of difference but a praxis that exceeds the state's categories of difference. In the end, however, SRKs are an attempt to use violence as a means to claim the right to define who is a member of a political community and worthy of protection.

There is another kind of response from the grassroots in which the question of recognition is deliberately left open. One example of this comes from the wider public debate over Zurenuoc's decision to remove carvings from Parliament Haus. At the time, many editorials and opinion essays condemned the removal of the carvings. In letters to the editor of the PNG *Post-Courier*, however, readers took a variety of stands. Some accepted, or at least were willing to entertain, the possibility that the carvings were demonic. Others agreed that Christian symbols would be more appropriate for a national institution than neotraditional decorations (and for many years public opinion has questioned the overtly Sepik origin of the building's profile since the first prime minister was a Sepik man).

Among these varying opinions, one compromise solution was proposed by two correspondents: the decorations that had been removed should not be destroyed but deposited in the National Museum and Art Gallery. As the authors explained, these decorations may not be appropriate for the national Parliament, but traditional styles of carving are still an important part of PNG's history as a nation and so should be preserved.

This compromise solution is, on reflection, more nuanced than it may appear. The decorations of Parliament are not in fact examples of any one specific carving style and thus are not artifacts of a particular culture or region in a narrow sense. Indeed, they were meant to be a deliberate fusion of styles, like many other parts of the building. They were the work of a team of art students at a national institution: that is, new artists in a new environment who drew on tradition but were not themselves beholden to it. More to the point, the carvings were not meant to serve any function other than decoration. If they were linked to traditional cultures it was only as ethnographic works in their own right. That is, they were mimetic of traditional forms but also added meaning to these by bringing them into a new context. In the intervening years, Parliament Haus had also taken on a new meaning. Rather than being read as a symbol of popular sovereignty as intended, for good or ill, most PNG people now saw it as a symbol of state power. If Zurenuoc promised, as so many leaders had, to renew this institution, then the former decorations are apt historical artifacts of a previous generation's leadership of the country.

Throughout their history, museums have often been called on not only to provide stories of the national unity of a people (e.g., Adedze 1995; Schildkrout 1995) but also to inculcate patrons in the "rituals of citizenship," especially by making it possible to imagine one's identity as an innerness: that is, as an attribute of an individual self in a rational order (Duncan 1995). In more recent years, and in plural societies, museums may expand to tell another story of a society's diversity, but this story also maps diversity to discrete, identifiable groups who each possess innerness from their past (Pieterse 1997). The PNG national museum could be read then as buttressing the ethnographic citizenship of the early PNG state. Those supporting Christian citizenship for PNG are also well served by a cultural museum as a repository for the past, because they as Christians can define themselves in opposition to it. This is entirely consistent with the political ritual of cultural museums in the West: museumgoers are never on display. Rather as an audience, they are the conclusion of the story exhibits tell, because their political membership is based on possessing the knowledge of history but not being beholden to it as an enduring reality.

Yet museums are also public institutions in a very specific sense. For Bonnie Honig, "democracy is rooted in common love for and contestation of public things" such as public schools, health services, and museums (2013, 60). These are all real places and resources in whose "thingness" people with common interests in the value they provide can create enduring relationships of belonging in spite of their differences (Honig 2013, 61). As public things, many people can bring different agendas to bear on ethnographic museums, and that seems to be what one sees in the proposal to deposit parliamentary decorations.[6] The letter writers say, "Our contemporary political history is also a source of our identity. Here is one group's attempt at representing us as a nation." I would argue that those who advocated for the museum solution were also arguing for suspending the question of epistemic authority over citizenship, rather than allowing one faction to decide finally whether ethnographic citizenship or Christian citizenship would be the only possible answer. The museum solution is, more precisely, a desire to make use of another public institution as the basis for belonging, but through the participation of many people who don't agree, rather than only those whom others deem eligible.

When citizens write letters proposing to move demonic carvings from the halls of government to a national museum, they do not want to force everyone to agree that PNG consists of many different traditions of material culture or to require everyone to deny the possibility that PNG's cultures may each make contact with different kinds of occult forces. Rather, they suggest instead that people of PNG can bring different interpretations to the same symbols of national unity in another kind of public institution. PNG is, in this framework, a land of many cultures, but what difference this makes is to be determined and is a question that many can participate in deciding. Ethnographic museums sit at the crossroads of many different paradigms of difference within anthropology and other human sciences, not to mention being meeting places of scientists and the public. Given this, they are similar to Auhelawa yam houses in that they serve as boundary objects that can coordinate divergent maps of difference. As public institutions, ideally they also grant access to epistemic authority to many and can potentially create dialogues across different perspectives on difference as well.

Making public institutions into public things, and hence spaces of dialogue, is particularly relevant for postcolonial societies like PNG. As I discussed at the outset of this book, contemporary PNG is characterized by not simply an ontological multiplicity but pervading ontological insecurity. Rather than being incorporated fully into the conquering culture as was promised, modernity is permanently on hold. People of Auhelawa and other societies of PNG face the possibility of the end of the world, not in the sense of history's final destination but rather the loss of any one single authoritative source of meaning. How can they respond? Jonathan Lear (2008) finds one possibility in the dreams of Crow prophet Plenty-Coups. At the end of the Indian Wars, Plenty-Coups prophesied the collapse of the Crow way of life. His prophecies, Lear argues, are an attempt to render meaningful the possibility of meaninglessness. Plenty-Coups dreams of a chickadee who is a "good listener" (Lear 2008, 70). For Lear, the chickadee is an ethical model for life for Crow in a world where one's culture can no longer serve as an absolute normative guide (or, in terms more acceptable to Harold Garfinkel, where one cannot reliably read in others' actions their natural accountability nor be assured that others will account for one's own actions in terms of the processes of which they form a part). The chickadee is a subject that does not seek to translate foreign forms into familiar terms but rather is committed to a "radical openness" to otherness (McDougall 2016, 21). If museums become truly public things, then they can also serve as places where people can practice this kind of openness.[7] A history in which the present is a time when things become mikisi (mixed) is similarly a way to realize a space in which people can grapple productively with ontological insecurity.

In the book I show that this history is one among many, and that Christian narratives, colonial narratives, and folk models of historical change all play a part in sustaining each other, even in spite of their contradictions. This I call postculturalism, by which I mean not so much the death of a culture or a transition to an acultural state, but rather a position from which the credibility of symbolic codes—e.g., graves stand for descent groups, descent groups stand for a traditional order, or prayer stands for Christianity and in turn modernity—is questioned. Sustaining particular narratives of change hinges on the knowledge people produce about themselves. While political elites seek to advance a vision of the nation in terms of either ethnographic citizenship and Christian citizenship, Auhelawa represent a postcultural belonging to community grounded in their own partial, practical models of social process and their own ways of deploying these as a basis for making certain kinds of relationships visible. Thus commitment to the possibility of future transformation, even after years of failed promises of the same, is a postcultural position from which Auhelawa can remain skeptical of the present.

Notes

Introduction

1. Uttering the names of the deceased and of affines is generally prohibited, but this seems not to be the reason why no names were recalled. I often suggested skipping questions that were taboo, but many just brushed it off: "Ah, that's just *kastam* (traditional rules)! It's for your study, right?" If I asked people to tell me who the first daughter of the founder had married and where was his village, people would giggle and whisper it or just ask someone sitting nearby to utter it for them.

2. The turn to political economy as a frame for ethnographic analysis hinges on, as Sahlins says, one of two ways of reading Marxist social theory and has been complemented in anthropology by another paradigm in which the social order is an integrated, structured whole that mediates material and practical conditions (1976, chap. 1; see also Friedman 1998 [1979]; Bashkow 2004; Otto and Bubandt 2011).

3. Likewise, Joel Robbins (2007) argues that anthropology generally remains committed to an epistemology of continuity, presuming that social patterns are fundamentally linked to processes of reproduction, and deviations and innovations are always treated as a noisy signal. According to Robbins, rarely do ethnographers entertain the possibility that people organize their own lives around rupture, or as a project of rejecting one form over another. That is to say, because they seek to recover continuity above all, ethnographers ignore the times and places when a culture invests meaning in exogenous forces, and ensure that they have consequences (see also Hirsch 2001; Knauft 2008; Tomlinson 2009; Ballard 2014). Robbins concludes that this makes most ethnographies blind to forms of life in which change itself is a

value, the most important for him being charismatic Christianity. When born-again Christians take hold of Christianity's own value of decisive change, for good or ill, their encounter with other kinds of forces then comes to signify change.

4. Melissa Demian (2006) makes a similar argument and has influenced my thinking on this issue.

5. For a related analysis of line formation as a logical calculation of precedence, see Hutchins 2005, 1560.

6. For a few scholars, this description of an indigenous model and its application is also a characteristic of a particular type of social system, associated with a particular cultural construction of the person as a microcosm of the whole—a dividual person or partible person rather than an individual (e.g., Mosko 2000).

7. To critics of this approach like David Graeber (2015), this may be an overly generous reading. Graeber criticizes Viveiros de Castro and others for invoking the term "ontology" to denote, on the one hand, different kinds of entities and, on the other, different systems of classifications based on different premises about reality. While recognizing his point that these two aspects are often confused by scholars making these arguments, I want to discuss the strengths and weaknesses of coherent versions, rather than give undue weight to flawed ones. It seems more consistent with the insights of Wagner and Strathern to hold that alternative ontologies, whether explicit or implicit, reveal the blind spots in Western social theory, which potentially obscure alternative forms of being (that is, ontic alterity), and that alternative ontologies and the models of society derived from them might be a basis for exegesis that would lead to new social theories.

8. In some ways, thinkers in this school already see this point and thus do not call for comparison of cultures but, to quote Marilyn Strathern (2005), seek to forge "partial connections." Rather than arbitrarily isolating one specific indigenous model of reality and setting it against a Western model, they wish to draw on ethnographic moments taken from great distances to reveal unseen dimensions within everyone's world. For arguments along these lines, see Henare, Holbraad, and Wastell 2007, Alberti et al. 2011, Candea 2012, Holbraad 2012, and Lebner 2016.

9. While I take the term "ontological insecurity" from R. D. Laing (1965, 39) and Giddens (1991, 36), unlike them, I do not assume that it is a necessary feature of the actors' experience of their social environment or any one type of social environment. Nor do I, like them, believe that the only response to ontological insecurity is to work to establish or reestablish ontological security. I wish to highlight here a specific aspect of cultural domination. One could also argue that many different kinds of historical conditions besides colonialism also produce ontological insecurity. What seems crucial to this condition is not so much the foreignness of a dominant culture or its superior power over the subordinate culture but conditions in which the power of the dominant culture fails to establish a firm stratification of identities, and both sides in a relation of domination are forced to confront the fact that they are in conflict. It is the crisis induced by domination, rather than the relation of domination itself, that I want to highlight.

10. Also, in her study of Egyptian Muslim women's participation in the Islamic revival, Saba Mahmood (2005) breaks with Bourdieu's habitus to argue that her informants made use of disciplines of daily prayer and observing Islamic codes of behavior to create an alternative basis for public politics, one not grounded in the Western liberal conception of secular modernity. Each of these ritual and discursive forms contains within itself the same kind of shifting social analyses that Gershon talks about.

Chapter 1. Natives and Travelers

1. Local-level government (LLG) areas are divisions within a province, comparable to council areas in Australia or counties in the United States. An LLG council consists of elected representatives of wards. In rural areas, wards correspond more or less with districts first set

down in the colonial period by patrolling police officers. Hence the people who speak Auhelawa live in one of two wards, Kurada and Bwasiyaiyai. LLG councils have some power to regulate local businesses—for instance, issuing licenses to trade fuel or alcohol—but for the most part serve as administrative units within provinces. The seat of Duau LLG was on the opposite side of the island of Normanby and so always seemed rather remote to people of Auhelawa, who could much more easily access government services in the provincial capital town of Alotau.

2. It is worth noting that the words *nuwatuwu'avivini* and *nuwapwanopwano* both have some connection to the word for "mind" (*nuwa*). The verb meaning *to remember* can be decomposed into *nuwatuwu* (thought, idea) and *avivini* (grasp with one's hand, restrain). *Nuwatuwu* itself can also be further decomposed into *nuwa* and *tuwu* (root, stem, trunk). Likewise, combining *nuwa* and *pwanopwano* (lose) produces a verb meaning *to forget*. The nuwa is conceptualized as being in one's chest and is the seat of one's individual thoughts. (The heart organ of humans and animals is called the *nuwa'epo*.) People often gesture to the midchest when speaking personally, for instance, when stating their opinion in a meeting. It contrasts with *ate*, the liver, which similarly is used in combination with other words to form many emotion words. It is tempting to treat words like *nuwa* and *ate* as primarily terms for organs and infer that speakers of the Auhelawa language actually see these organs as the physical locations of different mental states (Mallett 2003, 124). They may or may not. For instance, *nuwa* is also distinct from the rarely used word for the brain, *uto*, and yet one of the cruelest insults in Auhelawa is to say "you don't have a brain" (*nige utom*) (see also Kuehling 2005, 44). While Auhelawa use body parts as idioms for some mental states and use inalienable possessive pronouns as they do for body parts generally, they speak of other sensations as being alienable possessions. Given this, it seems more important to observe that, whether or not body parts are used to express mental states idiomatically, Auhelawa talk about and understand many if not all of their subjective states as inner, private, and intrinsic to the person as an individual. In that respect, Auhelawa ethnopsychology does seem to contain some form of mind-body dualism even though it is expressed in different terms. (And so it seems reasonable to translate *nuwa* as mind in the sense of the seat of reason.) Matrilineal descent is a fact, but an individual as a thinking subject may not be aware of this fact. Hence one's identity hinges on both one's kinship and one's knowledge and memory of this kinship.

3. The word *duluva* literally means *cave* and is commonly used as a synecdoche for a susu's shrine, since this is the most common location for a shrine.

4. It was Francis who told me this story (many times). He took it as a point of pride that his marriage to Lucy conformed to both traditional rules of exogamy and to Catholic doctrine, and he saw the Catholics' teaching on matrimony as affirming the importance of both traditional customary rules as well as the rules of the church.

5. The plural form of *natuleiya* is *natunatuleiya*, as *tubutubuni* is the plural of *tubuni* (the child of a *natuleiya*). For ease of reading in English, I have used the singular form for both singular and plural throughout.

6. This derived sense of connection based on having a congruent relationship to a third person or thing comes up often in many forms of relationship (see also Kelly 1977; Schieffelin 2005 [1976]). This is also the same kind of logic which underlies the pan-Melanesian concept of *wantok*, or a friendship based on one's shared origin, usually from the same language group or province (Schram 2015). Considering that such perceptions of similarity are necessarily relative to something else that is not the same, we can also say that this is basically a logic of segmentary structures (Evans-Pritchard 1940; Merlan and Rumsey 1991). Unlike the nested levels of membership in Nuer patrilineages, however, Auhelawa segmentary identities can derive from many different possible bases.

7. Roy Wagner makes a similar argument about the nature of symbolic meaning itself, saying that symbols are not decoded in the sense of simply substituting a referent. Rather, the

meaning of a symbol is "a perception within what could call the 'value space' set up by symbolic points of reference" (Wagner 1986, 18). He compares this to how visual signals from each eye must be synthesized in the mind to form a single image. It is from this argument that I take my own understanding of how people come to perceive magai as a sign of unity of a susu, and of the co-totemic association of two bu'una individuals. In each case, the magai, as a symbol, does not stand for this unity like a code, but to use Wagner's terms, it elicits a reading in which it is such a sign. The magai has a specific connection to each individual as the burial site of a relative, and as a common reference point it also facilitates the perception of congruence among all these specific ties to the site, which in turn can be apprehended stereoscopically as an abstract group (a susu) or abstract category of totemic relatives (bu'una).

Chapter 2. You Cannot Eat Your Own Blood

1. The connection between prohibition and the imperative to give will be familiar to readers of Claude Lévi-Strauss's *Elementary Structures of Kinship* (1969). As he argues, the prohibition on incest also entails a prescription to marry out of one's group, or as he says, for a man to offer his sister in exchange for a wife. Not only would the same mechanism be seen were genders reversed, but the same principle also explains why abstaining from what is given leads the recipient to reciprocate (see also Rubel and Rosman 1978).

2. This form of adoption is called *awatoutougu*. It amounts to labeling a person as a member of a susu rather than taking him in as a coresident, as is often described as the basis for a bu'una relationship among two susu in a tetela, or adopting a child and caring for it as one's own. These forms of adoption are both called *amwewe*.

Chapter 3. Hunger and Plenty

1. This comment was spontaneously transcribed. I later translated this statement in my fieldnotes for that day, June 8, 2006.

2. Quotations were spontaneously transcribed, and then synthesized in a narrative account of the exchange in my fieldnotes from the same day, June 8, 2006.

3. I offered to contribute the household's food budget whenever necessary, including by buying 20 kilograms of rice about once a month when I went to Alotau. I also paid Francis and Lucy 100 kina every month as rent (although they tended to view it as a gift). Only rarely did my presence require me to supplement our food stores. For most of the time I have lived in New Home, our household has consisted of mainly adults who could work in the garden, and thus we probably had more food than other families with fewer gardens and fewer garden workers. A more typical type of household, as I describe below, consists of a married couple, its children, and possibly another adult, including often an elderly parent or parents.

4. The colonization of New Guinea occurred slowly in several stages and by several different powers, leading to many different names for the territories that now compose independent Papua New Guinea. British and Australian colonial control began with the unrecognized annexation of the southern coasts and southeastern islands by Queensland in 1883, motivated in part by the perceived threat of German encroachment in the South Seas. This eventually became recognized as a Protectorate of the British Crown known as British New Guinea the following year. In 1888 William Macgregor became the first administrator of the Possession of British New Guinea (and later its first lieutenant governor). While "native protection" was an important element of his mission, he also sought to compel indigenous subjects to plant and harvest coconut for export, hoping that involvement in a colonial cash economy would contribute to their welfare. In 1906, government control passed to Australia's new federal government with its passage of the Papua Act, making the colony into an external territory. J.H.P. Murray became lieutenant governor in 1908. New ordinances were passed making it easier

to for the government to acquire land from indigenous owners for the development of mines and plantations, and indigenous subjects were drawn even more into the colonial economy. Murray and Macgregor, though different in their approaches, more or less took up the same dual mandate of economic development and so-called native protection (Edmonds 2006). Unlike Macgregor, Murray presided over a more liberal period in which settler colonialism was encouraged. Still, both Macgregor and Murray saw native protection in terms of intervention in indigenous people's lives to improve what they believed to be declining health and welfare and to stop depopulation. Murray also inherited and improved on the system of governance created by Macgregor, including especially patrols by officers and police from outstations to inspect indigenous communities. For histories of this period, see Legge 1946, Joyce 1953, Roe 1961, Oke 1975, and Lewis 1996.

5. In a 1914 report, a patrol officer named N.K. Bushell described his activities on an early patrol through Kurada. Walking by foot with a group of armed native constables, he spoke with people in each village. He took two people into custody who had been accused of adultery. He then writes in an entry of May 14, "I made enquiries for venereal disease, but found no cases. I explained to the people the Government's wishes for a bigger birth-rate and had the printed leaflets distributed" (Bushell 1914). He goes on to describe how he ordered that all the "old houses" be pulled down and burned by his officers. He makes a positive comment about the apparent health of the people and notes that local people told him that the coming yam harvest was expected to be a big one. He notes that the water supply in this area is excellent because of its many "fine, flowing creeks." He also took two women into custody for treatment for venereal disease. Although it is unclear from his report, it appears that he and his officers made camp in Bwasiyaiyai and kept the venereal disease patients and the men charged with adultery overnight in camp. In the morning he held a court for resolving local disputes, treated the women, and discharged the men. This early contact between the colonial state and Auhelawa, though perhaps excessive, is also representative in many ways. The police power of colonial administration was sporadic. Indeed, according to patrol officers' reports, from 1891 to 1941, patrols in this area occurred no more than once a year. When a patrol appeared, it was swift, quite intrusive, and somewhat brutal and could appear capricious. At the same time, officers were very paternalistic and concerned with the well-being of the residents. An officer intervened in practically every domain of people's domestic existence, inquiring about marital problems, sexual activity, and food supplies and apparently giving the residents no choice but to comply with his supposedly benevolent delivery of government services.

6. Some examples of this are the articles "Papuan Gardens" (April 15, 1929), "Better Villages" (September 16, 1929), "Population and Depopulation" (January 15, 1930), in *The Papuan Villager, 1929–1941.*

7. In his history of public health in Papua New Guinea, Donald Denoon (2002) notes that although many government programs have sought to improve the conditions for childbirth, few have considered women as social beings or acknowledged that women's social status influenced their pregnancy and successful delivery. Hence much attention has been paid to encouraging women to prepare for childbirth and care for children in particular ways, and little attention has been given to the social causes for women's nutrition and health.

8. As yaheyahe fallow, one can still often harvest food from some of the plantings still growing.

9. In this context, yabayaba is properly the object of the activity of lauyaba, or the daily provisioning of one's own household. Any yam that has not matured enough to be harvested, let alone given as a gift, is also called yabayaba. Such yams are left in the ground and can be harvested at any time afterward when one needs food. In naming this activity as lauyaba, though, Auhelawa are emphasizing its unimportance. The word *yabayaba* also forms part of

a verb meaning to insult or to belittle, *awayabayaba*, with the verbal prefix *awa-*, which signifies an action performed by speaking. In this sense, yabayaba is any food that is so small or worthless that it is only useful as one's own food.

10. In this regard, Auhelawa's agricultural shift toward more productive crops involving less labor is consistent with changes throughout PNG. See Bourke 2001.

11. Several people said that they planted taro in its own garden. Many others explained that they did not have the right kind of land to grow taro or could not be bothered with inspecting it regularly, especially if the appropriate sites were too far from their houses.

12. One exception is taro. While some varieties of taro have been introduced, and these are considered to be "new," like other crops brought by missionaries, taro in general is considered to be a traditional crop and has its own special kind of gardening work, known as *wegavi*. All varieties of taro require a different kind of soil than yams, and so a taro cultivator will dig completely separate gardens for it and then frequently visit this garden to care for the plants and to protect it from parrots, which eat the flowers. Many people told me that they did not grow taro, either because they lacked access to the kind of land on which it can grow or potential gardening sites are too far from their villages to make it worthwhile, since they would have to regularly tend the plants. A blight killed much of the taro in recent years, after which many others stopped planting it. The decline of taro in Auhelawa is attributed to these factors, whereas perceived declines in yam harvests are attributed solely to social factors. In my household survey in 2006, 58 percent of households reported planting any taro that year, much lower than 'wateya, halutu, and cassava (planted by 100 percent of households) or sweet potato (planted by 96 percent of households). *Musa* banana of various species, including one traditional species called pona'e, was planted by 79 percent of households (see Schram 2009, 122). Explaining this change would require more research into gardening and would likely lead to a very different story about that change. Nonetheless, taro's decreasing importance in general is still sometimes taken as a sign of the same broad trend away from tradition.

Chapter 4. Banks, Books, and Pots

1. Bohannan goes on to argue that money would ultimately erode these categories of goods and establish a "unicentric" economy in which any kind of value could be measured in money and be exchanged for money without any repercussions (1959, 498, 501). This prediction has not always been the most influential part of the model, and so I want to highlight the compelling fact that the initial classification of money in Tiv was in the lowest sphere along with foodstuffs, utensils, chickens, goats, and tools.

2. Although common, reselling fuel in this way exists in a gray area of the law. Local councils require sellers to pay a fee to obtain a license to trade fuel, and most sellers in Auhelawa did not have one.

3. Tobacco was introduced to New Guinea by Portuguese traders and spread throughout the region through trade. Perhaps speaking to its age, Auhelawa has many different names for tobacco. It is known as *mabele, tapwa'e, kasiya* (supposed to be borrowed from a Goodenough Island language), *ligu* (possibly a play on *lugu* [leaf]), *yawayawai* (possibly a play on *yawahi* [breath]), and *sadua* (specifically refers to rolled tobacco, and is supposed to derived from the English word *cigar*). Tobacco is also strongly associated with the colonial period, and it was an important medium of exchange between Australians and indigenous people at that time. Tobacco is now grown locally for sale, and several areas within Milne Bay Province have specialized in its production. Producers cure the leaves and braid them into long ropes, which can be coiled into a large disk. Some also pound the cured leaves into a hollow bamboo tube. These bulk quantities of tobacco are produced outside Auhelawa and sold to local

sellers. Auhelawa sellers then sell segments of the braided rope for several kina or chop it into loose flakes and roll it in strips of newspaper to make cigarettes. The trade in tobacco is much like betel nut in that it is a very common way for rural residents to make money, but it is interesting to note that there is a higher degree of specialization in the division of labor, in part due to the fact that only certain regions can grow tobacco.

4. In addition to the complex play of signals conveyed by one's bag as a container, Lucy's bilum is also another kind of sign. Most women and men carry a peha (personal basket) woven from pandanus or coconut fronds. Women who have Highlands bilums woven from yarn usually receive them as gifts from relatives working in Port Moresby and other big PNG cities, where they are sold by women weavers.

5. While Auhelawa usually translate the word buka into English as *credit*, no interest is added to the debt. The seller simply accepts a promise of a deferred payment but otherwise has nothing to gain. This practice, known as *dinau* in PNG Pidgin English, is widespread among informal sellers in the region (van der Grijp 2003; Silverman 2005; Maclean 2013). Some of the elements of the Auhelawa practice of buka, particularly the keeping of written accounts, appear to have been established by an agricultural cooperative begun in the colonial period after the Second World War. Members of the cooperative produced copra, and each member was credited money earned from copra sales to an account which they could spend in a cooperative-owned trade store. Like today's trade stores, they would order goods on display from a counter and then give the clerk their account number who would record the total to debit from their account. According to the memories of many of the cooperative members, this store and other similar ventures among voluntary associations eventually closed because of either unpaid debts or theft. People assume that this kind of slow depletion of a store's money is an inherent risk in any business where customers are allowed to defer payment. While these enterprises may have very clear, widely understood and accepted rules and procedures, they ultimately rest on nothing more than the personal trust between customers and seller. Likewise, today, buka is understood as working like a contract in theory but in practice requires an appeal to shared moral ideas. Francis, for instance, only permitted teachers to book by signing over paychecks, and as a former teacher himself was very well known to and respected by his customers.

6. My conversation with this man (who did not give permission for his name to be used) was summarized in my field notes for October 29, 2006.

7. This is not to say that Francis and Lucy did not share resources as a married couple. They were in fact completely economically interdependent in all respects, including cash income. At times, Lucy gave money to Francis when he needed some to put in an order for the store. At other times, Francis lent or gave Lucy money or store goods to finance her baking. The method of accounting, in this case literally, though is different from a joint bank account. This method of accounting through hidden banks, much like yam houses, facilitates a different kind of imagination of what is valuable about money.

8. It is also worth noting that, at least ideally, visitors in a pot-to-pot event offer financial credit to their hosts, and the cooperation of hosts and visitors is like a very small rotating credit association (see Kavanamur 2003). In both their pageantry and in the facilitation of credit, they also recall the *wok meri* (women's work) organizations described by Sexton (1982).

9. In 1978, the Women's International League for Peace and Freedom printed bumper stickers exclaiming, "It will be a great day when our schools get all the money they need and the Air Force has to hold a bake sale to buy a bomber." For them, bake sales for schools were not simply means of generating revenue but themselves political statements about public spending bordering on protest. Each sale at a bake sale potentially sends the implicit message that it is wrong for schools not to receive "all the money they need," since schools are a public good.

Chapter 5. One Mind

1. In 1890, the colonial administration of William Macgregor established separate territories within British New Guinea for each of the three main Protestant mission bodies, the London Missionary Society, the Anglican Mission, and the Australasian Wesleyan Methodist Missionary Society (Langmore 1989, 3; Trompf 1991, 149).

2. I have mentioned to many people of Auhelawa that some anthropologists hold the view that Christianity has made an insignificant impact on indigenous societies of PNG. For the most part, they reject this as it applies to them and to other people of the region. In their minds, there are still many areas of PNG that have only recently had contact with Christianity, and they may not have yet *nuwamasele* (mind-light, or the Auhelawa idiom for conversion), but many other people like themselves had it over a century ago. In other contexts, people thought that some forms of Pentecostalism were too extreme in their piety. Discussing the recent, religiously motivated destruction of traditionally styled decorations in the national parliamentary building in 2014, an Auhelawa man told me, "We are not holy people!" Christianity isn't everything, that is; leave the carvings alone. In my observation, not only are there many degrees of piety and involvement, Christianity serves many different purposes and involves people equally as social beings as well as individual believers.

3. Bromilow and his fellow missionaries scrupulously documented their progress on Dobu and throughout their sphere of influence in their annual reports to the Australasian Wesleyan Methodist Missionary Society (after 1902, the Methodist Missionary Society of Australasia), including counts of the number of preaching places they established and the numbers of hearers who attended services there. The reports were circulated to churches in Australia and individuals who had paid subscriptions, and each of whose names were listed in pages at the back of the report along with the amount of his donation. In both their counts of attendees at worship and in the report itself, missionary progress was measured quantitatively.

4. The date for the establishment of a church at Kurada by a Samoan pastor named Pati is mainly based on Auhelawa oral history. The first mention of Kurada by the Methodist missionaries comes in their report for 1910 in which it is noted that a catechist is present there, supervised by an Australian missionary named Gordon Burgess at a new station at Bunama, several hours walk east from Kurada (Gilmour 1911, 112). In the report of the following year, Gordon Burgess notes that Pati Isaia is living in "Kulada" (Burgess 1912, 114; Gilmour 1912, 102). He writes: "At Kulada [sic] we have a fine large native church nearly finished. Our Catechist, Pati Isiah [sic], who has been in New Guinea for nineteen years, has been recommended as a candidate for the Native Ministry. Pati is our best worker, and well deserves the honour" (1912, 114). Reports suggest that it is possible that a preacher or catechist like Pati was in regular contact with Auhelawa from around 1902, but that a church and permanent pastor were not present until at least 1910. Like many oral historical narratives, Auhelawa stories of Pati have condensed many different events and simplified the process of establishing relationships with the new mission into a single dramatic encounter.

5. Auhelawa distinguishes between inclusive and exclusive plural first person, which I note in transcripts with "we(incl.)" and "we(excl.)," and plural and singular second person, which I note with "you" and "you(pl.)." This story was told by David Magisubu of Alogawa Village on May 16, 2006.

6. These are spontaneously transcribed statements.

7. This is from a recording of a prayer by Opa in the Sowala United Church on January 29, 2006.

8. This is from a recording of a prayer by Alimita in the Sowala United Church on March 26, 2006.

9. This is taken from a recording of a prayer by Loise in the Sowala United Church on April 23, 2006. The speaker uses three different words, *no'o*, *tupu*, and *wasa*, which all can be essentially translated as "praise" or "esteem" in English. Tangentially, Auhelawa language does have a great many synonymous words. Speakers often attribute this to the "mixing" of neighboring languages and the influence of Dobu as a Bible language and regional lingua franca. What one sees here is the kind of rhetorical resource this provides to a speaker who is otherwise speaking "pure" Auhelawa. United religious language in Auhelawa can be seen as a distinct, formal register, using many set phrases and Dobuan words that index the sacredness of the topic. It is outside the scope of this book to describe this register in detail, although it is worth noting that it is one way that people distinguish United Christianity from the newer Pentecostal fellowships.

10. Money was itself relatively new and yet was already widely used as a means to commensurate values in exchanges across cultural boundaries. In this usage, money is fungible and quantifiable and so facilitates what Fredrik Barth calls "incorporation," or contributions to a common pool, as opposed to a balanced transaction between parties (1981, 38). Individual contributions of money can be added up. In using money as a medium of value, the individual act of giving can be reframed as part of a collective action. Indeed, Bromilow also notes that the individual contributions of so-called native articles, which were presumably valuable in their own right, were later sold by missionaries (Bromilow 1900, lxxix).

11. Other examples of this connection between a "self-supporting" church and authentic individual conversion can be found in later annual reports from the Methodist missions, such as Methodist Missionary Society of Australasia 1919, 15; and Methodist Missionary Society of Australasia 1922, 55.

12. Conceptual blends are not, then, the outcome of blending two cultural constructions of reality. While syncretism or creolization of culture might be argued to also generate genuinely novel representations, Fauconnier and Turner see conceptual blending as a way that two ideal representations are merged to facilitate certain kinds of reasoning that are difficult to conceptualize within one representational frame. Syncretism is often invoked in discussions of religion, but as Stephan Palmié (2013) argues, such arguments tend to assume that certain instances of a religion are pure. In fact, as products of history all religions are syncretic in some way, but their borrowings from other cultures and religions are erased to support a claim to authority (see also Romberg 1998).

Chapter 6. The Weight of Tradition, the Children of Light

1. Throughout many parts of PNG, the Pidgin word *kastom*, derived from the English word *custom*, is a way in which people talk about the institutions, rules, and values of a local village community with respect to its difference from foreign ideas and values introduced since the colonial period. Early discussions of kastom in PNG and other parts of colonial and postcolonial Melanesia emphasized how it functioned as a form of resistance to foreign influence or as a generic conception of cultural distinctiveness on which an independent national identity could be crafted (Keesing 1982; Tonkinson 1982; Babadzan 1988; see also Lindstrom 2008). While claims about kastom undoubtedly have a political dimension, for many indigenous peoples of Melanesia, kastom discourse has become naturalized as a way to talk about historical change. For instance, Robert Foster (1995) shows how Tanga Island people differentiate their own mortuary feasting complex as kastom from what they call *bisnis* (business). Most Auhelawa people do not use Pidgin, yet the concept of *kastam* seems to have been borrowed from Pidgin to draw a similar metacultural distinction. In Auhelawa, kastam is generally opposed to *tapwalolo*, or more commonly *masele* (light) as a word to refer to Christian

attitudes and morality (see also Otto 1992). In fact, the informant who told me he wished that people would simply "sit, cook, eat, full stop" also said that masele was "Christian kastam" (see Schram 2007). For him, individuals are capable of choosing either masele or kastam, yet for many other Auhelawa, kastam is associated with the past and society as a whole is gradually shifting toward masele. The present is dominated by both kastam and masele, making many situations uncertain.

2. This terminology does not perfectly translate the terms Auhelawa use in these contexts, but it does accurately describe the two sides in any mortuary feast. It is also consistent with ethnographic terminology used to describe similar mortuary complexes throughout the region (e.g., Damon and Wagner 1989).

3. Everyone immediately recognized that Tagelani was leading a *tapwalolo*, and they all switched from their roles as owners and visitors to the role of congregant.

4. These terms are both derived from synonymous words for aibika (*Abelmoschus manihot*), an edible leafy green vegetable, *ipatu* or *welolo*. I was not able to find out why this would be the basis for the name of the feast.

5. Although not precisely recorded in my notes, in my memory of this early period of fieldwork I recall asking questions that were phrased in terms of social norms, institutions, and rules and in this sense also resonated with the local discourse of bwabwale as a form of kastam. Indeed, and although my fieldnotes and diaries from this time were not very introspective, I wonder now in retrospect if, as a newcomer, foreigner, and person interested in cultural differences, my presence itself elicited the frame of bwabwale in spite of Lorenzo's statements.

6. *Bagi* (or in other parts of the region *soulava*) is a type of necklace made from ground discs of red *Spondylus* shells. Very long decorated bagi are one of two types of ceremonial valuable (*une*) that partners exchange for each other in a practice Auhelawa people call *awa'une* (to ask for valuables) and anthropologists know as kula exchange. Auhelawa people do not participate in kula and have always been relatively marginal to these networks. The valuables of kula, especially bagi, are generally important as items of wealth and prestige. Auhelawa can give bagi and pigs for land in some exceptional cases, although it is not clear if the land becomes permanently transferred through this payment. While some people and susu possess long, decorated bagi as heirlooms, and hold clear ideas about the "road" (*eda*, or a chain of exchange partners) on which these items must travel, it is far more common today for people take a long bagi, often acquired for money, and cut it into several segments that can be distributed among kin as personal decorations. In fact, Elobi (mentioned above) once gave me a small personal bagi segment as a *pwaoli*, a gift thanking me for my dou (wailing) as a mourner for her brother. In this case, I interpret the daughter's presentation of the bagi to her father as a very lavish and generous gift of love, rather than a specific kind of exchange. To my knowledge, bagi are not traditionally transacted as part of bwabwale exchange and are not used in this way today.

7. To be clear, in making this decision, Lucy was not banishing these natuleiya either. Indeed, she invited the children to visit her in the village and accompanied one of her brother's daughters to the market quite often. It may be that in so firmly ruling out the demonstration of respect, she risked the perception by her natuleiya that she was also voiding their kinship altogether, which in her mind, she was not.

8. The sketch, entitled "The $65 Funeral," was first performed on *Tonight Starring Jack Paar* in the early 1960s and can be seen in full in Schopper 1996.

9. This quotation is taken from a taped interview conducted on May 28, 2004.

10. One exception would be the case of a stillborn baby delivered to a mother in the health center at the Catholic mission in Mwademwadewa Village. Although there was no mourning beyond the immediate family and susu segment, the natuleiya of this susu,

did demonstrate respect to the susu by avoiding the village for a time, even though this was not requested.

11. I want to acknowledge Jukka Siikala for this way of thinking about these issues.

Conclusion

1. In contrasting African cultural citizenship and PNG ethnographic citizenship, I am grossly oversimplifying the politics of citizenship in both places. One can easily find examples of either in each region. In particular, since I discuss separatist movements in African states as a result of cultural citizenship, it is also important to note that there have also been many separatist movements in PNG's postcolonial history as well (see, e.g., May 1982). I exaggerate the differences between the regions to better develop ideal types of solution to the problem of citizenship in multicultural societies. Actual cases will always exhibit a mix of several elements, but I believe that my formulation of the contrast will highlight important features of postcoloniality in PNG today.

2. In calling PNG an "ethnographic state," I draw on work by Nicholas Dirks (2001), Edmund Burke III (2014), and Townsend Middleton (2015). It is important to note key differences between their uses of the term and my own. Burke uses the phrase to denote the ideological representation of a generic national version of Islam in Morocco, which the Moroccan state inherits from French ethnographers. The Moroccan case thus resembles what I call cultural citizenship but is similar to the PNG case of ethnographic citizenship insofar as the state grants epistemic authority over national identity to the ethnographic gaze. Dirks describes the appeal to supposedly scientific principles of governance in the British colonial rule of India. Middleton writes about a similar system of government through "state anthropology" in contemporary India. He also describes how the ethnographic representations of government anthropologists create the conditions for the political recognition of tribal peoples in Darjeeling state. Dirks and Middleton each develop cases which could possibly be compared to the work of W. E. Armstrong and Francis Williams. While latter-day anthropologists have long flocked to PNG, actual anthropological research has never entered into official deliberations over citizenship or national identity in a substantive way (see Ritchie 2003). Rather, Narokobi's Melanesian Way is premised on a particular theory of society as a total, integrated system and, in that sense, asks PNG citizens to see themselves as a foreign ethnographer might.

3. In her article on the history of Parliament House's decorations, Pamela Rosi (1991) translates *Bung Wantaim* as *Coming Together* (303). Andrew Moutu (personal communication) proposes that a more accurate translation of the title is *Unity*. This is particularly relevant since Zurenuoc proposed to replace the assemblage with what he called a Unity Pole.

4. The epithets describing PNG as an "island of gold floating on a sea of oil" or a "mountain of gold floating on a sea of oil" are well known in the country and have been continuously updated (see Mydans 1997; Gomez 2006; Elapa 2011). Its most recent version, invoked by Zurenuoc himself, states that PNG is "a green island of gold, floating on a sea of oil, powered by gas" (Zurenuoc 2015). Besides foregrounding natural resources as the country's wealth, the image alienates the natural landscapes from the people who occupy and own them. It contrasts with another familiar group of caricatures of PNG: a "land of a thousand tribes," a country where "over 800 languages are spoken," and where the population is overwhelmingly rural, and presumably also living in traditional communities. By rendering all of PNG in terms of its colors and commodities, the image dispossesses the people who live in this landscape of the basis for their real livelihoods (West 2016).

5. For the most extensive discussion of his vision for reforming Parliament, see Zurenuoc's speech on July 17, 2013 at the Crawford School of Public Policy, Australian National

University. In this speech, he distinguished himself from the independence generation of Michael Somare, the first prime minister. He argues that their approach to policymaking was based on the traditional cultural values of Melanesian villages and clashed with the principles of democracy. Their traditional ethos had led to official corruption and ethnic favoritism, and Zurenuoc promised to break with this mindset and build a parliament based on formal procedures. Months later, he ordered the removal of the carved faces on the lintel and *Bung Wantaim*. Arguably, this action was a visual symbol of his broader aim of "modernization" presented in the speech.

6. In this regard, the letter writers proposing a museum solution to the Zurenuoc affair can also be seen as working in the same spirit as museums which now seek to go beyond multiculturalism and "decolonize" themselves, for instance, by designing exhibits to serve multiple simultaneous audiences, and by creating spaces of collaboration between curators and communities whose lives are represented by exhibits (Lonetree 2012, 5).

7. Alice Street (2014) argues that public hospitals in PNG are already becoming this kind of public thing, although she treats this as an unanticipated result born of practical necessity. Intended as embodiments of a modern, liberal state, chronically underfunded public hospitals create spaces in which sick patients wait for extended periods to see a doctor and receive a diagnosis. Many are willing to accept the subject position required by the scientific rationality of biomedicine, but nonetheless never learn the "name" of their malady in the eyes of doctors (Street 2014, chap. 5). In the spaces of waiting, many theories of illness contend and circulate, bringing patients, their kin, hospital workers, and fellow patients into new kinds of relationships of responsibility to one another.

REFERENCES

Adedze, Agbenyega. 1995. "Museums as a Tool for Nationalism in Africa." *Museum Anthropology* 19 (2): 58–64. doi:10.1525/mua.1995.19.2.58.

Alberti, Benjamin, Severin Fowles, Martin Holbraad, Yvonne Marshall, and Christopher Witmore. 2011. "'Worlds Otherwise': Archaeology, Anthropology, and Ontological Difference." *Current Anthropology* 52 (6): 896–912. doi:10.1086/662027.

Appadurai, Arjun. 1996. *Modernity at Large: Cultural Dimensions of Globalization.* Minneapolis: University of Minnesota Press.

Armstrong, W. E. 1922a. "Native Taxation." In *Native Taxes Ordinance, 1917–1922, Anthropology Report No. 2: Native Taxation,* 32–36. Port Moresby: Government Printer.

——. 1922b. *Native Taxes Ordinance, 1917–1922, Anthropology Report No. 1: Report on the Suau-Tawala.* Port Moresby: Government Printer.

Austen, Leo. 1945. "Cultural Changes in Kiriwina." *Oceania* 16 (1): 15–60.

Austin, J. L. 1975 [1962]. *How to Do Things with Words: The William James Lectures.* Edited by J. O. Urmson and Marina Sbisà. 2nd ed. Cambridge, Mass.: Harvard University Press.

Babadzan, Alain. 1988. "Kastom and Nation Building in the South Pacific." In *Ethnicities and Nations: Processes and Interethnic Relations in Latin America, Southeast Asia, and the Pacific,* edited by Remo Guidieri, Francesco Pellizzi, and S. J. Tambiah, 199–228. Austin: University of Texas Press.

Ballard, Chris. 2014. "Oceanic Historicities." *Contemporary Pacific* 26 (1): 96–124. doi:10.1353/cp.2014.0009.
Barclay, Kate, and Fiona McCormack, eds. 2013. *Engaging with Capitalism: Cases from Oceania*. Research in Economic Anthropology 33. Bingley, UK: Emerald Group Publishing.
Barker, John. 1990. "Mission Station and Village: Religious Practice and Representations in Maisin Society." In *Christianity in Oceania: Ethnographic Perspectives*, edited by John Barker, 173–96. Lanham, Md.: University Press of America.
———. 2012. "Secondary Conversion and the Anthropology of Christianity in Melanesia." *Archives de Sciences Sociales des Religions* 157: 67–87. doi:10.4000/assr.23633.
Barth, Fredrik. 1981. "Models of Social Organization, I." In *Process and Form in Social Life: Selected Essays of Fredrik Barth*, 1:32–47. London: Routledge and Kegan Paul.
Bashkow, Ira. 2004. "A Neo-Boasian Conception of Cultural Boundaries." *American Anthropologist* 106 (3): 443–58. doi:10.1525/aa.2004.106.3.443.
Bateson, Gregory. 1958. "Epilogue 1958." In *Naven: A Survey of the Problems Suggested by a Composite Picture of the Culture of a New Guinea Tribe Drawn from Three Points of View*, 2nd ed., 280–303. Stanford, Calif.: Stanford University Press.
———. 1972. *Steps to an Ecology of Mind: Collected Essays in Anthropology, Psychiatry, Evolution, and Epistemology*. Chicago: University of Chicago Press.
Battaglia, Debbora. 1985. "'We Feed Our Father': Paternal Nurture among the Sabarl of Papua New Guinea." *American Ethnologist* 12 (3): 427–41.
Bayliss-Smith, Tim. 2014. "Colonialism as Shell-Shock: William Rivers's Explanations for Depopulation in Melanesia." In *The Ethnographic Experiment: A. M. Hocart and W. H. R. Rivers in Island Melanesia, 1908*, edited by Cato Berg and Edvard Hviding, 179–213. New York: Berghahn Books.
Beidelman, Thomas O. 1986. *Moral Imagination in Kaguru Modes of Thought*. Washington, D.C.: Smithsonian Institution Press.
Benediktsson, Karl. 2002. *Harvesting Development: The Construction of Fresh Food Markets in Papua New Guinea*. Ann Arbor: University of Michigan Press.
Bennett, Judy. 2014. "A Vanishing People or a Vanishing Discourse?: W. H. R. Rivers's 'Psychological Factor' and the Depopulation of the Solomon Islands and the New Hebrides." In *The Ethnographic Experiment: A. M. Hocart and W. H. R. Rivers in Island Melanesia, 1908*, edited by Cato Berg and Edvard Hviding, 214–51. New York: Berghahn Books.
Bialecki, Jon. 2012. "Virtual Christianity in an Age of Nominalist Anthropology." *Anthropological Theory* 12 (3): 295–319. doi:10.1177/1463499612469586.
Bielo, James S. 2012. "Belief, Deconversion, and Authenticity among U.S. Emerging Evangelicals." *Ethos* 40 (3): 258–76. doi:10.1111/j.1548-1352.2012.01257.x.
Blackburn, Carole. 2009. "Differentiating Indigenous Citizenship: Seeking Multiplicity in Rights, Identity, and Sovereignty in Canada." *American Ethnologist* 36 (1): 66–78. doi:10.1111/j.1548-1425.2008.01103.x.
Blaser, Mario. 2013. "Ontological Conflicts and the Stories of Peoples in Spite of Europe: Toward a Conversation on Political Ontology." *Current Anthropology* 54 (5): 547–68. doi:10.1086/672270.
Bloch, Maurice. 1993 [1971]. *Placing the Dead: Tombs, Ancestral Villages, and Kinship Organization in Madagascar*. Prospect Heights, Ill.: Waveland Press.

Boddy, Janice. 1998. "Afterword: Embodying Ethnography." In *Bodies and Persons: Comparative Perspectives from Africa and Melanesia*, edited by Michael Lambek and Andrew M. Strathern, 252–73. Cambridge: Cambridge University Press.

Bohannan, Paul. 1955. "Some Principles of Exchange and Investment among the Tiv." *American Anthropologist*, New Series 57 (1): 60–70.

———. 1959. "The Impact of Money on an African Subsistence Economy." *Journal of Economic History* 19 (4): 491–503. doi:10.1017/S0022050700085946.

Bolyanatz, Alexander H. 2000. *Mortuary Feasting on New Ireland: The Activation of Matriliny among the Sursurunga*. Westport, Conn.: Bergin and Garvey.

Boserup, Ester. 2007 [1970]. *Woman's Role in Economic Development*. London: Routledge.

Bourdieu, Pierre. 1977. *Outline of a Theory of Practice*. Cambridge: Cambridge University Press.

Bourke, R. Michael. 2001. "Intensification of Agricultural Systems in Papua New Guinea." *Asia Pacific Viewpoint* 42 (2–3): 219–35. doi:10.1111/1467-8373.00146.

Briggs, Charles L. 1984. "Learning How to Ask: Native Metacommunicative Competence and the Incompetence of Fieldworkers." *Language in Society* 13 (1): 1–28.

Brison, Karen J. 1999. "Hierarchy in the World of Fijian Children." *Ethnology* 38 (2): 97–119. doi:10.2307/3773978.

———. 2007. *Our Wealth Is Loving Each Other: Self and Society in Fiji*. Lanham, Md.: Lexington Books.

Bromilow, William E. 1892. "British New Guinea District: Dobu Circuit Report and Panaeti Section." In *Report of the Australasian Wesleyan Methodist Missionary Society for the Year Ending March, 1892*, xlv–xlvii. Sydney: Samuel E. Lees, Printer.

———. 1895. "British New Guinea District: Dobu Circuit Report." In *Report of the Australasian Wesleyan Methodist Missionary Society for the Year Ending March, 1895*, lviii–lx. Sydney: Samuel E. Lees, Printer.

———. 1896. "British New Guinea District: Dobu Circuit Report." In *Report of the Australasian Wesleyan Methodist Missionary Society for the Year Ending March, 1896*, lxi–lxv. Sydney: Epworth Printing and Publishing House.

———. 1897. "British New Guinea District: Dobu Circuit Report." In *Report of the Australasian Wesleyan Methodist Missionary Society for the Year Ending March, 1897*, lxv–lxx. Sydney: Epworth Printing and Publishing House.

———. 1900. "British New Guinea District: Dobu Circuit Report." In *Report of the Australasian Wesleyan Methodist Missionary Society for the Year Ending March, 1900*, lxxix–lxxxvi. Sydney: Epworth Printing and Publishing House.

———. 1929. *Twenty Years among Primitive Papuans*. London: Epworth Press.

Brown, George. 1908. *George Brown, D.D.: Pioneer-Missionary and Explorer, an Autobiography*. London: Hodder and Stoughton.

Burgess, Gordon. 1912. "Papua (British New Guinea District): Duau Circuit Report." In *Report of the Australasian Wesleyan Methodist Missionary Society for the Year Ending March, 1911*, 113–15. Sydney: Samuel E. Lees, Printer.

Burke, Edmund, III. 2014. *The Ethnographic State: France and the Invention of Moroccan Islam*. Berkeley: University of California Press.

Burridge, Kenelm. 1975. "The Melanesian Manager." In *Studies in Social Anthropology*, edited by J. Beattie and G. Lienhardt, 86–104. Oxford: Clarendon Press.

———. 1978. "Introduction: Missionary Occasions." In *Mission, Church and Sect in Oceania*, edited by James A. Boutilier, Daniel T. Hughes, and Sharon W. Tiffany, 1–30. Ann Arbor: University of Michigan Press.

Burt, Ben. 1994. *Tradition and Christianity: The Colonial Transformation of a Solomon Islands Society*. London: Routledge.

Busby, Cecilia. 1997. "Permeable and Partible Persons: A Comparative Analysis of Gender and Body in South India and Melanesia." *Journal of the Royal Anthropological Institute* 3 (2): 261–78. doi:10.2307/3035019.

Bushell, N.K. 1914. "Report of a Police Patrol of D'Entrecasteaux Group of Islands, March 11th to May 16th 1914." Files of Correspondence, Journals, and Patrol Reports from Outstations of British New Guinea and Papua, 1890–1941 (CRS G91), Item 627.

Cahn, Miranda. 2008. "Indigenous Entrepreneurship, Culture, and Micro-Enterprise in the Pacific Islands: Case Studies from Samoa." *Entrepreneurship and Regional Development* 20 (1): 1–18. doi:10.1080/08985620701552413.

Candea, Matei. 2012. "Different Species, One Theory: Reflections on Anthropomorphism and Anthropological Comparison." *Cambridge Journal of Anthropology* 30 (2): 118–35.

Cannings, David. 2016. "Somare v. Zurenuoc." National Court of Papua New Guinea, docket no. N6308, May 30.

Carr, E. Summerson. 2011. *Scripting Addiction: The Politics of Therapeutic Talk and American Sobriety*. Princeton, N.J.: Princeton University Press.

Carrier, James G. 1994. *Gifts and Commodities: Exchange and Western Capitalism since 1700*. Routledge.

Carsten, Janet. 1989. "Cooking Money: Gender and the Symbolic Transformation of Means of Exchange in a Malay Fishing Community." In *Money and the Morality of Exchange*, edited by Maurice Bloch and Jonathan Parry, 117–41. Cambridge: Cambridge University Press.

———. 1995. "The Substance of Kinship and the Heat of the Hearth: Feeding, Personhood, and Relatedness among Malays in Pulau Langkawi." *American Ethnologist* 22 (2): 223–41. doi:10.2307/646700.

Chakrabarty, Dipesh. 2000. *Provincializing Europe: Postcolonial Thought and Historical Difference*. Princeton, N.J.: Princeton University Press.

Chowning, Ann. 1990. "God and Ghosts in Kove." In *Christianity in Oceania: Ethnographic Perspectives*, edited by John Barker, 33–58. Lanham, Md.: University Press of America.

Clifford, James. 1981. "On Ethnographic Surrealism." *Comparative Studies in Society and History* 23 (4): 539–64.

Coleman, Simon. 2006. "Studying 'Global' Pentecostalism: Tensions, Representations, and Opportunities." *PentecoStudies* 5 (1): 1–17.

———. 2011. "Introduction: Negotiating Personhood in African Christianities." *Journal of Religion in Africa* 41 (3): 243–55. doi:10.1163/157006611X592296.

Comaroff, John L., and Jean Comaroff. 1992. *Ethnography and the Historical Imagination*. Boulder, Colo.: Westview Press.

Damon, Frederick H., and Roy Wagner, eds. 1989. *Death Rituals and Life in the Societies of the Kula Ring*. DeKalb: Northern Illinois University Press.

Daswani, Girish. 2011. "(In-)Dividual Pentecostals in Ghana." *Journal of Religion in Africa* 41 (3): 256–79. doi:10.1163/157006611X586211.

De la Cadena, Marisol. 2010. "Indigenous Cosmopolitics in the Andes: Conceptual Reflections beyond 'Politics.'" *Cultural Anthropology* 25 (2): 334–70. doi:10.1111/j.1548-1360.2010.01061.x.

Demian, Melissa. 2006. "Reflecting on Loss in Papua New Guinea." *Ethnos* 71 (4): 507–32. doi:10.1080/00141840601050692.

———. 2015. "Dislocating Custom." *PoLAR: Political and Legal Anthropology Review* 38 (1): 91–107. doi:10.1111/plar.12088.

Denoon, Donald. 2002. *Public Health in Papua New Guinea: Medical Possibility and Social Constraint, 1884–1984*. Cambridge: Cambridge University Press.

Dewey, Susan. 2011. "Markets and Women's Market Trading in the Pacific Islands: An Overview of Social Contexts and Ongoing Challenges." *Asian Women* 27 (3): 1–23.

Dirks, Nicholas B. 2001. *Castes of Mind: Colonialism and the Making of Modern India*. Princeton, N.J.: Princeton University Press.

Dumont, Louis. 1980. *Homo Hierarchicus: The Caste System and Its Implications*. 2nd ed. Chicago: University of Chicago Press.

Duncan, Carol. 1995. *Civilizing Rituals: Inside Public Art Museums*. London: Psychology Press.

Duranti, Alessandro. 1988. "Intentions, Language, and Social Action in a Samoan Context." *Journal of Pragmatics* 12: 13–33.

Edmonds, Penelope. 2006. "Dual Mandate, Double Work: Land, Labour, and the Transformation of 'Native' Subjectivity in Papua, 1908–1940." In *Collisions of Cultures and Identities: Settlers and Indigenous Peoples*, edited by Patricia Grimshaw and Russell McGregor, 163–86. Melbourne: RMIT Publishing.

Elapa, Jeffrey. 2011. "Ex-PM Fights for Resources." *The National*. April 20. http://www.thenational.com.pg/ex-pm-fights-for-resources/.

Englund, Harri, and James Leach. 2000. "Ethnography and the Meta-Narratives of Modernity." *Current Anthropology* 41 (2): 225–48. doi:10.1086/ca.2000.41.issue-2.

Ernst, Manfred. 2012. "Changing Christianity in Oceania: A Regional Overview." *Archives de Sciences Sociales des Religions* 157: 29–45. doi:10.4000/assr.23613.

Escobar, Arturo. 1994. "Welcome to Cyberia: Notes on the Anthropology of Cyberculture." *Current Anthropology* 35 (3): 211–321. doi:10.1086/204266.

Evans-Pritchard, Edward Evan. 1940. *The Nuer: A Description of the Modes of Livelihood and Political Institutions of a Nilotic People*. Oxford: Oxford University Press.

Evara, Rosalyn Albaniel. 2013. "Zurenuoc Banishes 'Ungodly Images and Idols' from Parliament: Speaker 'Cleanses' House." *The Papua New Guinea Post-Courier*, December 6. Port Moresby.

Evers, Hans-Dieter, and Heiko Schrader, eds. 1994. *The Moral Economy of Trade: Ethnicity and Developing Markets*. London: Routledge.

Eves, Richard. 2011. "Pentecostal Dreaming and Technologies of Governmentality in a Melanesian Society." *American Ethnologist* 38 (4): 758–73. doi:10.1111/j.1548-1425.2011.01335.x.

Eves, Richard, Nicole Haley, R. J. May, John Cox, Philip Gibbs, Francesca Merlan, and Alan Rumsey. 2014. "Purging Parliament: A New Christian Politics in Papua New Guinea." State, Society, and Governance in Melanesia Working Paper. Canberra, Australia.

Ewing, Katherine P. 1990. "The Illusion of Wholeness: Culture, Self, and the Experience of Inconsistency." *Ethos* 18 (3): 251–78.

Eyoh, Dickson. 1998. "Through the Prism of a Local Tragedy: Political Liberalisation, Regionalism, and Elite Struggles for Power in Cameroon." *Africa* 68 (3): 338–59. doi:10.2307/1161253.

Fauconnier, Gilles, and Mark Turner. 2002. *The Way We Think: Conceptual Blending and the Mind's Hidden Complexities*. New York: Basic Books.

Feil, Daryl Keith. 1984. *Ways of Exchange: The Enga Tee of Papua New Guinea*. St. Lucia: University of Queensland Press.

Fletcher, Ambrose. 1901. "British New Guinea District: Duau Circuit Report." In *Report of the Australasian Wesleyan Methodist Missionary Society for the Year Ending March, 1901*, lxxxvi–lxxxviii. Sydney: Samuel E. Lees, Printer.

Foale, Simon. 2005. "Sharks, Sea Slugs, and Skirmishes: Managing Marine and Agricultural Resources on Small, Overpopulated Islands in Milne Bay, PNG." RMAP Working Paper. Canberra, Australia.

Fortes, Meyer. 1953. "The Structure of Unilineal Descent Groups." *American Anthropologist* 55 (1): 17–41. doi:10.2307/664462.

———. 1969. "Kinship and the Axiom of Amity." In *Kinship and the Social Order: The Legacy of Lewis Henry Morgan*, 219–49. Chicago: Aldine.

Fortune, R. F. 1963 [1932]. *Sorcerers of Dobu: The Social Anthropology of the Dobu Islanders of the Western Pacific*. London: Routledge and Kegan Paul.

Foster, Robert John. 1990. "Nurture and Force-Feeding: Mortuary Feasting and the Construction of Collective Individuals in a New Ireland Society." *American Ethnologist* 17 (3): 431–48. doi:10.1525/ae.1990.17.3.02a00020.

———. 1995. *Social Reproduction and History in Melanesia: Mortuary Ritual, Gift Exchange, and Custom in the Tanga Islands*. Cambridge: Cambridge University Press.

———. 2002. *Materializing the Nation: Commodities, Consumption, and Media in Papua New Guinea*. Bloomington: Indiana University Press.

Foucault, Michel. 1991. "Governmentality." In *The Foucault Effect: Studies in Governmentality*, edited by Graham Burchell, Colin Gordon, and Peter Miller, 87–104. Chicago: University of Chicago Press.

Fox, Liam. 2011. "PNG 'Repentance Day' a Bolt from the Blue." *ABC News*. http://www.abc.net.au/news/2011-08-26/png-marks-repentance-day/2856522.

Friedman, Jonathan. 1998 [1979]. *System, Structure, and Contradiction: The Evolution of Asiatic Social Formations*. Walnut Creek, Calif.: Altamira Press.

Garfinkel, Harold. 1967. *Studies in Ethnomethodology*. Englewood Cliffs, N.J.: Prentice-Hall.

———. 1988. "Evidence for Locally Produced, Naturally Accountable Phenomena of Order, Logic, Reason, Meaning, Method, Etc. in and as of the Essential Quiddity of Immortal Ordinary Society (I of IV): An Announcement of Studies." *Sociological Theory* 6 (1): 103–9. doi:10.2307/201918.

Garfinkel, Harold, and Anne Warfield Rawls. 2002. *Ethnomethodology's Program: Working Out Durkheim's Aphorism*. Lanham, Md.: Rowman and Littlefield.

Gershon, Ilana. 2012. *No Family Is an Island: Cultural Expertise among Samoans in Diaspora*. Ithaca, N.Y.: Cornell University Press.

Geschiere, Peter. 2009. *The Perils of Belonging: Autochthony, Citizenship, and Exclusion in Africa and Europe*. Chicago: University of Chicago Press.

Giddens, Anthony. 1979. *Central Problems in Social Theory: Action, Structure, and Contradiction in Social Analysis*. Berkeley, Calif.: University of California Press.

——. 1991. *Modernity and Self-Identity: Self and Society in the Late Modern Age*. Stanford, Calif.: Stanford University Press.

Gilmour, M. K. 1911. "Papua (British New Guinea District)." In *Report of the Australasian Wesleyan Methodist Missionary Society for the Year Ending March, 1910*, 102. Sydney: Samuel E. Lees, Printer.

——. 1912. "Papua (British New Guinea District)." In *Report of the Australasian Wesleyan Methodist Missionary Society for the Year Ending March, 1911*, 102. Sydney: Samuel E. Lees, Printer.

Goffman, Erving. 1967a. "On Face-Work." In *Interaction Ritual: Essays in Face to Face Behavior*, 1–46. New York: Doubleday.

——. 1967b. "The Nature of Deference and Demeanor." In *Interaction Ritual: Essays in Face to Face Behavior*, 47–96. New York: Doubleday.

——. 2009 [1971]. *Relations in Public*. New Brunswick, N.J.: Transaction Publishers.

Golub, Alex. 2007. "Ironies of Organization: Landowners, Land Registration, and Papua New Guinea's Mining and Petroleum Industry." *Human Organization* 66 (1): 38–48.

——. 2014. *Leviathans at the Gold Mine: Creating Indigenous and Corporate Actors in Papua New Guinea*. Durham, N.C.: Duke University Press.

Gomez, Brian. 2006. "Mountain of Gold Floating in a Sea of Oil." *Energy News Bulletin*. June 29. http://www.energynewsbulletin.net/energynewsbulletin/news/1064935/mountain-of-gold-floating-in-a-sea-of-oil.

Graeber, David. 2015. "Radical Alterity Is Just Another Way of Saying 'Reality': A Reply to Eduardo Viveiros de Castro." *HAU: Journal of Ethnographic Theory* 5 (2): 1–41. doi:10.14318/hau5.2.003.

Gregory, Chris A. 1980. "Gifts to Men and Gifts to God: Gift Exchange and Capital Accumulation in Contemporary Papua." *Man* 15 (4): 626–52. doi:10.2307/2801537.

——. 1997. *Savage Money: The Anthropology and Politics of Commodity Exchange*. Chur, Switzerland: Harwood Academic Press.

Guyer, Jane I. 2004. *Marginal Gains: Monetary Transactions in Atlantic Africa*. Chicago: University of Chicago Press.

Habermas, Jürgen. 2015 [1991]. *The Philosophical Discourse of Modernity: Twelve Lectures*. Translated by Frederick Lawrence. Malden, Mass.: Polity Press.

Handman, Courtney. 2015. *Critical Christianity: Translation and Denominational Conflict in Papua New Guinea*. Berkeley: University of California Press.

Hannerz, Ulf. 1987. "The World in Creolisation." *Africa* 57 (4): 546–59. doi:10.2307/1159899.

Harvey, David. 1998. "The Body as an Accumulation Strategy." *Environment and Planning D-Society and Space* 16 (4): 401–21. doi:10.1068/d160401.

Haynes, Naomi. 2012. "Pentecostalism and the Morality of Money: Prosperity, Inequality, and Religious Sociality on the Zambian Copperbelt." *Journal of the Royal Anthropological Institute* 18 (1): 123–39. doi:10.1111/j.1467-9655.2011.01734.x.

Heekeren, Deborah Van. 2004. "Feeding Relationship: Uncovering Cosmology in Christian Women's Fellowship in Papua New Guinea." *Oceania* 75 (2): 89–108.

Henare, Amiria, Martin Holbraad, and Sari Wastell, eds. 2007. *Thinking through Things: Theorising Artefacts Ethnographically*. London: Routledge.

Hertz, Robert. 2006 [1960]. *Death* and *The Right Hand*. London: Routledge.

Hess, Sabine. 2006. "Strathern's Melanesian 'Dividual' and the Christian 'Individual': A Perspective from Vanua Lava, Vanuatu." *Oceania* 76 (3): 285–96.

Hirsch, Eric. 1994. "Between Mission and Market: Events and Images in a Melanesian Society." *Man* 29 (3): 689–711. doi:10.2307/2804349.

———. 2001. "When Was Modernity in Melanesia?" *Social Anthropology* 9 (2): 131–46. doi:10.1111/j.1469-8676.2001.tb00142.x.

Holbraad, Martin. 2012. *Truth in Motion: The Recursive Anthropology of Cuban Divination*. Chicago: University of Chicago Press.

Hollan, D. 1992. "Cross-Cultural Differences in the Self." *Journal of Anthropological Research* 48 (4): 283–300.

Honig, Bonnie. 2013. "The Politics of Public Things: Neoliberalism and the Routine of Privatization." *No Foundations* 10: 59–76.

Hutchins, Edwin. 2005. "Material Anchors for Conceptual Blends." *Journal of Pragmatics* 37 (10): 1555–77. doi:10.1016/j.pragma.2004.06.008.

Jebens, Holger. 2005. *Pathways to Heaven: Contesting Mainline and Fundamentalist Christianity in Papua New Guinea*. New York: Berghahn Books.

Jolly, Margaret. 1998. "Other Mothers: Maternal 'Insouciance' and the Depopulation Debate in Fiji and Vanuatu, 1890–1930." In *Maternities and Modernities: Colonial and Postcolonial Experiences in Asia and the Pacific*, edited by Kalpana Ram and Margaret Jolly, 177–212. Cambridge: Cambridge University Press.

Jorgensen, Dan. 2005. "Third Wave Evangelism and the Politics of the Global in Papua New Guinea: Spiritual Warfare and the Recreation of Place in Telefolmin." *Oceania* 75 (4): 444–61.

———. 2007. "Clan-Finding, Clan-Making and the Politics of Identity in a Papua New Guinea Mining Project." In *Customary Land Tenure and Registration in Australia and Papua New Guinea: Anthropological Perspectives*, edited by James F. Weiner and Katie Glaskin, 57–72. Canberra, Australia: ANU E Press.

———. 2014. "Preying on Those Close to Home: Witchcraft Violence in a Papua New Guinea Village." *Australian Journal of Anthropology* 25 (3): 267–86. doi:10.1111/taja.12105.

Joyce, R. B. 1953. "The Administration of British New Guinea." MLitt thesis, University of Cambridge.

Kahn, Miriam. 1983. "Sunday Christians, Monday Sorcerers: Selective Adaptation to Missionization in Wamira." *Journal of Pacific History* 18 (2): 96–112. doi:10.1080/00223348308572461.

———. 1986. *Always Hungry, Never Greedy: Food and the Expression of Gender in a Melanesian Society*. Cambridge: Cambridge University Press.

Kallinen, Timo. 2016. *Divine Rulers in a Secular State*. Helsinki: Finnish Literature Society.

Kavanamur, David. 2003. "Re-Positioning Non-Bank Service Strategy in Papua New Guinea." *Labour and Management in Development Journal* 3 (6): 1–24. http://digital collections.anu.edu.au/handle/1885/40630.

Keane, Webb. 2007. *Christian Moderns: Freedom and Fetish in the Mission Encounter*. Berkeley: University of California Press.

———. 2015. *Ethical Life: Its Natural and Social Histories*. Princeton, N.J.: Princeton University Press.

Keesing, Roger M. 1982. "Kastom and Anticolonialism on Malaita: 'Culture' as Political Symbol." *Mankind* 13 (4): 357–73. doi:10.1111/j.1835-9310.1982.tb01000.x.

Kelly, Raymond. 1977. *Etoro Social Structure: A Study in Structural Contradiction*. Ann Arbor: University of Michigan Press.

Knauft, Bruce M. 1994. "Pushing Anthropology Past the Posts: Critical Notes on Cultural-Anthropology and Cultural-Studies as Influenced by Postmodernism and Existentialism." *Critique of Anthropology* 14 (2): 117–52. doi:10.1177/0308275X 9401400202.

———. 2008. "After Modern: Decline at Nomad Station, Papua New Guinea." Presented at the Annual Meeting of the American Anthropological Association, November 19-23, San Francisco, Calif.

Koczberski, Gina. 2007. "Loose Fruit Mamas: Creating Incentives for Smallholder Women in Oil Palm Production in Papua New Guinea." *World Development* 35 (7): 1172–85. doi:10.1016/j.worlddev.2006.10.010.

Kohn, Eduardo. 2015. "Anthropology of Ontologies." *Annual Review of Anthropology* 44 (1): 311–27. doi:10.1146/annurev-anthro-102214-014127.

Kopytoff, Igor. 1986. "The Cultural Biography of Things: Commoditization as Process." In *The Social Life of Things: Commodities in Cultural Perspective*, edited by Arjun Appadurai, 64–91. Cambridge: Cambridge University Press.

Kuehling, Susanne. 2005. *Dobu: Ethics of Exchange on a Massim Island, Papua New Guinea*. Honolulu: University of Hawai'i Press.

Kulick, Don. 1993. "Speaking as a Woman: Structure and Gender in Domestic Arguments in a New-Guinea Village." *Cultural Anthropology* 8 (4): 510–41. doi:10.1525/can.1993.8.4.02a00050.

Kymlicka, Will. 1996. *Multicultural Citizenship: A Liberal Theory of Minority Rights*. Oxford: Clarendon Press.

Laing, R.D. 1965. *The Divided Self*. London: Penguin Books.

Lambert, Sylvester Maxwell. 1934. *The Depopulation of Pacific Races*. Special Publication 23. Honolulu: Bernice P. Bishop Museum.

Langmore, Diane. 1989. *Missionary Lives: Papua, 1874–1914*. Honolulu: University of Hawai'i Press.

Larson, Gerald James. 1990. "India through Hindu Categories: A Sāṃmkhya Response." *Contributions to Indian Sociology* 24 (2): 237–49. doi:10.1177/00699669002400 2006.

Latour, Bruno. 1993. *We Have Never Been Modern*. Cambridge, Mass.: Harvard University Press.

———. 2005. *Reassembling the Social: An Introduction to Actor-Network Theory.* Oxford: Oxford University Press.
Lear, Jonathan. 2008. *Radical Hope: Ethics in the Face of Cultural Devastation.* Cambridge, Mass.: Harvard University Press.
Lebner, Ashley. 2016. "La redescription de l'anthropologie selon Marilyn Strathern." *L'homme* 218: 117–50.
LeFevre, Tate A. 2013. "Turning Niches into Handles: Kanak Youth, Associations, and the Construction of an Indigenous Counter-Public Sphere." *Settler Colonial Studies* 3 (2): 214–29. doi:10.1080/2201473X.2013.781933.
Legge, J. D. 1946. "Australian Colonial Policy: A Survey of European Development and Native Administration in Papua." MA thesis, University of Melbourne.
Lepowsky, Maria. 1990. "Gender in an Egalitarian Society: A Case Study from the Coral Sea." In *Beyond the Second Sex: New Directions in the Anthropology of Gender*, edited by Ruth Gallagher Goodenough and Peggy Reeves Sanday, 171–226. Philadelphia: University of Pennsylvania Press.
———. 1993. *Fruit of the Motherland: Gender in an Egalitarian Society.* New York: Columbia University Press.
Lévi-Strauss, Claude. 1963. *Structural Anthropology.* Vol. 1. New York: Basic Books.
———. 1969. *The Elementary Structures of Kinship.* Boston: Beacon Press.
Lewis, D. C. 1996. *The Plantation Dream: Developing British New Guinea and Papua, 1884–1942.* Canberra, Australia: Journal of Pacific History.
Lindstrom, Lamont. 2008. "Melanesian Kastom and Its Transformations." *Anthropological Forum* 18 (2): 161–78. doi:10.1080/00664670802150208.
LiPuma, Edward. 1998. "Modernity and Forms of Personhood in Melanesia." In *Bodies and Persons: Comparative Perspectives from Africa and Melanesia*, edited by Michael Lambek and Andrew Strathern, 53–79. Cambridge: Cambridge University Press.
Lonetree, Amy. 2012. *Decolonizing Museums: Representing Native America in National and Tribal Museums.* Chapel Hill, N.C.: University of North Carolina Press.
Macintyre, Martha. 1987. "Nurturance and Nutrition: Change and Continuity in Concepts of Food and Feasting in a Southern Massim Community." *Journal de la Société des océanistes* 84 (1): 51–59. doi:10.3406/jso.1987.2561.
———. 1989. "The Triumph of the Susu: Mortuary Exchanges on Tubetube." In *Death Rituals and Life in the Societies of the Kula Ring*, edited by Frederick H. Damon and Roy Wagner, 133–52. DeKalb: Northern Illinois University Press.
———. 1990. "Christianity, Cargo Cultism and the Concept of the Spirit in Misiman Cosmology." In *Christianity in Oceania: Ethnographic Perspectives*, edited by John Barker, 81–100. Lanham, Md.: University Press of America.
Maclean, Neil. 2013. "Fenced In: Intimacy and Mobility in Highlands Papua New Guinea." *Oceania* 83 (1): 31–48. doi:10.1002/ocea.5006.
Mahmood, Saba. 2005. *Politics of Piety: The Islamic Revival and the Feminist Subject.* Princeton, N.J.: Princeton University Press.
Malinowski, Bronislaw. 1932 [1922]. *Argonauts of the Western Pacific: An Account of Native Enterprise and Adventure in the Archipelagoes of Melanesian New Guinea.* London: Routledge and Sons.

———. 1935. *Coral Gardens and Their Magic: A Study of the Methods of Tilling the Soil and of Agricultural Rites in the Trobriand Islands*. Vol. 1: *Soil-Tilling and Agricultural Rites in the Trobriand Islands*. London: Allen and Unwin.

Mallett, Shelley. 2003. *Conceiving Cultures: Reproducing People and Places on Nuakata, Papua New Guinea*. Ann Arbor: University of Michigan Press.

Marcus, George E., and Dick Cushman. 1982. "Ethnographies as Texts." *Annual Review of Anthropology* 11 (1): 25–69. doi:10.1146/annurev.an.11.100182.000325.

Marriott, McKim. 1992. "Alternative Social Sciences." In *General Education in the Social Sciences: Centennial Reflections on the College of the University of Chicago*, edited by John MacAloon, 262–78. Chicago: University of Chicago Press.

Marriott, McKim. 1976. "Hindu Transactions: Diversity without Dualism." In *Transaction and Meaning: Directions in the Anthropology of Exchange and Symbolic Behavior*, edited by Bruce Kapferer, 109–42. Philadelphia: Institute for the Study of Human Issues.

Marx, Karl. 1972 [1852]. "The Eighteenth Brumaire of Louis Bonaparte." In *The Marx-Engels Reader*, edited by Robert C. Tucker, 594–617. New York: W. W. Norton.

Mauss, Marcel. 1985. "A Category of the Human Mind: The Notion of Person, the Notion of Self." In *The Category of the Person: Anthropology, Philosophy, History*, edited by Michael Carrithers, Steven Lukes, and Steven Collins, translated by W. D. Halls, 1–25. Cambridge: Cambridge University Press.

———. 1990 [1925]. *The Gift: The Form and Reason for Exchange in Archaic Societies*. Translated by W. D. Halls. New York: W. W. Norton.

May, Ronald James, ed. 1982. *Micronationalist Movements in Papua New Guinea*. Political and Social Change Monograph 1. Canberra: Department of Political and Social Change, Research School of Pacific Studies, Australian National University.

McDougall, Debra. 2003. "Fellowship and Citizenship as Models of National Community: United Church Women's Fellowship in Ranongga, Solomon Islands." *Oceania* 74 (1/2): 61–80.

———. 2009. "Christianity, Relationality, and the Material Limits of Individualism: Reflections on Robbins's *Becoming Sinners*." *Asia Pacific Journal of Anthropology* 10 (1): 1–19. doi:10.1080/14442210802706855.

———. 2016. *Engaging with Strangers: Love and Violence in the Rural Solomon Islands*. New York: Berghahn Books.

Merlan, Francesca. 1998. *Caging the Rainbow: Places, Politics, and Aborigines in a North Australian Town*. Honolulu: University of Hawai'i Press.

———. 2005. "Explorations towards Intercultural Accounts of Socio-Cultural Reproduction and Change." *Oceania* 75 (3): 167–82.

Merlan, Francesca, and Alan Rumsey. 1991. *Ku Waru: Language and Segmentary Politics in the Western Nebilyer Valley, Papua New Guinea*. Cambridge: Cambridge University Press.

Metcalf, Peter, and Richard Huntington. 1991. *Celebrations of Death: The Anthropology of Mortuary Ritual*. 2nd ed. Cambridge: Cambridge University Press.

Methodist Missionary Society of Australasia. 1919. *Annual Report and List of Contributions for the Year 1918*. Sydney: Samuel E. Lees, Printer.

———. 1922. *Annual Report and List of Contributions for the Year 1921*. Sydney: Samuel E. Lees, Printer.
Middleton, Townsend. 2015. *The Demands of Recognition: State Anthropology and Ethnopolitics in Darjeeling*. Stanford, Calif.: Stanford University Press.
Miller, Daniel. 1998. *A Theory of Shopping*. Ithaca, N.Y.: Cornell University Press.
Miller, Joan G. 1984. "Culture and the Development of Everyday Social Explanation." *Journal of Personality and Social Psychology* 46 (5): 961–78. doi:10.1037/0022-3514.46.5.961.
Monnerie, Denis. 2010. "Following the Pathways: Contemporary Ceremonies, Representations of the Past and Catholicism in Northern New Caledonia." In *Religious Dynamics in the Pacific/Les dynamiques religieuses dans le Pacifique*, edited by Gabriele Weichart and Francoise Douaire-Marsudon, 85–111. Paris: Cahiers du Credo.
Mosko, Mark S. 1989. "The Developmental Cycle among Public Groups." *Man* 24 (3): 470–84. doi:10.2307/2802702.
———. 1992. "Motherless Sons: Divine Kings and Partible Persons in Melanesia and Polynesia." *Man* 27 (4): 697–717. doi:10.2307/2804170.
———. 2000. "Inalienable Ethnography: Keeping-While-Giving and the Trobriand Case." *Journal of the Royal Anthropological Institute* 6 (3): 377–96.
———. 2010. "Partible Penitents: Dividual Personhood and Christian Practice in Melanesia and the West." *Journal of the Royal Anthropological Institute* 16 (2): 215–40. doi:10.1111/j.1467-9655.2010.01618.x.
Munn, Nancy D. 1992. *The Fame of Gawa: A Symbolic Study of Value Transformation in a Massim (Papua New Guinea) Society*. Durham, N.C.: Duke University Press.
Murray, Hubert. 1933. "The Scientific Aspect of the Pacification of Papua." *Report of the Australian New Zealand Association for the Advancement of Science* 1933: 1–11.
Muru-Lanning, Marama. 2016. *Tupuna Awa: People and Politics of the Waikato River*. Auckland: Auckland University Press.
Mydans, Seth. 1997. "As Election Nears, More Than Politics Divides Islands." *The New York Times*, April 27, sec. World. https://www.nytimes.com/1997/04/27/world/as-election-nears-more-than-politics-divides-islands.html.
Narokobi, Bernard. 1975. *Foundations for Nationhood*. Port Moresby: Papua New Guinea Press and Bookshop.
———. 1980. *The Melanesian Way: Total Cosmic Vision of Life*. Boroko, Papua New Guinea: Institute of Papua New Guinea Studies.
National Community Transformation Network. ca. 2015. "Tear Down the Idols: A Call to the People of Papua New Guinea to Destroy All Idolatrous Objects." National Community Transformation Network. PDF scanned copy of pamphlet in files of author.
Niehaus, I. 2002. "Bodies, Heat, and Taboos: Conceptualizing Modern Personhood in the South African Lowveld." *Ethnology* 41 (3): 189–207. doi:10.2307/4153025.
Nkrumah, Kwame. 1965. *Consciencism, Philosophy, and Ideology for Decolonization and Development: With Particular Reference to the African Revolution*. New York: Monthly Review Press.
Nyamnjoh, Francis, and Michael Rowlands. 1998. "Elite Associations and the Politics of Belonging in Cameroon." *Africa* 68 (3): 320–37. doi:10.2307/1161252.

Nyerere, Julius Kambarage. 1968. *Ujamaa: Essays on Socialism*. Oxford: Oxford University Press.

Ochs, Elinor, and Bambi B. Schieffelin. 1984. "Language Acquisition and Socialization: Three Developmental Stories and Their Implications." In *Culture Theory: Essays on Mind, Self, and Emotion*, edited by Richard A. Schweder and Robert A. LeVine, 276–320. Cambridge: Cambridge University Press.

Oke, Christine. 1975. "The Native Administrations of MacGregor, Murray, and Hasluck in Papua/New Guinea: Continuity and Contrast." *Historical Journal* 1 (1): 7–41.

Ong, Aihwa. 1987. *Spirits of Resistance and Capitalist Discipline: Factory Women in Malaysia*. Albany: State University of New York Press.

———. 1999. *Flexible Citizenship: The Cultural Logics of Transnationality*. Durham, N.C.: Duke University Press.

Ortner, Sherry B. 1984. "Theory in Anthropology since the Sixties." *Comparative Studies in Society and History* 26 (1): 126–66.

———. 2016. "Dark Anthropology and Its Others: Theory since the Eighties." *HAU: Journal of Ethnographic Theory* 6 (1): 47–73.

Otto, Ton. 1992. "The Ways of Kastam: Tradition as Category and Practice in a Manus Village." *Oceania* 62 (4): 264–83. doi:10.1002/j.1834-4461.1992.tb00357.x.

Otto, Ton, and Nils Bubandt, eds. 2011. *Experiments in Holism: Theory and Practice in Contemporary Anthropology*. Malden, Mass.: John Wiley and Sons.

Palmié, Stephan. 2013. *The Cooking of History: How Not to Study Afro-Cuban Religion*. Chicago: University of Chicago Press.

Parmentier, Richard J. 1987. *The Sacred Remains: Myth, History, and Polity in Belau*. Chicago: University of Chicago Press.

———. 1994. *Signs in Society: Studies in Semiotic Anthropology*. Bloomington: Indiana University Press.

Pieterse, Jan Nederveen. 1997. "Multiculturalism and Museums: Discourse about Others in the Age of Globalization." *Theory, Culture, and Society* 14 (4): 123–46. doi:10.1177/026327697014004006.

Piot, Charles. 1992. "Wealth Production, Ritual Consumption, and Center-Periphery Relations in a West African Regional System." *American Ethnologist* 19 (1): 34–52. doi:10.1525/ae.1992.19.1.02a00030.

The Papuan Villager, 1929–1941. Port Moresby: Government Printer. http://png.athabascau.ca/VirAboutPapuanVillager.php.

PNG *Post-Courier*. 2013. "Time for Leaders to Condemn Sorcery Killings." *Papua New Guinea Post-Courier*, February 7, 2.

Polanyi, Karl. 1947. "Our Obsolete Market Mentality." *Commentary* 3 (February): 109–17.

Povinelli, Elizabeth A. 2006. *The Empire of Love: Toward a Theory of Intimacy, Genealogy, and Carnality*. Durham, N.C.: Duke University Press.

Radcliffe-Brown, A. R. 1952 [1935]. "Patrilineal and Matrilineal Succession." In *Structure and Function in Primitive Society*, 32–48. New York: The Free Press.

Reed, Adam. 1997. "Contested Images and Common Strategies: Early Colonial Sexual Politics in the Massim." In *Sites of Desire/Economies of Pleasure: Sexualities in Asia and the Pacific*, edited by Margaret Jolly and Lenore Manderson, 48–71. Chicago: University of Chicago Press.

Richards, Audrey I. 1950. "Some Types of Family Structure among the Central Bantu." In *African Systems of Kinship and Marriage*, edited by A.R. Radcliffe-Brown and Daryll Forde, 207–51. London: Oxford University Press.

Ritchie, Jonathan. 2003. "Making Their Own Law: Popular Participation in the Development of Papua New Guinea's Constitution." PhD diss., Melbourne, Australia: University of Melbourne.

Rival, Laura. 2005. "The Attachment of the Soul to the Body among the Huaorani of Amazonian Ecuador." *Ethnos* 70 (3): 285–310. doi:10.1080/00141840500294300.

Robbins, Joel. 2001. "God Is Nothing but Talk: Modernity, Language, and Prayer in a Papua New Guinea Society." *American Anthropologist* 103 (4): 901–12.

——. 2004. *Becoming Sinners: Christianity and Moral Torment in a Papua New Guinea Society*. Berkeley: University of California Press.

——. 2007. "Continuity Thinking and the Problem of Christian Culture: Belief, Time, and the Anthropology of Christianity." *Current Anthropology* 48 (1): 5–38.

——. 2008. "On Not Knowing Other Minds: Confession, Intention, and Linguistic Exchange in a Papua New Guinea Community." *Anthropological Quarterly* 81 (2): 421–29. doi:10.1353/anq.0.0007.

——. 2009. "Pentecostal Networks and the Spirit of Globalization: On the Social Productivity of Ritual Forms." *Social Analysis* 53 (1): 55–66. doi:10.3167/sa.2009.530104.

Robbins, Joel, Bambi B. Schieffelin, and Aparecida Vilaça. 2014. "Evangelical Conversion and the Transformation of the Self in Amazonia and Melanesia: Christianity and the Revival of Anthropological Comparison." *Comparative Studies in Society and History* 56 (3): 559–90. doi:10.1017/S0010417514000255.

Roe, Margriet. 1961. "A History of South-East Papua to 1930." PhD diss., Canberra: Australian National University.

Rollason, Will. 2014. "Introduction: Pacific Futures, Methodological Challenges." In *Pacific Futures: Projects, Politics, and Interests*, edited by Will Rollason, 1–27. New York: Berghahn Books.

Romberg, Raquel. 1998. "Whose Spirits Are They? The Political Economy of Syncretism and Authenticity." *Journal of Folklore Research* 35 (1): 69–82.

Rosi, Pamela C. 1991. "Papua New Guinea's New Parliament House: A Contested National Symbol." *Contemporary Pacific* 3: 289–324.

Rowlands, Michael. 1993. "The Role of Memory in the Transmission of Culture." *World Archaeology* 25 (2): 141–51.

Rubel, Paula, and Abraham Rosman. 1978. *Your Own Pigs You May Not Eat*. Chicago: University of Chicago Press.

Rumsey, Alan. 2000. "Agency, Personhood, and the 'I' of Discourse in the Pacific and Beyond." *Journal of the Royal Anthropological Institute* 6 (1): 101–15.

——. 2006. "The Articulation of Indigenous and Exogenous Orders in Highland New Guinea and Beyond." *Australian Journal of Anthropology* 17 (1): 47–69. doi:10.1111/j.1835-9310.2006.tb00047.x.

Sahlins, Marshall. 1976. *Culture and Practical Reason*. Chicago: University of Chicago Press.

——. 1992. "The Economics of Develop-Man in the Pacific." *Res* 21: 13–25.

——. 2011a. "What Kinship Is (Part One)." *Journal of the Royal Anthropological Institute* 17 (1): 2–19. doi:10.1111/j.1467-9655.2010.01666.x.

———. 2011b. "What Kinship Is (Part Two)." *Journal of the Royal Anthropological Institute* 17 (2): 227–42. doi:10.1111/j.1467-9655.2011.01677.x.

Sartre, Jean Paul. 1963. Preface to *The Wretched of the Earth*, by Frantz Fanon, 7–34. New York: Grove Press.

Schieffelin, Bambi B. 2007. "Found in Translating: Reflexive Language across Time and Space in Bosavi, Papua New Guinea." In *Consequences of Contact: Language Ideologies and Sociocultural Transformations in Pacific Societies*, edited by Miki Makihara and Bambi B. Schieffelin, 140–65. Oxford: Oxford University Press.

Schieffelin, Edward. 2005 [1976]. *The Sorrow of the Lonely and the Burning of the Dancers*. 2nd ed. New York: Palgrave Macmillan.

Schildkrout, Enid. 1995. "Museums and Nationalism in Namibia." *Museum Anthropology* 19 (2): 65–77. doi:10.1525/mua.1995.19.2.65.

Schneider, David M. 1968. *American Kinship: A Cultural Account*. Chicago: University of Chicago Press.

Schopper, Phillip. 1996. "Nichols and May: Take Two." *American Masters* (season 10, episode 5), May 22. Eagle Rock Entertainment and WNET Channel 13 New York.

Schram, Ryan. 2007. "'Sit, Cook, Eat, Full Stop': Religion and Rejection of Ritual in Auhelawa (Papua New Guinea)." *Oceania* 77 (2): 172–90.

———. 2009. "Feast of Water: Christianity and the Economic Transformation of a Melanesian Society." PhD diss., San Diego: University of California, San Diego.

———. 2014. "Only the Names Have Changed: Dialectic and Differentiation of the Indigenous Person in Papua New Guinea." *Anthropological Theory* 14 (2): 133–52. doi:10.1177/1463499614534100.

———. 2015. "Notes on the Sociology of Wantoks in Papua New Guinea." *Anthropological Forum* 25 (1): 1–18. doi:10.1080/00664677.2014.960795.

———. 2016. "Birds Will Cover the Sky: Humiliation and Meaning in Two Historical Narratives from Auhelawa, Papua New Guinea." *Ethnohistory* 63 (1): 95–117. doi:10.1215/00141801-3325422.

Scott, Michael. 2005. "'I Was Like Abraham': Notes on the Anthropology of Christianity from the Solomon Islands." *Ethnos* 70 (1): 101–25. doi:10.1080/00141840500048565.

Sexton, Lorraine. 1982. "Wok Meri: A Women's Savings and Exchange System in Highland Papua New Guinea." *Oceania* 52 (3): 167–198. doi:10.1002/j.1834-4461.1982.tb01493.x.

Sharp, Timothy L. M. 2013. "Baias, Bisnis, and Betel Nut: The Place of Traders in the Making of a Melanesian Market." In *Engaging with Capitalism: Cases from Oceania*, edited by Kate Barclay and Fiona McCormack, 227–56. Bingley, UK: Emerald Group Publishing.

———. 2016. "Trade's Value: Relational Transactions in the Papua New Guinea Betel Nut Trade." *Oceania* 86 (1): 75–91. doi:10.1002/ocea.5116.

Shipton, Parker. 1989. *Bitter Money: Cultural Economy and Some African Meanings of Forbidden Commodities*. Washington, D.C.: American Anthropological Association.

Silverman, Eric. 2005. "Sepik River Selves in a Changing Modernity: From Sahlins to Psychodynamics." In *The Making of Global and Local Modernities in Melanesia: Humiliation, Transformation and the Nature of Cultural Change*, edited by Holly Wardlow and Joel Robbins, 85–101. Aldershot, UK: Ashgate Publishing, Ltd.

Silverstein, Paul A. 2009. "Of Rooting and Uprooting: Kabyle Habitus, Domesticity, and Structural Nostalgia." In *Bourdieu in Algeria: Colonial Politics, Ethnographic Practices, Theoretical Developments*, edited by Jane E. Goodman and Paul A. Silverstein, 164–98. Lincoln: University of Nebraska Press.

Spiro, Melford E. 1993. "Is the Western Conception of the Self 'Peculiar' within the Context of the World Cultures?" *Ethos* 21 (2): 107–53. doi:10.1525/eth.1993.21.2.02a00010.

Star, Susan Leigh, and James R. Griesemer. 1989. "Institutional Ecology, 'Translations,' and Boundary Objects: Amateurs and Professionals in Berkeley's Museum of Vertebrate Zoology, 1907–39." *Social Studies of Science* 19 (3): 387–420. doi:10.1177/030631289019003001.

Stasch, Rupert. 2003. "Separateness as a Relation: The Iconicity, Univocality, and Creativity of Korowai Mother-in-Law Avoidance." *Journal of the Royal Anthropological Institute* 9 (2): 317–37. doi:10.1111/1467-9655.00152.

———. 2009. *Society of Others: Kinship and Mourning in a West Papuan Place*. Berkeley: University of California Press.

Strathern, Andrew. 1971. *The Rope of Moka: Big-Men and Ceremonial Exchange in Mount Hagen, New Guinea*. Cambridge: Cambridge University Press.

Strathern, Marilyn. 1988. *The Gender of the Gift: Problems with Women and Problems with Society in Melanesia*. Berkeley: University of California Press.

———. 1991. "One Man and Many Men." In *Big Men and Great Men: Personifications of Power in Melanesia*, edited by Maurice Godelier and Marilyn Strathern, 197–214. Cambridge: Cambridge University Press.

———. 2005. *Partial Connections*. Walnut Creek, Calif.: Altamira Press.

Strauss, Claudia. 1997. "Partly Fragmented, Partly Integrated: An Anthropological Examination of 'Postmodern Fragmented Subjects.'" *Cultural Anthropology* 12 (3): 362–404. doi:10.1525/can.1997.12.3.362.

Street, Alice. 2014. *Biomedicine in an Unstable Place: Infrastructure and Personhood in a Papua New Guinean Hospital*. Durham, N.C.: Duke University Press.

Territory of Papua. 1949 [1936]. "Native Taxes (Funds) Regulations." *The Laws of the Territory of Papua, 1888–1945*, 3434–3445. Sydney: Halstead Press.

Thune, Carl. 1990. "Fathers, Aliens, and Brothers: Building a Social World in Loboda Village Church Services." In *Christianity in Oceania: Ethnographic Perspectives*, edited by John Barker, 101–25. Lanham, Md.: University Press of America.

Tilly, Charles. 1984. *Big Structures, Large Processes, Huge Comparisons*. New York: Russell Sage Foundation.

Tomlinson, Matt. 2009. *In God's Image: The Metaculture of Fijian Christianity*. Berkeley: University of California Press.

Tomlinson, Matt, and Matthew Engelke. 2006. "Meaning, Anthropology, and Christianity." In *The Limits of Meaning: Case Studies in the Anthropology of Christianity*, edited by Matthew Engelke and Matt Tomlinson, 1–38. New York: Berghahn Books.

Tonkinson, Robert. 1982. "National Identity and the Problem of Kastom in Vanuatu." *Mankind* 13 (4): 306–15.

Toren, Christina. 1989. "Drinking Cash: The Purification of Money through Ceremonial Exchange in Fiji." In *Money and the Morality of Exchange*, 142–64. Cambridge: Cambridge University Press.

Trompf, Garry. 1991. *Melanesian Religion*. Cambridge: Cambridge University Press.
Trouillot, Michel-Rolph. 2016. *Global Transformations: Anthropology and the Modern World*. New York: Palgrave Macmillan.
Tsing, Anna. 2009. "Supply Chains and the Human Condition." *Rethinking Marxism* 21 (2): 148–76. doi:10.1080/08935690902743088.
Turner, Terence. 1995. "Social Body and Embodied Subject: Bodiliness, Subjectivity, and Sociality among the Kayapo." *Cultural Anthropology* 10 (2): 143–70.
Tuzin, Donald F. 1997. *The Cassowary's Revenge: The Life and Death of Masculinity in a New Guinea Society*. Chicago: University of Chicago Press.
———. 1972. "Yam Symbolism in the Sepik: An Interpretative Account." *Southwestern Journal of Anthropology* 28 (3): 230–54.
Uzendoski, M. A. 2004. "Manioc Beer and Meat: Value, Reproduction, and Cosmic Substance among the Napo Runa of the Ecuadorian Amazon." *Journal of the Royal Anthropological Institute* 10 (4): 883–902.
Van der Grijp, Paul. 2003. "Between Gifts and Commodities: Commercial Enterprise and the Trader's Dilemma on Wallis ('Uvea)." *Contemporary Pacific* 15 (2): 277–307.
Verdery, Katherine. 1998. "Transnationalism, Nationalism, Citizenship, and Property: Eastern Europe since 1989." *American Ethnologist* 25 (2): 291–306. doi:10.1525/ae.1998.25.2.291.
Viveiros de Castro, Eduardo. 1998. "Cosmological Deixis and Amerindian Perspectivism." *Journal of the Royal Anthropological Institute* 4 (3): 469–88. doi:10.2307/3034157.
———. 2004. "Exchanging Perspectives: The Transformation of Objects into Subjects in Amerindian Ontologies." *Common Knowledge* 10 (3): 463–84. doi:10.1215/0961754X-10-3-463.
Wagner, Roy. 1977. "Analogic Kinship: A Daribi Example." *American Ethnologist* 4 (4): 623–42.
———. 1986. *Symbols That Stand for Themselves*. Chicago: University of Chicago Press.
———. 1991. "The Fractal Person." In *Big Men and Great Men: Personifications of Power in Melanesia*, edited by Maurice Godelier and Marilyn Strathern, 159–73. Cambridge: Cambridge University Press.
Wallerstein, Immanuel. 1974. *The Modern World-System*. Vol. 1: *Capitalist Agriculture and the Origins of the European World-Economy in the Sixteenth Century*. New York: Academic Press.
Walsh, Andrew. 2003. "'Hot Money' and Daring Consumption in a Northern Malagasy Sapphire-Mining Town." *American Ethnologist* 30 (2): 290–305.
Wardlow, Holly. 2006. *Wayward Women: Sexuality and Agency in a New Guinea Society*. Berkeley: University of California Press.
Webb, Michael. 2011. "Palang Conformity and Fulset Freedom: Encountering Pentecostalism's 'Sensational' Liturgical Forms in the Postmissionary Church in Lae, Papua New Guinea." *Ethnomusicology* 55 (3): 445. doi:10.5406/ethnomusicology.55.3.0445.
Weichart, Gabriele. 2010. "'We Are All Brothers and Sisters': Community, Competition, and the Church in Minahasa." In *Religious Dynamics in the Pacific/Les dynamiques religieuses dans le Pacifique*, edited by Gabriele Weichart and Francoise Douaire-Marsudon, 213–33. Paris: Cahiers du Credo.

Weiner, James F. 1993. "Anthropology Contra Heidegger 2: The Limit of Relationship." *Critique of Anthropology* 13 (3): 285–301. doi:10.1177/0308275X9301300306.

Werbner, Richard. 2011. "The Charismatic Dividual and the Sacred Self*." *Journal of Religion in Africa* 41 (2): 180–205. doi:10.1163/157006611X569247.

Wesch, Michael. 2007. "A Witch Hunt in New Guinea: Anthropology on Trial." *Anthropology and Humanism* 32 (1): 4–17. doi:10.1525/ahu.2007.32.1.4.

West, Paige. 2006. *Conservation Is Our Government Now: The Politics of Ecology in Papua New Guinea*. Durham, N.C.: Duke University Press.

———. 2012. *From Modern Production to Imagined Primitive: The Social World of Coffee from Papua New Guinea*. Durham, N.C.: Duke University Press.

———. 2016. *Dispossession and the Environment: Rhetoric and Inequality in Papua New Guinea*. New York: Columbia University Press.

Williams, Francis Edgar. 1933. *Depopulation of the Suau District*. Port Moresby: W. A. Bock, Acting Government Printer.

Wolf, Eric R. 1982. *Europe and the People without History*. Berkeley: University of California Press.

Young, Michael. 1971. *Fighting with Food: Leadership, Values, and Social Control in a Massim Society*. Cambridge: Cambridge University Press.

———. 1995. "South Normanby Island: A Social Mapping Study." *Research in Melanesia* 17: 1–70.

Young, Michael W., and Julia Clark. 2001. *An Anthropologist in Papua: The Photography of F. E. Williams, 1922–39*. London: Crawford House.

Zelizer, Viviana A. 1994. *The Social Meaning of Money*. New York: Basic Books.

Zurenuoc, Theo. 2013. "The Hon. Theo Zurenuoc Lecture: Restoring the People's Parliament." June 5. Crawford School of Public Policy, The Australian National University.

———. 2014. "Reformation of the National Parliament as a Symbol of National Unity: A Tribute to the Founding Fathers Sir Michael Somare and Sir Julius Chan." *Business Melanesia* 1 (5): 36–38.

———. 2015. "2015: The Year of Crossing Over to the Other Side." *The National Parliament of Papua New Guinea News*. February 11. http://www.parliament.gov.pg/index.php/news/view/2015-the-year-of-crossing-over-to-the-other-side.

INDEX

Note: Page numbers in bold show where an explanation of the local language term can be found.

adoption, 27, 39, 42, 60, 218n2
aemehelino, 49–52, **171–172**, 175
Africa
   agricultural change in, 99–100
   postcolonial states in, 200–201, 204
agency
   anthropologists on, 7, 12–13
   of deceased person, 189, 192–194, 195
   displacement of, 121, 128, 150
   framing of mourning and, 182
   submission of, 91
agriculture. *See* gardens and gardening
alawata, **67**, 74, 95–96
Alogawa
   history, 27
   location and layout, 27fig, 32–33
ancestral names, 3, 15–16, 42, 43–44

Armstrong, W.E., 85, 86
asiyebwa, **34–35**, 48–55, 171, 177
Auhewala
   kinship organization (overview), 30–34
   language, 30, 197–198, 223n9
   location and tetela, 26–27
Austin, J.L., 186
Australia, Aboriginal people of, 200–201
avoidance, 73–74
   in burial/mourning practices, 35, 36, 37, 50, 54, 66, 73, 171, 178
   of burial sites *(magai),* 37, 56, 171, 188
   fathers and, 55–56, 58, 71–72, 73
   of gardens/yams, 91
   of names, 55–56, 71–72, 74, 215n1
awawa'uhi, **30**

bale'u, 33
Barker, John, 136
Bateson, Gregory, 11–12, 70
besobeso, **31**, 58, 66
betel nuts, 107, 111, 113, 114, 117–118, 120, 121–122, 129
Bialecki, Jon, 161–162
bird totems, 41–43, 45
birth certificates, 78
birthplaces, 30
boda ehebo, 30
body gloss, 72–73
Bohannan, Paul, 108, 220n1
Boserup, Ester, 81, 99–100
boundary objects
  museums as, 211–212
  yam houses as, 101–104
Bourdieu, Pierre, 17, 63–68
bridewealth, 108
Brison, Karen, 8
Bromilow, William, 131, 136–139, 143–145, 151, 167, 222n3
Brown, George, 132
buka, **115**–117, 120, 121, 130, 221n5
Bung Wantaim artwork, 205–207, 209–210, 225n3
burial and mourning practices, 34–38, 48–55, 168–176
  asiyebwa, **34**–35, 48–55, 171, 177
  bu'una and, 19, 29, 41, 44, 170
  bwabwale and *masele*, 23, 169–170, 174–182, 188–196
  fathers, mourning of, 59–60, 170–171, 179–180, 194
  gift giving, 49–52, 67, 70, 72–73, 169, 170, 175, 179
  history of, 191–196
  kinship divide at, 170–174, 193
  knowledge preservation and, 19, 29, 31, 37–38
  person, location of in, 182–191
  skull enshrinement, 3–4, 29, 33, 35–36, 38, 40–41
  susu and, 31, 33–35, 40–41, 44, 170–171, 217–218n7

Burke, Edmund III, 225n2
Burridge, Kenelm, 96, 166
bu'una, **3**, **19**
  active maintenance of relationships, 29, 44
  burial and, 19, 29, 41, 44, 170
  discovery of, 43, 45
  as network, 31
  organization and recognition of, 38–47
  trading within, 105–106, 109
  as uncertain/controversial, 39–40, 45
  validation of, 41–44, 45
bwabwale, **59–60**
  dividual person and, 186
  gift giving, 49–52, 67–68, 70, 72–74, 169, 170, 175, 179
  kinship divide at, 170–174, 193
  masele and, 23, 169–170, 174–182, 188–196
bwalesi yam tubers, 91, 107

Cannings, David, 206
Carr, E. Summerson, 17
cassava, 21, 77, 97–98
Catholics and Catholic missions
  acceptance of, 159
  fundraising and, 122–123, 150, 152–159
Chakrabarty, Dipesh, 6–7
child census, 78
children
  fathers and, 55–60, 71, 73
  intertemporality and, 194
  state policies and, 78–79, 82–86
Christianity
  metaphors and, 139–143, 160–167
  mourning and, 23, 169–170, 174–176, 194, 199
  "one mind" and, 22–23, 134–136, 142–143, 152, 158–160, 164–165, 198
  politicization of, 205–207
  See also churches; missionaries; mission stations

churches
    fundraising and, 22, 23, 122–128, 150–157, 165, 198
    tapwalolo (services), **134–136,** 140–150, 158–160, 164–167, 188–189, 196
cigarette selling, 114–115
citizenship, conceptions of, 200–213
coalitions, 121–122
Coleman, Simon, 162
colonial governments
    agricultural change and, 100
    brief history of, 218n4
    burial regulations, 3–4, 33
    families/women, narratives on, 82–86, 100
    indigenous people, vision of, 7–8, 20
    missions, coordination with, 131
    monetization by, 109
    perceptions of change and, 4–5, 6–7
conceptual blends, 163–165, 223n12
credit *(buka),* **115**–117, 120, 121, 130, 221n5
cross-relatives. *See* father's *susu; natuleiya*
cultural identity, and citizenship, 200–213

da'eda'e, **35**
Dawatai shrine, 29
death. *See* burial and mourning practices
debts, gifts as, 50–53, 60, 72. *See also* reciprocity
decline, perceived
    agricultural, 20, 21, 77–80, 98–99
    of gift giving, 74–75, 77, 99, 107, 169
    money as sign of, 107
    social and moral, 79, 112
depopulation, colonial fears of, 82–86
diagrammatic icons, 146
difference, and citizenship, 200–213
Dioscorea alata, 34, 49, 89, 129
Dirks, Nicholas, 225n2
dividuals. *See* personhood
domination, 216n9
dualism (Western), 183–184

Duau island, description of, 25–26
Duduwega, Christopher, 139–140
duluva, **35**, **217n3**. *See also* skulls
Duranti, Alessandro, 186
Durkheim, Émile, 13
Durkheimian theory, 13, 47, 71, 185

earmarking, 118–122, 127, 129
ebe laoma, **39**
ebe towolo, **33**, **88**, 90, 92. *See also* gardens
ecology of mind, 11–12
Edahosi, Kevin, 1–2, 32
ehebo, **31**
Ekalesiya Sowala. *See* Sowala
Ela Beach, 26–27
emergent typification, 195–196
enao, **89**–96, 100, 101–102, 128–129
    of money, 116–117, 128–130
ethical life, 18
ethnographic citizenship, 203–207, 225n2
ethnographic museums, 210–212
ethnographic state, 204, 225n2

face, 71
fathers
    children, relationships with, 55–60, 71, 73
    mourning of, 59–60, 170–171, 179–180, 194
father's *susu*
    active maintenance of relationships, 60–63
    burial and mourning practices, 49–55, 62, 63, 66, 72–73, 168, 171, 172, 178, 187
    church offerings and, 153
    debts/reciprocity, 52–55
    gifts and, 49–52, 67–68, 70, 72–74, 169, 170, 175, 179
    land rights and, 60, 62, 63, 66, 67, 88, 180
    marriage prohibition and, 44
    See also bwabwale; natuleiya

248 Index

Fauconnier, Gilles, 163–164, 223n12
fear, 55, 57–58
feasts. *See* burial and mourning practices; pot-to-pot events
Fiji, 16
Fletcher, Ambrose, 139
Foster, Robert, 223n1
Foucault, Michel, 83
fractal images, 187–188
framing, of mourning, 188–191, 192
fundraising (churches), 22, 23, 122–128, 150–157, 165, 198

galiyauna, 35–36, 42, 44, 170, 173, 174, 178
gardens and gardening
  agricultural decline, perceived, 20, 21, 77–80, 98–99
  dual division of, 77, 80–81, 87–88, 94, 95–97, 100–102
  mental labor of, 102–104
  process, 87–96
  secondary/new crops, 77, 80, 81, 87, 97–100, 101
  timing and, 91–92
  See also yams
Garfinkel, Harold, 11, 18, 74, 190, 212
Gershon, Ilana, 16–17
Ghana, 201–202, 204
Giddens, Anthony, 17
gift economies, money and, 108–109
gifts
  bwabwale, 49–52, 67–68, 70, 72–74, 169, 170, 175, 179
  decline of, perceived, 74–75, 77, 99, 107, 169
  to forge bonds, 62–63, 64
  motivations for, 65–73
  at pot-to-pot events, 123–128
  timing of, 64, 65, 66–67
  velau, 152, 154, 155–156, 157, 161, 165
  yams as, 49–52, 59, 67–68, 94–95, 107, 179
  See also reciprocity

gimwala, 21, 106, 198. *See also* money and markets
Goffman, Erving, 69–73
gogo/dalava, 32
Golub, Alex, 203
government. *See* colonial governments; PNG government
Graeber, David, 216n7
graves. *See* burial and mourning practices; *magai*
Gregory, C.A., 109
Griesemer, James, 103–104
guguya, 147–148, 160–161
Guyer, Jane, 108–109

Habermas, Jürgen, 200
habitus, 17, 63–69, 80–81
hagu, 34, 68, **68**, 165
halutu yams, **89**, 98, 125, 129
harvests. *See* gardens and gardening; yams
hau, 10
hauga isesens, **4**, 197
Haus Parliament artwork, 205–207, 209–210
Hertz, Robert, 40
hilauwa, 172–173, 175
Hindu society, 183, 185
hinihinini, 68
historicism, 6–7
Honig, Bonnie, 211
human rights violations, 207–209
humiliation, 16
hymns, 119, 135, 143–146, 153, 172, 174

indigenous models, 10–15
individuals, and "one mind," 134–136, 158–159, 162–167
in-laws, 61
intention, 186, 190
intercultural situations, 8–10
ipa'ipatu, 173–174
Isaia, Pati story, 222n4
  conversion of Auhelawa and, 139–140

Jolly, Margaret, 82
Jorgensen, Dan, 208–209

kastam (custom), 4, **168–169**, 199, 223n1
  bwabwale and *masele*, 23, 169–170, 174–182, 188–196
Keane, Webb, 18
Kehelala, 27, 29
kinship
  division of, in mourning, 170–174, 193
  organization and recognition of, 30–34, 38–47
  reflexive sociality and, 19
  See also bu'una; father's *susu;* matrilineage; *susu*
Kiriwina, Trobriand Islands, 87, 106, 122
Kohn, Eduardo, 14
Korowai people, 194–195
Kuehling, Susanne, 191
kula exchange, 106, 224n6
Kurada ward, map of, 28fig
Kymlicka, Will, 201

land claims/rights
  citizenship and, 203–204
  increasing interest in, 46
  susu and, 30, 60, 62, 63, 66, 67, 88, 180
language
  of Auhewala, 30, 197–198, 223n9
  of church services, 143–144, 145
  meaning and, 186
  as metaphor for cultural difference, 207
lateness, 92, 133–135
Latour, Bruno, 12
lauyaba, **96–97**, 100, 101–102, 106–107, 219n9
Lear, Jonathan, 212
Leniata, Kepari, 207–209
Lévi-Strauss, Claude, 11, 218n1
liberal modernity, 200–204
light and darkness metaphor, 139–143

Macgregor, William, 83–85, 86, 132, 218n4, 222n1
Macintyre, Martha, 191
magai (burial sites), **33**
  avoidance of, 37, 56, 171, 188
  knowledge preservation and, 29, 31–32, 34, 37–38
  skull shrines, 3–4, 29, 33, 35–38, 40–41
  See also burial and mourning practices
Mahmood, Saba, 216n10
maiha, **72**
malahilili, **49**, 171
Malinowski, Bronislaw, 10–11, 106
maps
  Kevin Edahosi's, 1–2
  as models, 15–16, 103, 129
  PNG and region, 26, 27
markets. *See* money and markets
marriage
  adoption and, 60
  bridewealth, 108
  death and, 73, 74, 170–171
  divorce, 61
  gardening practices and, 87–89
  in-laws, 61
  kinship prohibitions, 41–42, 44, 218n1
  prohibition on use of names, 55–56
  residence shifting and, 34, 56
Marriott, McKim, 183, 185
Marx, Karl, 6
masele, and *bwabwale*, **23, 169**–170, 174–182, 188–196
matrilineal descent, 2, 18, 19
  geographic distribution of groups and, 33
  susu and, 30, 34
  two forms of (networks and groups), 31, 38–39, 43
  yam culture and, 34, 80–82, 88, 100
  See also bu'una; susu
Mauss, Marcel, 185
mehe'uhi, **55**, 57–58
Melanesia
  cultural identity in, 202
  social theory and, 13, 184–185, 187

mental space, 164–165
Merlan, Francesca, 7–8, 200–201
metaphors, and Christianity, 139–143, 160–167
Methodist missions and missionaries, 131–132, 136–139, 143–145, 151, 167. *See also* United Church missions
Middleton, Townsend, 225n2
migration, 30
mikisi, **197–213**
mind
  child development and, 57–58
  conversion and, 163
  memory and, 34, 217n2
  See also "one mind"
minorities, and citizenship, 200–213
missionaries, 22, 85, 98, 131–132, 136–139, 167
mission stations
  early/colonial, 131–132, 137–139, 151, 222n1, 222n4
  fundraising and, 122–124, 150–157, 165
  services at, 132–135, 141–150
modernity, 200–204
money and markets
  bu'una, trade within, 105–106, 109
  church offerings and, 151, 198
  earmarking, 118–122, 127, 129
  marketplaces, 111–114, 117
  performance of morality and, 21–22, 115–117, 120–130, 157, 198
  practices, 112–118
  stigma of, 21–22, 104, 106–111
  widespread use of, 107, 110–111, 128
  women and, 21–22, 109, 110
mothers
  state narratives on, 82–86, 100, 219n7
  yams and, 20–21, 80–81, 88, 94, 100, 102, 104, 198
mourning. *See* burial and mourning practices
Moutu, Andrew, 205–206, 225n3

mulolo, **150–157**, 165
mumuga, 39
murders, sorcery-related, 207–209
Murray, J.H.P., 83–84, 86, 218n4
museums, 210–212, 226n7
mwadimwadi, 35, 36, 37

names
  ancestral, 3, 15–16, 42, 43–44
  avoidance of, 55–56, 71–72, 74, 215n1
Narokobi, Bernard, 202–203, 225n2
natuleiya, **42, 44, 56**
  burials and, 49–55, 62, 63, 66, 72–73, 168, 171, 172, 178, 187
  definitions, **42, 44, 56**
  land rights and, 62, 63, 88, 180
  marriage prohibition and, 44
  reciprocity and, 60, 62, 69, 88, 187
  respect (*ve'ahihi*) and, 61–63, 66, 68–69, 71–73, 88, 178
  taliya natuleiya, **44, 56**
New Home (village), 26, 27, 28fig, 29, 77, 93fig
nibai, **56**, 59–60, 69
Nkrumah, Kwame, 201–202, 204
Normanby Island, 28fig
nuwapwanopwano, 34, 217n2
nuwatuwu'avivini, 34, 217n2
nuwatuwu ehebo, **134**. *See also* "one mind"
Nyerere, Julius, 201–202

observer effects, 15
"one mind," **22, 134**
  burial and, 33–34, 173
  the individual and, 134–136, 158–159, 162–167
  offerings and, 152, 198
  at *tapwalolo* (services), 22–23, 134–135, 142–143, 146, 148–150, 158–160, 162
ontological anthropology, 14, 15
ontological insecurity, 16–18, 216n9
ontology, use of term, 216n7

overpopulation, perceptions of, 79, 99, 106–107
oya, 87–96. *See also* gardening; yams
oyama, 40, 45, **158**
oya'oyama, **158**, 159

Pade, Francis, 1, 26, 133fig
  economic activities of, 115, 221n5, 221n7
  kinship networks of, 41–42, 62, 217n4
Pade, Lucy, 1, 26, 51fig
  economic activities of, 114–115, 118–119, 121–122, 221n7
  kinship networks of, 27–29, 32, 41–42, 61–63, 217n4
  at mortuary feasts, 49–53, 180, 224n7
Palmié, Stephan, 223n12
parish feast days, 122–123
Parliament House artwork, 205–207, 209–210
Parmentier, Richard, 146
Pentecostals, 159–160, 163, 166, 206, 222n2, 223n9
pepper, 107, 111, 114, 120
personhood, 40, 46
  dividual, 52–53, 182–188
Plenty-Coups, 212
PNG government
  children/families, policies on, 78–79, 219n7
  citizenship, conceptions of, 200, 202–204
Polanyi, Karl, 204
politics, 24
politiki, **40**
population growth/decline, 79, 82–86, 99, 106–107
postcolonial citizenship, 200–213
postcultural consciousness, 8–10, 16
postculturalism, 212–213
pots, and gift exchanges, 49, 50
pot-to-pot events, 124–128, 221n8
poverty, perceptions of, 20, 21, 77–80, 86–87, 99
Povinelli, Elizabeth, 46–47

prayers, 141–142, 147–148
prices, 113–114
public institutions, 210–211, 226n7

Ranapiri, Tamati, 10, 11
reciprocal recognition, 188, 189
reciprocity
  church offerings and, 151–152, 157
  dividuals, association with, 185
  father's *susu* and, 30, 50–54
  garden work and, 88–89
  masele and, 175
  motivation for, 62–73
  as normative action, 53–55
  parish fundraising and, 123–128
  as a strategy, 62–64
  timing of, 64, 66–67
  yams and, 21, 81, 89, 94, 100
  See also gifts
Reed, Adam, 82
reflexivity, 8–10, 17–18, 20, 73–75, 130
respect. *See ve'ahihi*
ritual, as symbolic communication, 186–187
Robbins, Joel, 162–163, 215n3
Rosi, Pamela, 225n3
Rumsey, Alan, 195

Sahlins, Marshall, 16, 45, 46, 215n2
Samoan diaspora, 16–17
Schieffelin, Bambi, 163
Schneider, David, 14
schools, 79
scientific knowledge, 12
script flipping, 17, 22
selfishness, perceptions of, 21–22
sementi, **180**–182
sens, 4, 5–6, 9–10
shame, 66
skulls, enshrinement of, 3–4, 29, 33, 35–38, 40–41
social action theories
  Bourdieu's, 63–69
  Goffman's, 69–73
social media, 207–208

sorcery-related killings (SRK), 207–209
Sowala
  church fundraising at, 123
  church services at, 132–133, 143–150
  location, 28fig
  marketplace at, 111, 112, 113
  story about church founding, 139–141, 222n4
spheres of exchange, models of, 108–109
Star, Susan Leigh, 103–104
Stasch, Rupert, 73, 194–195
state, the. *See* colonial governments; PNG government
Strathern, Marilyn, 13, 14–15, 52–53, 182–187, 216n7, 216n8
Street, Alice, 226n7
structuration, 17
subsistence societies, money and, 107
susu, **2**, **27**, 30
  assistance and, 34, 68
  burial sites and, 31, 33, 40–41, 44, 171, 217–218n7
  land rights and, 30, 88
  organization and recognition of, 38–47
  as owners of mourning events, 33–35, 170–171
  tetelas, change, and, 27, 29, 38–39, 41, 43–44
  as uncertain/controversial, 39–40
  See also father's *susu*
sweet potatoes, 21, 77, 97, 98–99
symbolic capital, 66

tagwala, **48**, 91, 94, 98, 101, 106–107
taliya, 31, **31**, 44
taliya natuleiya, **44**, **56**
Tanzania, 201–202
tapwalolo, **134–136**, 140–150, 164–167, 188–189, 196
  at burials/mourning, 50, 173, 175, 177, 182
  in daily life, 135, 141
  "one mind" at, 22–23, 134–135, 142–143, 146, 148–150, 158–160, 162

tapwalolo oya'oyama, **158–160**
taro, 220n11, 220n12
taxes, 84–86
tetela, **3**, **27**, 29, 38–39, 41–47
Thune, Carl, 160–161
Tilly, Charles, 9
Tiv people, 108–109
tobacco, 114–115, 120, 220n3
Tomlinson, Matt, 16
totems, 41–43, 45
totoleana, **35**, 37–38. *See also* skulls
trade stores, 115–117
transpersonal praxis, 46–47
Trobriand Islands. *See* Kiriwina
Turner, Mark, 163–164, 223n12
Tuzin, Donald, 101

United Church missions
  fundraising at, 122–123, 150–152, 165
  services, 119, 142, 143–150
Unity Pole proposed artwork, 205–207, 209–210

vaga, 50, 60, 72
ve'ahihi (respect), **19**, 171
  fathers and children, 55–60, 71, 73;
    during mourning, 59–60, 170–171, 179–180, 194
  father's *susu* and, 19–20, 50, 54–63, 71–73, 187
  to form bonds, 62–63
  natuleiya and, 61–63, 66, 68–69, 71–73, 88, 178
  reflexivity and, 20, 73–74
  towards yams and gardens, 90–91, 96
  See also avoidance
velau, **152**, 154, 155–156, 157, 161, 165
Viveiros de Castro, Eduardo, 13–14, 216n7

Wagner, Roy, 12–13, 52–53, 187–188, 216n7, 217n7
'wahi ehebo, 30

wasawasa, 67, 74, 92, 95–96
'wateya yams, 34, **49**, 89, 129
   earmarking of, 129
   as gifts, 50, 125
   matrilineage and, 34
Weiner, James, 185
welowelolo, **173–174**
Williams, Francis, 85
women
   dual roles of, 81, 100, 104, 198
   gardening and, 20–21, 81–82, 89, 92, 94–95, 99–100, 102–104, 198
   matrilineage and, 34
   money earning and, 21–22, 109, 110
   state narratives on, 82–86, 100, 219n7
   violence against, 207–209

yabayaba, **94**, 97, 98, 129, 219n9
yaheyahe, **87**, 96–98, 101, 219n8

yams
   gardening practices, 87–98
   as gifts, 49–52, 59, 67–68, 94–95, 107, 179
   matrilineage and, 34, 80–82, 88, 100
   as metaphor for moral order, 5–6, 82, 198
   mothers and, 20–21, 80–81, 88, 94, 100, 102, 104, 198
   reciprocity and, 21, 81, 88–89, 94, 100
   ve'ahihi (respect) and, 90–91, 96
   yam houses: as boundary objects, 101–104; curating and earmarking in, 20–21, 92–96, 127, 129–130, 198; reading of, 80–82
   See also gardens and gardening

Zelizer, Viviana, 119–120
Zurenuoc, Theo, 205–207, 209–210, 225n4, 225n5

CPSIA information can be obtained
at www.ICGtesting.com
Printed in the USA
FSHW04n1432070318
45163FS